General equilibrium analysis

WITHDRAWN

What is the nature of the intellectual enterprise – general equilibrium analysis – that so many economists regard as the centerpiece of their discipline? In this book, Roy Weintraub considers both the modern history of the analysis and the methodological puzzles that it, and mathematical economic theory in general, pose.

General Equilibrium Analysis: Studies in Appraisal argues that previous writings on the history and method of general equilibrium theory have been curiously biased and misleading. Weintraub provides a clear and careful presentation of the development of the theory from the 1930s through to the Arrow–Debreu work of the 1950s. This historical analysis is the center of the book: a case study that permits the author to justify the status of general equilibrium theory in economics and the activity in which economic theorists engage. Weintraub argues that previous methodological investigations have been distorted by the use of inappropriate models taken from the philosophy of science that were developed to appraise work in the physical sciences.

This is a highly readable and original work that, by examining general equilibrium analysis, casts a light on the very basis of most theoretical and applied work in the "neoclassical" tradition. As such, it will be of interest not only to economists but also to students and to philosophers of science.

Historical Perspectives on Modern Economics

General Editor: Professor Craufurd D. Goodwin, Duke University

This series contains original works that challenge and enlighten historians of economics. For the profession as a whole it promotes a better understanding of the origin and content of modern economics.

Other books in the series:
Don Lavoie: *Rivalry and central planning: the Socialist calculation debate reconsidered*
Takashi Negishi: *Economic theories in a non-Walrasian tradition*

General equilibrium analysis

Studies in appraisal

E. Roy Weintraub
Duke University

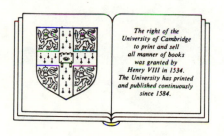

The right of the
University of Cambridge
to print and sell
all manner of books
was granted by
Henry VIII in 1534.
The University has printed
and published continuously
since 1584.

CAMBRIDGE UNIVERSITY PRESS

Cambridge
London   New York   New Rochelle
Melbourne   Sydney

Published by the Press Syndicate of the University of Cambridge
The Pitt Building, Trumpington Street, Cambridge CB2 1RP
32 East 57th Street, New York, NY 10022, USA
10 Stamford Road, Oakleigh, Melbourne 3166, Australia

© Cambridge University Press 1985

First published 1985

Printed in the United States of America

Library of Congress Cataloging in Publication Data
Weintraub, E. Roy.
General equilibrium analysis.
(Historical perspectives on modern economics)
Bibliography: p.
Includes index.
1. Equilibrium (Economics) I. Title. II. Series.
HB145.W427 1985 339.5 84–23260
ISBN 0 521 25968 1 hard covers

Contents

Contents

Preface

Although I am a teacher, I am not the Teacher whom you will presently meet. Neither are my students to be confused with A, B, and C (or with their later instantiations as α, β, and γ).

The conversations raise, but do not settle, many issues. They are meant to engage you, the reader, in a dialogue with the text. As I may quarrel with what the teacher and students say to each other, so too should you be able to say, "Wait just one minute – what about ...?" Nor does my setting of the conversations in a classroom imply that the issues concern only economics graduate students.

One of the values of an intellectual enterprise is attention, which infrequently results in publication, to the worth of the project itself. That attention may be stimulated by a colleague who does not respect the success of economic analysis. Alertness may be engaged by one's students who seek clarity in their own lives, who seek coherence between their desire for self-esteem and their growing awareness that the work of professional economists is evaluated by other professional economists. And attention to the enterprise is forced on each of us as we seek spiritual nourishment in the human activity called "doing economics."

In such ways does the enterprise itself become the subject of discussion. "What use is economics?" and "How may it be justified as an activity?" require, for most of us, more of an answer than "It pleases me" or "If I'm paid to do economics, it must be of value."

To appraise is "to evaluate the worth, significance, or status of: especially to give an expert judgment on the value or merit of." This dictionary definition ought to be kept in mind.

In economics, appraisals take many forms. Technical work, built on other technical work, necessarily appraises the foundations of the structures being erected. Differences in opinion on matters of theory and policy are manifest in arguments designed to convince the reader; the rhetorical convention of appraising an opponent's argument and finding it wanting is common. We all, as economists, appraise what we read, hear, and learn. Appraisals are the goods we produce, consume, and distribute.

Yet for so ubiquitous an activity, it is curiously disreputable. Among economists, appraisal activity is usually called "methodology," and methodological studies are not prized. Methodologists are regarded as gnats buzzing and flitting around the ears of those professionals who are "getting on with it," where the "it" refers to expanding the disciplinary corpus.

Sir Roy Harrod, long ago, opened a piece of *his* on methodology with an apology for writing on such a disreputable subject; he claimed that, nonetheless, he wished to *say something*. I too wish to say some things. In particular, I want to examine general equilibrium analysis. I shall provide, if not an appraisal of it as an enterprise, at least a framework in which such an appraisal may be proffered by others. Thus what follows is best read as variations on the theme, How are we to appraise general equilibrium analysis?

This book began to take form in 1978. It grew out of conversations with my colleague Neil deMarchi and several of our graduate students, particularly Rodney Maddock and Arjo Klamer. It was initially conceived as a joint enterprise; deMarchi was to focus on philosophical topics, and I was to examine general equilibrium analysis. My concern that I could not write on the topic without understanding its history led to the work that here stands as Chapter 6 (which appeared in a slightly different form in the *Journal of Economic Literature*, in March 1983).

Colin Day, editorial director of the Cambridge University Press, guided this project to its current form. As my material on general equilibrium analysis expanded, and deMarchi found that he had two books growing out of our joint work, we separated, and I restructured the project again. It is now time to send it forth to be itself appraised.

A number of individuals have read, heard, and commented on various portions of this work. Duke's Craufurd Goodwin, David Nickerson, Marjorie McElroy, Dale Stahl, and Dan Graham have been helpful, as has an interdisciplinary faculty seminar on "The Growth of Knowledge" initially chaired by the historian Seymour Mauskopf.

Anthony A. Brewer, visiting Duke from the University of Bristol, nurtured the various revisions of Chapter 6. That chapter could not have been written without the cooperation of Kenneth Arrow, Lionel McKenzie, Gerard Debreu, and Tjalling Koopmans, who most graciously searched their memories, and files, at my behest.

In the fall of 1982 I visited UCLA and had the privilege of co-teaching a seminar on economic thought with Bob Clower. He, Axel Leijonhufvud, Earlene Craver Leijonhufvud, Joseph Ostroy, and others there encouraged me to confront the appraisal issue directly. Correspondence with Warren Samuels, Mark Blaug, Daniel Hausman, Douglas Wade Hands, Paul Davidson, and Jan Kregel helped shape what is offered here, and its completion was made possible by Victor Zinn and Barrie J. Hurwitz.

Patricia Johnson and Wanda Jedierowski produced manuscript from scrawl and printout, with my grateful appreciation. No grant or agency funded this project, as usual.

This book is dedicated to the memory of my father, Sidney Weintraub (April 28, 1914–June 19, 1983).

E.R.W.

Part I

The five chapters of Part I provide a number of entry points to the appraisal issue. Chapter 1 presents an overview of general equilibrium arguments by developing a simple model of exchange. Chapter 2, the first classroom interlude, then raises many questions about general equilibrium analysis. They will be echoed in later chapters.

Chapter 3 introduces the reader to the idea of appraisal and sketches some philosophical problems that appear in the various literatures. Chapter 4, a second classroom interlude, introduces another set of problems and perspectives on the nature of general equilibrium analysis; these too prefigure arguments in later chapters. Finally, Chapter 5 links the discussion of appraisal with the general equilibrium analysis itself by examining recent work on the nature and role of general equilibrium analysis.

CHAPTER 1

A general equilibrium model

I shall begin the examination of general equilibrium analysis as simply as I know how. I shall proceed from the specific to the general by developing a general equilibrium model that can motivate much of the subsequent discussion. As I proceed, I shall make various remarks that will point to the complications, problems, and unresolved issues associated with research in general equilibrium analysis.

Consider a three-agent (or household), three-commodity world in which agents hold different initial stocks of the three goods. Assume that agents have similar tastes. They come to market to barter their goods in order to attain a more desirable consumption bundle.

Remark: Three goods give substance to the problem. With only two, it is hard to study the interdependence that characterizes the general equilibrium approach.

Remark: Production is not allowed in this simple model. Including production will be an "agenda item." Historically, pure exchange models have proved more tractable than production–exchange models.

Remark: Similar tastes will entail that aggregation is simple. Thus there is only one effective agent.

Our problem is to ascertain whether there exists a set of three prices, one for each good, such that were all traders to maximize utility subject to their incomes (computed at these prices), their buy and sell offers in the market would lead, through market supplies and demands, to just those prices at which they optimized. Suppose such an equilibrium price vector exists. If we postulate a dynamic process of price adjustment, we can then ask whether prices approach equilibrium over time.

Remark: "Maximizing utility" is the way we describe why the agents wish to trade.

Remark: We want to know whether the choices that the agents make are even *potentially* consistent. The search for the existence of equilibrium prices is equivalent to a search for a mutually consistent set of decisions.

Remark: If an equilibrium exists, the problem of its attainment is called the *stability problem.*

Let us formalize the model in the following way. Let p_j be the price of the jth good. Let $\bar{x}_{ij}$ be the initial stock of good j held by individual i, and let x_{ij} be the quantity demanded of good j by individual i, where p_j, $\bar{x}_{ij}$, and x_{ij} are non-negative real numbers.

Remark: We are now beginning to *model* the problem. The first step, defining notation, is not neutral. In stating that prices and quantities can be modeled as real numbers, we assume that prices and quantities are continuously divisible. The mathematics influences the economic reasoning.

For the purposes of the example, let each individual i's preferences be represented by a log-linear utility function:

$$U^i(x_i) = \sum_{k=1}^{3} a_k \log x_{ik}, \qquad 0 < a_k < 1, \quad \Sigma a_k = 1,$$

where $x_i = (x_{i1}, x_{i2}, x_{i3})$, and a_k is the same for each individual.

Remark: A specific utility function illustrates the methods better than a general function. This particular function implies that i's utility depends on the quantities of the goods that i has, that more of any good increases utility, that utility is a continuously differentiable function of the quantities, and that the law of diminishing marginal utility holds. The a_k are *preference weights* that show how the goods contribute to utility. The assertion that a_k is unchanged across individuals models the assumption that the individuals have identical preferences.

Because the income of the ith agent is associated with the value of that agent's initial bundle, letting μ denote income yields

$$\mu^i = \sum_{k=1}^{3} p_k \bar{x}_{ik}.$$

Remark: The income of individuals is the imputed value of their marketable goods. Their income is thus a variable, in the sense that only some prices (equilibrium prices) will emerge as correct (consistent). Hence traders, taking prices as given, propose trades that may or may not sustain the initial valuation of their stock of goods.

The budget constraint for individual i is

$$\mu^i = \sum_{j=1}^{k} p_k x_{ik}.$$

Remark: Individuals thus spend all their income, perhaps including an imputed expenditure on their own marketable stock.

Maximizing the utility function subject to the budget constraint and solving for x_{ij} yields the demand function of agent i for good j:

$$x_{ij} = \frac{a_j \mu^i}{p_j}.$$

Remark: This equation is obtained using a calculus technique of optimization subject to constraints, the technique of Lagrange multipliers.

Remark: The assumption that the utility function had the form it did allowed use of the optimization argument. The demand function was derived under the condition that the utility function was twice continuously differentiable. That a maximum of utility, not a minimum, was involved, was inferred from the assumption of diminishing marginal utility.

Remark: The properties of this individual's demand function thus flow from the utility function, the budget constraint, and optimization. Notice that the demand for good j by individual i depends directly on i's income and inversely on the price of good j. And since the prices of goods other than j are in μ^i, i's demand for good j depends directly on the prices of those other goods.

To obtain market demand it is necessary to aggregate – to sum over all agents. Thus

$$x_j = \sum_{i=1}^{3} x_{ij} = \sum_{i=1}^{3} a_j \frac{\mu^i}{p_j} = \frac{a_j}{p_j} \sum_{i=1}^{3} \left(\sum_{k=1}^{3} p_k \bar{x}_{ik} \right)$$

$$= \frac{a_j}{p_j} \sum_{k=1}^{3} \left(\sum_{i=1}^{3} p_k \bar{x}_{ik} \right) = \frac{a_j}{p_j} \sum_{k=1}^{3} p_k \bar{x}_k.$$

Remark: The assumption that agents are identical was used here to perform the aggregation.

To recapitulate, under fairly standard (to the economist) assumptions about the preferences, constraints, and rationality of economic agents, we have derived expressions for the market demand for each of the three commodities. We now begin to study the possibility of coherent market outcomes, the existence of equilibrium for the model, by combining the demands just identified with the (productionless) supply available in this exchange market world.

Because the market supply of good j is simply $\bar{x}_j$, letting the excess demand for good j be denoted E_j, we have

$$E_j(p_1, p_2, p_3) = \frac{a_j}{p_j}\left(\sum_{k=1}^{3} p_k\bar{x}_k\right) - \bar{x}_j,$$

since $\bar{x}$ and a_k are parameters of the model and $p = (p_1, p_2, p_3)$ defines the state variables.

Remark: Equilibrium is defined by the supply–demand balance. In other words, an equilibrium is defined when the excess demand functions simultaneously equal zero. For the specific model we are working with, equilibrium is associated with a price vector $p^* = (p_1^*, p_2^*, p_3^*)$ such that $E_1(p^*) = E_2(p^*) = E_3(p^*) = 0$. If such a p^* exists, it is called equilibrium.
Remark: Not just any p^* that balances supply and demand can be an equilibrium. It must be the case that $p^* \geqslant 0$. If $p_i^* = 0$, then good i is a free good, which may or may not make sense for any particular problem.

For these particular excess demand functions, it is easy to check that (1) the E_j are continuously differentiable for $p > 0$, (2) the E_j are homogeneous of degree zero in prices, and (3) Walras's Law holds, i.e.,

$$\Sigma\, p_j x_j = \Sigma\, p_j \bar{x}_j \text{ or } \sum_{i=1}^{3} p_j E_j(p_1, p_2, p_3) \equiv 0.$$

Remark: Because analysis of a competitive equilibrium is often analysis of a set of excess demand functions, one standard problem, which may appear in different guises in different models, is to establish properties 1–3 in various special cases.

To complete the model, we must define the dynamic system with reference to which equilibration may be studied. The standard dynamic process, the Walrasian tatonnement, assumes that prices change directly with excess demand.

Specifically, we postulate the dynamic system

$$\dot{p}_1 = \frac{a_1}{p_1}\left[p_1\bar{x}_1\left(1 - \frac{1}{a_1}\right) + p_2\bar{x}_2 + p_3\bar{x}_3\right],$$

$$\dot{p}_2 = \frac{a_2}{p_2}\left[p_1\bar{x}_1 + p_2\bar{x}_2\left(1 - \frac{1}{a_2}\right) + p_3\bar{x}_3\right],$$

$$\dot{p}_3 = \frac{a_3}{p_3}\left[p_1\bar{x}_1 + p_2\bar{x}_2 + p_3\bar{x}_3\left(1 - \frac{1}{a_3}\right)\right].$$

Remark: The equation for $\dot{p}_3$ is actually redundant. It can be derived from the first two equations by differentiating Walras' Law.

Remark: This approach to the analysis of equilibrium builds on the Walrasian tatonnement, which interprets the *law of supply and demand*. This law states that the price of a good in excess demand tends to rise, whereas the price of a good in excess supply tends to fall. [Mathematically, $\dot{p}_i > 0$ if $E_i(p) > 0$.] The tatonnement assumption is subject to many caveats. Attempts to justify it, explore it, or replace it have generated a considerable analytic corpus, involving "fast-versus-slow adjustment," nontatonnement price dynamics, partial price adjustment theories, search and information theories of price adjustment, and other theories. Such research had an analytic stimulus during the years of controversy over labor-markets adjustments in the debates over the interpretation of Phillips curve.

For our special model it is possible to find the values of p_1^*, p_2^*, and p_3^* such that $\dot{p}_1 = \dot{p}_2 = \dot{p}_3 = 0$. Indeed, the simplicity of our system allows us to find the equilibrium directly. It is easy to check that

$$p_i^* = \frac{a_i}{\bar{x}_i}$$

defines an equilibrium for the system. If $a_i > 0$, then $p_i^* > 0$. *It is also easy to verify that any scalar multiple of this p^* vector is also an equilibrium. The model thus determines relative prices.*

Remark: If the utility function did not have such a nice closed-form representation, the excess demand functions would not be so simple and equilibrium would be inferred, not found. Studies of the existence of equilibrium in more general economic models thus often require sophisticated proofs based on mathematical theorems of the form "If A, B, and C hold, then *there exists a D such that....*"

Remark: We have found a relative price equilibrium. Without money in the model, macroeconomic inferences about the price level are invalid. Much modern work, under the title "microfoundations of macroeconomics," develops appropriate modeling strategies that permit macroeconomic inferences to be drawn.

Having determined that there does indeed exist an equilibrium price vector (a set of three prices) that *could* reconcile in advance the choices of the agents, we next ask whether the dynamics of the tatonnement allow us to conclude that the equilibrium will, in fact, be reached if prices start at nonequilibrium values. This type of analysis is called *stability analysis*. Do prices, starting at some initial vector $p(t)$, eventually converge to p^* under the dynamic laws that are described by the p equations? Those p equations are termed the dynamic equations, and (in the language of mathematical systems theory) the equations form a dynamic system.

Stability analysis is easier if we can write the dynamic system in vector–matrix form:

$$
\begin{bmatrix} \dot{p}_1 \\ \dot{p}_2 \\ \dot{p}_3 \end{bmatrix} = \begin{bmatrix} \dfrac{a_1}{p_1} & 0 & 0 \\ 0 & \dfrac{a_2}{p_2} & 0 \\ 0 & 0 & \dfrac{a_3}{p_3} \end{bmatrix}
$$

$$
\times \begin{bmatrix} \bar{x}_1\left(1 - \dfrac{1}{a_1}\right) & \bar{x}_2 & \bar{x}_3 \\ \bar{x}_1 & \bar{x}_2\left(1 - \dfrac{1}{a_2}\right) & \bar{x}_3 \\ \bar{x}_1 & \bar{x}_2 & \bar{x}_3\left(1 - \dfrac{1}{a_3}\right) \end{bmatrix} \begin{bmatrix} p_1 \\ p_2 \\ p_3 \end{bmatrix}.
$$

It would appear that an answer to the stability question would involve solving the differential equations that define the dynamic system. This would require producing solution equations for $p_1(t)$, $p_2(t)$, and $p_3(t)$ and then seeing whether, as $t \to \infty$, $p_1(t) \to p_1^*$, say. There is, fortunately, an easier way.

The Liapunov Second Method, or indirect method, of stability analysis is particularly useful for analysis of this system. Define

$$V(p) = \tfrac{1}{2}[(p_1 - p_1^*)^2 + (p_2 - p_2^*)^2 + (p_3 - p_3^*)^2].$$

Remark: This function V measures the distance between arbitrary price vectors $p = (p_1, p_2, p_3)$ and the equilibrium price vector $p^* = (p_1^*, p_2^*, p_3^*)$. If such a function is also continuously differentiable (and of course is zero only when $p = p^*$), then it is called a Liapunov function.

Certainly if $\dot{V}(p) < 0$, then over time $V(p)$ is decreasing. In that case, over time the distance between arbitrary prices and equilibrium (relative) prices is getting smaller. Our strategy is thus to define $V(p)$ for our system and then to compute $\dot{V}(p)$. If we can infer from our various assumptions that $\dot{V}(p) < 0$, then the equilibrium is *stable*; i.e., prices converge over time to equilibrium relative prices, the equilibrium price ray, under the systemic laws of motion.

It is easy to verify that $V(p)$ defines a Liapunov function. It remains to show that $\dot{V}(p) < 0$ for the system.

$$\dot{V}(p) = (p_1 - p_1^*)\dot{p}_1 + (p_2 - p_2^*)\dot{p}_2 + (p_3 - p_3^*)\dot{p}_3$$
$$= p_1 E_1 - p_1^* \dot{p}_1 + p_2 E_2 - p_2^* \dot{p}_1 + p_3 E_3 - p_3^* \dot{p}_3$$
$$= \sum_{i=1}^{3} p_i E_i - (p_1^*, p_2^*, p_3^*)(\dot{p}_1, \dot{p}_2, \dot{p}_3)^T.$$

Remark: Even for simple analyses, some tedious algebra may intrude.

By Walras's Law, the first term on the right side is identically zero, so

$$-\dot{V}(p) = \begin{bmatrix} \dfrac{a_1}{\bar{x}_1} & \dfrac{a_2}{\bar{x}_2} & \dfrac{a_3}{\bar{x}_3} \end{bmatrix} \begin{bmatrix} \dfrac{a_1}{p_1} & 0 & 0 \\[2ex] 0 & \dfrac{a_2}{p_2} & 0 \\[2ex] 0 & & \dfrac{a_3}{p_3} \end{bmatrix}$$

$$\times \begin{bmatrix} \bar{x}_1\left(1 - \dfrac{1}{a_1}\right) & \bar{x}_2 & \bar{x}_3 \\[2ex] \bar{x}_1 & \bar{x}_2\left(1 - \dfrac{1}{a_2}\right) & \bar{x}_3 \\[2ex] \bar{x}_1 & \bar{x}_2 & \bar{x}_3\left(1 - \dfrac{1}{a_3}\right) \end{bmatrix} \begin{bmatrix} p_1 \\[2ex] p_2 \\[2ex] p_3 \end{bmatrix}.$$

Multiplying the vectors and matrices on the right-hand side yields

$$-\dot{V}(p) = \left[a_1(a_1 - 1) + p_1\bar{x}_1 \frac{a_2^2}{p_2\bar{x}_2} + p_1\bar{x}_1 \frac{a_3^2}{p_3\bar{x}_3} \right]$$

$$+ \left[p_2\bar{x}_2 \frac{a_1^2}{p_1\bar{x}_1} + a_2(a_2 - 1) + p_2\bar{x}_2 \frac{a_3^2}{p_3\bar{x}_3} \right]$$

$$+ \left[p_3\bar{x}_3 \frac{a_1^2}{p_1\bar{x}_1} + p_3\bar{x}_3 \frac{a_2^2}{p_2\bar{x}_2} + a_3(a_3 - 1) \right].$$

The problem is now to show that the right-hand side of this equation is strictly positive. This expression is complicated. We can simplify it using the following argument.

Suppose $p^* = u^* = (1, 1, 1)$. Define $h_i(p) = h_i(p_1, p_2, p_3) = p_1^* E_i(p_1^* p_1,$

$p_2^* p_2, p_3^* p_3)$. By the definition of equilibrium, since $E_i(p^*) = 0$, $h_i(u^*) = 0$. Furthermore, $\Sigma u_i^* h_i(p) > 0$ for $p \neq \lambda u^*$ if and only if $\Sigma p_i^* E_i(p) = \Sigma p_i^* p_i > 0$ for $p \neq \lambda p^*$. Consequently, there is no loss in generality in the stability analysis if we assume $p^* = (1, 1, 1)$. Because $p_i^* = ka_i/\bar{x}_i$, this observation allows considerable simplification. It permits us to set $a_i = k\bar{x}_i$.

Hence

$$-\dot{V}(p) = \left[a_1(a_1 - 1) + \frac{p_1}{p_2} a_1 a_2 + \frac{p_1}{p_3} (a_1 a_3) \right]$$

$$+ \left[\frac{p_2}{p_1} a_1 a_2 + a_2(a_2 - 1) + \frac{p_2}{p_3} a_2 a_3 \right]$$

$$+ \left[\frac{p_3}{p_1} a_3 a_1 + \frac{p_3}{p_2} a_3 a_3 + a_3(a_3 - 1) \right].$$

Because $a_1 + a_2 + a_3 = 1$, further algebra yields

$$1 - \dot{V}(p) = \left(a_1^2 + \frac{p_2}{p_1} a_1 a_2 + \frac{p_3}{p_1} a_3 a_1 \right)$$

$$+ \left(a_2^2 + \frac{p_1}{p_2} a_1 a_2 + \frac{p_3}{p_2} a_3 a_2 \right)$$

$$+ \left(a_3^2 + \frac{p_1}{p_3} a_1 a_3 + \frac{p_2}{p_3} a_2 a_3 \right).$$

Notice now that society's total income is defined by $\mu = \mu^1 + \mu^2 + \mu^3$ where $\mu^i = \Sigma_{k=1}^3 p_k \bar{x}_{ik}$. Thus since $a_i = k\bar{x}_i$,

$$a_1 p_1 + a_2 p_2 + a_3 p_3 = k(p_1 \bar{x}_1 + p_2 \bar{x}_2 + p_3 \bar{x}_3) = k\mu.$$

Multiplying this equation successively by a_1/p_1, by a_2/p_2, and by a_3/p_3 yields

$$a_1^2 + a_2 a_1 \frac{p_2}{p_1} + a_3 a_1 \frac{p_3}{p_1} = \frac{a_1}{p_1} \mu k,$$

$$a_2^2 + a_1 a_2 \frac{p_1}{p_2} + a_3 a_2 \frac{p_3}{p_2} = \frac{a_2}{p_2} \mu k,$$

$$a_3^2 + a_2 a_3 \frac{p_1}{p_3} + a_2 a_3 \frac{p_2}{p_3} = \frac{a_3}{p_3} \mu k,$$

which are precisely the parenthetical expressions found in the preceding equation for $1 - \dot{V}(p)$.

Thus

$$1 - \dot{V}(p) = \mu k \left(\frac{a_1}{p_1} + \frac{a_2}{p_2} + \frac{a_3}{p_3} \right).$$

Examine the right-hand side of this equation. It is easy to see that it has a minimum at $p_i = 1/(a_1 + a_2 + a_3) = 1 = p_i^*$. Thus

$$1 - \dot{V}(p) \geq 1, \qquad \text{with equality at} \quad p = kp^*,$$

and so

$$\dot{V}(p) < 0 \quad \text{. for} \quad p \neq kp^*.$$

Therefore prices converge to the equilibrium price ray.

   After so much algebra, recapitulation is in order. We have seen that, for the simple model (a) an equilibrium exists; (b) up to a scale factor, the equilibrium is unique; and (c) prices converge to the equilibrium price ray. These inferences were drawn about the model, not the world. Put another way, we have constructed a model in which a discussion about a stable set of equilibrium prices is nonvacuous. We now know that it is not outrageous to claim that, at least under one interpretation, a stable vector of equilibrium prices is a permissible analytic category.

Remark: This simple model contains within it many hints for generalization. For example, is it equally nonvacuous to speak of equilibrium in a framework that allows production? To answer this, we must model supply as the choice behavior of producers and not just as the behavior of consumers carrying stocks to market.

Remark: Further, we might ask about equilibrium in the context of time and assets. How, for instance, is a decision to purchase a capital good, which yields utility only in the future, to be integrated into a model in which equilibrium can be inferred? To answer such questions we must extend the model to allow the identification of commodities with dates. Time intrudes.

Remark: The analysis appears extendable. The theory, if such it is, may prove rich enough to answer interesting questions. On the other hand, it may be technically pretty but inapplicable.

CHAPTER 2

Classroom interlude I

Scene: Monday. A small classroom in the applied economics building.

Student A: Now that I've studied your lecture notes and read Debreu's (1959) *Theory of Value*, I'm even less sure that I want to continue to study economics. I suppose I don't much mind studying mathematics and working to understand proofs and theorems, but the kind of world Debreu sets up and analyzes bears no resemblance to the kind of economic system I observe.

Teacher: Now, let's be clear on your objections. Are you saying that Debreu's assumptions are demonstrably false, and thus for you the theory is irrelevant, or are you saying that the conclusions are unbelievable or that the writing style is opaque?

Student A: It goes beyond all of that. It seems to me that the *Theory of Value* makes no positive contribution to our understanding of any economic problem. For example, what possible relevance can there be in knowing that a certain mapping is upper semicontinuous? What economic problem is related to a theorem that states sufficient conditions for upper semicontinuity?

Student B: I'm as disturbed as A is, but let me phrase my problem a bit differently. I agree that Debreu's book is elegant, but what use is elegance in developing economic theory that is useful for explaining the real world?

Teacher: Is there an economic problem that Debreu has tried to solve?

Student A: No, I can't see one.

Student B: Not an economic problem, but rather an economist's problem. I'm aware that mathematical economists, from Walras on through von Neumann and Wald, were concerned to establish the existence of a competitive equilibrium. I'll even agree that Debreu's book presents a solution to the problem. But it seems that this problem is a highly derived one. The issue could have remained unsolved to today and very little that we know about real economic phenomena would be affected at all.

Student C: It is as though the puzzle of general equilibrium theory took on a mathematical life of its own as it became the plaything of some very smart mathematical economists who worked and worked and finally constructed a beautiful theory. But by the time they had finished, the construction was no longer relevant to the economic world.

Student B: You must admit, Teacher, that a theory that provides *n* conditions and axioms for consumers, *m* conditions and axioms for producers, and then says, "If these conditions hold, then a competitive equilibrium exists," is hardly a useful model.

Teacher: I don't want to belittle your concerns, but I am confused by the word "useful." Could you give me an example of a useful model?

Student A: Let's take a simple example. I want to pose the following problem: Let a country change its trade policy to allow the importation of beef where previously it had prohibited beef imports. What will happen to the price of beef in the importer country? I would use a supply–demand model for the beef market and argue that imports increase the supply, thus increasing beef purchases and lowering beef prices.

Teacher: Let's look a bit more closely at your simple model. Not only is it far from simple, but I shall contend that an understanding of Debreu's model is necessary to draw conclusions from your model. You begin by assuming given supply and demand curves for beef. Let's make things even simpler – let's assume the domestic supply of beef is perfectly inelastic. What are you assuming when you draw your demand curve for beef?

Student A: That demand curves are downward sloping.

Student C: A demand curve can be drawn under assumptions of fixed preferences, given income, and given prices of all other goods.

Teacher: Good. Now you are really making various assumptions about the behavior of consumers, are you not? You assume tastes are given, for instance. (Incidentally, we really need to say something about the income effect on the *suppliers* of beef. But I'll ignore this complication just as you have.) You further want, as A noted, the *market* demand curve to slope downward. When does this occur?

Student A: Whenever the good in question is *not* a Giffen good. Or, more specifically, whenever the commodity is one such that the substitution effect is not overwhelmed by a negative income effect.

Student B: In other words, the demand curve will slope downward whenever the indifference curves and budget constraints are regular enough that the solution of the consumer's optimization problem is well defined.

Teacher: And what are those conditions on individual indifference curves?

Student C: They must be continuous, convex, nonintersecting, etcetera.

Student B: In other words, they must satisfy Debreu's axioms for consumer behavior, right?

Student A: I'll grant the point, but I'm not going to grant that I didn't understand demand curves or indifference curves before I read Debreu.

Teacher: I think you're being a bit stubborn. Further, you may even be

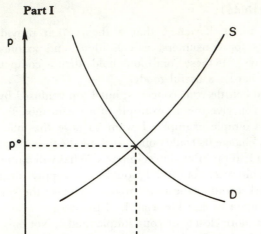

Figure 2.1

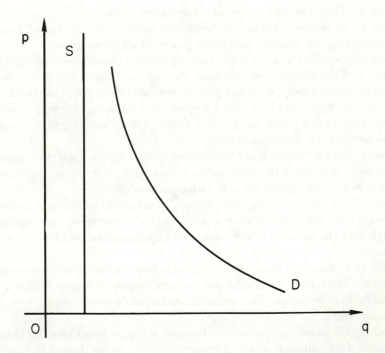

Figure 2.2

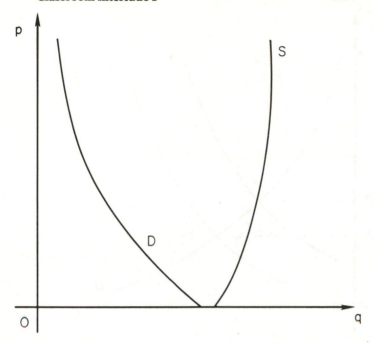

Figure 2.3

wrong, in the sense that demand curves are restricted by the optimization
theory, but I'll pass over your remark for today in order to go on a bit with
the beef market. You now have an inelastic supply curve and a continuous
downward-sloping demand curve. What do you argue next?

Student A: I argue that an initial market equilibrium exists, as in Figure
2.1, at price p^0.

Teacher: How do you rule out the situations depicted in Figures 2.2 and
2.3?

Student A: Figure 2.2 could not occur because I assumed that the demand
curve is continuous and downward sloping *for all p*, so that the *D* curve
gets closer and closer to the vertical axis as *p* gets large.

Teacher: Is it possible that a consumer might have to pay an infinite price
for a small amount of beef? Is there some consumer for whom beef is so
wonderful that the maximum amount he is willing to pay is infinite?

Student A: Not infinite, but perhaps a very large number. The point is that
you can't position a vertical supply curve between the vertical axis and the
demand curve without intersecting the demand curve at some finite
(perhaps large) price.

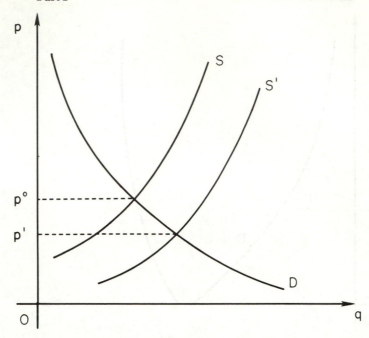

Figure 2.4

Teacher: All right, so far, but what about Figure 2.3?

Student A: I agree that this presents a problem. The way Figure 2.3 is drawn, beef is a free good, since it is always in excess supply. I will thus set the equilibrium price of such goods at zero.

Student C: But then an increase in supply might not induce a fall in the price of beef.

Student A: Correct. I suppose I have to assume, for my argument, that as the price falls, the amount of beef that people wish to purchase increases.

Teacher: What assumption on indifference curves gives you that result?

Student A: I suppose I must say Debreu's nonsatiation axiom.

Teacher: Correct. And now we can agree that Figure 2.1 models the problem, at least in the sense that, for price $p^0 > 0$, there is no discrepancy between the supply of beef and the amount of beef individuals wish to purchase. So proceed, A, to your argument about imports.

Student A: We model the increase in beef imports by a rightward shift in the supply curve to S'. Under our assumptions, it must be the case that the new equilibrium price is p', where p' is less that p^0, as in Figure 2.4.

Teacher: Are you sure that p' is the new equilibrium price?

Student A: Yes.

Teacher: Recall that you defined the demand curve under conditions of given tastes, given income, *and given other prices*. Are you still certain?

Student C: I think I see what you are saying. As the supply of beef changes, there will be a change in the price of beef, but there will also be a change in the price of pork, at least if there is a nonzero cross elasticity of demand. In that case, it must be true that the demand curve for beef shifts somewhere, which may negate the claim that p' is the new equilibrium price.

Student A: But I'm concerned only with the beef market. I'll invoke a *ceteris paribus* assumption to hold other prices constant, so they can't change.

Teacher: But then your model could be considered abstract and unrealistic. If you know that a change in beef supplies will change the demand for beef through market interdependencies, but you abstract from such effects in your model, aren't you open to the charge that your model is simply an elegant and precious abstraction of little explanatory power?

Student B: That's going a bit too far. Isn't A really saying that the influence of other markets is neglible?

Teacher: What if we were talking about the market for oil? Surely an increase in oil import quotas would affect the demand for oil through changes in the price of coal, electricity, and natural gas?

Student C: But not immediately. I think that A had better argue that his model is a short-run model, the short run here defined as a time period sufficiently short that the demand for beef is unaffected by changes in the price of pork, say.

Student B: But it is a period sufficiently long for the market to make the increased supply of beef available for purchase by consumers.

Teacher: I think your position can be caricatured too easily: "If the market interrelationships are sufficiently small, they may be ignored in the theory." If that is so, you have said no more than "if they are ignorable, ignore them." Your theory thus depends on the empirical magnitude of certain interrelationships. Yet your theory was expressly designed to provide us with a *qualitative* prediction about the effect on domestic beef prices of an increase in beef imports. You are now saying that in the real world no such prediction could be made and that your model is mute on any qualitative prediction.

Student A: I will admit I have a problem. And I suppose that you will say that the model presented in Debreu's *Theory of Value* solves my problem better than my own little model.

Teacher: Not exactly. The difficulty is that your model ignores known interrelationships.

Student C: Known?

Teacher: Interrelationships that cannot be ruled out a priori. Consequently

I want to ask under what conditions we can infer *your* conclusion that the price of beef will fall.

Student A: I thought you were working against me, but now you say you want to salvage my conclusion.

Teacher: I never said we weren't on the same side. General equilibrium analysis is well designed to frame questions like yours. As we saw with your model, there was an indeterminateness that appeared as you rushed to your conclusion. General equilibrium thinking, applied to your problem, suggests asking under what sorts of market interrelationships it would be true that an increase in supply of good *x* would lead, after all markets have adjusted, to an ultimate fall in the price of good *x*.

To answer this question, we need to know whether an equilibrium exists and, if it exists, whether it will continue to exist after the system of markets is "shocked" by a simple change in a parameter. That is, we need to know whether the system is stable, so that an increase in supply of good *x* will not lead to a price change for goods *y* and *z*, leading in turn to a demand change for good *x* that lowers the price of good *x* even more than it would have dropped were the markets for *y* and *z* not present. We need to be sure, in other words, that the market system is so constructed that a slight perturbation will not send some prices flying off to infinity while other prices go to zero.

Now it happens that mathematical economists do know some conditions – not many, but some – under which this messy situation *won't* occur. Recall that two goods are gross substitutes if an increase in the price of one good leads to an increase in demand for the other good. If *all* goods are gross substitutes, perturbations will die out fairly quickly and will not transmit disturbances throughout the system in an amplified fashion. Thus for your problem, if we increase the supply of beef, the price of beef will indeed fall, even if we consider the related pork, veal, lamb, chicken, and turkey markets.

But in a subtle way general equilibrium analysis does even more. It makes us aware of the conditions that must be true if we are to draw even the simplest of conclusions.

Student A: I appreciate your salvaging my argument. I can even understand a bit better how general equilibrium theory works behind the scenes as it were. But isn't all this simply common sense? Isn't my argument for ignoring cross effects among markets in practice equivalent to your telling me that the cross effects I chose to ignore are theoretically ignorable?

Scene: Wednesday. Same place.

Student B: I'd like to return to A's point about common sense. On Monday you seemed to suggest that one could not do economics successfully without a working knowledge of general equilibrium theory. But your use of general equilibrium theory simply reinforced the simple set of propositions with which we were comfortable. So I return to our initial query: Is it necessary for us to understand general equilibrium analysis to do economics?

Student C: For myself, I want to know whether we should spend much time on the various proofs in Debreu.

Student A: We're all apprentice economists, trying to become competent applied economists. Must we become expert mathematical theorists as well?

Teacher: Of course not. I am primarily interested that you become intelligent consumers of mathematical economic theory, especially general equilibrium analysis. So let's return to A's point about common sense. Can anyone sharpen the question a bit?

Student A: Let me try. It seems that most applied economists work with a set of partial equilibrium models, together with a batch of econometric skills to test the conclusions that their models generate. This is how most of us will earn our living. Last class you argued that our simple models worked *because* of some high-powered theory that lay behind our simple models. I'll grant that it's comforting to be told that my simple models work because *your* complicated theories work. Yet we're trained to work with our simple models, and their logical or formal justification, based on general equilibrium analysis, seems irrelevant.

A child learns to speak, to use the English language, in a wonderfully creative and imaginative way long before he is aware of gerunds, the subjunctive and the like.

Student B: With all apologies, sir, it seems as though general equilibrium theorists might as well as be locked up, away, out of sight, and left to indulge themselves in their proofs. Their work ultimately does no more than allow us working economists to feel easier (if we care to) about doing the work we do best.

Student A: I'm sorry if we seem to be ganging up on you, but you seem to be avoiding our basic question.

Teacher: Which was what?

Student A: Does a full understanding of general equilibrium theory ever violate the commonsense notions of our simple models?

Teacher: You've sharpened your question nicely. Let me begin by asking you a question: Will the world ever run out of oil?

Students A, B and C: (in chorus) No.

Teacher: Do you mean that sixty million Americans who watch television news are wrong to fear this? Are the environmentalists of "spaceship Earth" all stupid?

Student A: They're not stupid, just economically uneducated.

Student B: Just consider a simple supply and demand model. For a given supply curve, as demand increases, price rises. Rising price is a mechanism to ration demand, so the last oil will be very expensive. At a billion American dollars a gallon, we'll walk instead of riding in cars. At that price, it's probably cheap to raise and train grasshoppers to pull carriages from the suburbs to the city.

Student B: But that's a silly question coming from a general equilibrium theorist anyway. You, if anyone, should know that the price system works to clear markets and that the resulting competitive equilibrium is Pareto efficient.

Teacher: So you are saying that the depletion of oil stocks will be efficient over the time it takes to pump out the oil.

Student C: Yes, at least to the degree that we allow the oil industry to be competitive and don't allow governments to regulate it into oblivion.

Teacher: Let's leave regulation questions aside.

Student A: Are you satisfied with our answers? Are you convinced?

Teacher: No, not at all.

Student A: But all economists agree with what we've said.

Teacher: Let's examine exactly what you *have* said. You argued that the world oil industry is competitive, the price of oil at any time is the competitive equilibrium price, and thus the rate of depletion of oil stocks at any time is Pareto efficient.

Student C: Don't caricature our statements so baldly. Certainly the oil companies have acted in concert; their history is a history of monopoly power. I, for one, took your question more generally to be, "Is it necessary that the world run out of oil?" Many environmentalists say yes, because there is a finite stock and a constant increase in growth of demand outstripping new discoveries. They argue that there is no mechanism that will "save" oil reserves. We as economists reply that the price mechanism will do the job. And these questions are apart from the issue of monopoly pricing.

Teacher: Why do you have such confidence that the price mechanism will *efficiently* allocate the increasingly scarce oil reserves?

Student C: Because all equilibrium prices are efficient.

Teacher: Which particular price are you talking about?

Student C: The price of oil.

Teacher: Which oil?

Student C: Who cares? Perhaps Arabian light crude f.o.b. Ras Tanura.

Teacher: On January 17, 1993?

Student C: No, today.

Teacher: So a commodity is given by a position in time and space, and there is a market for each such commodity.

Student A: Well, of course, there must be if we're talking of market prices.
Teacher: But I asked about the efficiency of oil allocation over time.
Comparing the price system and, say, government allocation by fiat,
you argued that the price system would be more efficient over time. Specifically you argued that the price system would allocate oil to competing
uses in an intertemporally efficient manner. Intuitively, your price system
guarantees that we are not pumping out more today than we should
relative to tomorrow.
Student B: Yes, that's what we're saying. The collection of prices – today's,
tomorrow's, next year's – forms an intertemporal price system. If those
prices are competitive equilibrium prices, then the quantities of dated oil
are being allocated in an efficient manner over time.
Teacher: How do you know there are such prices as you describe? Does
there even exist an intertemporal competitive equilibrium set of prices?
Student A: All right, I suppose that just as in our last class, we should
appeal to general equilibrium theory. Using Debreu's definition of a
commodity as a spatial–temporal object, tomorrow's oil is simply oil_{t+1}
and our equilibrium prices will yield relative prices for oil_t/oil_{t+1} for all
choices of t. Implicitly we've defined the one-period "oil rate of interest."
To show that such equilibrium prices exist, we have simply to apply
general equilibrium theory, where we must interpret oil_t and oil_{t+1} as
different commodities.
Student C: Does this imply, A, that since we're forced to appeal to general
equilibrium theory, the teacher's point is established? Are we just
repeating the previous discussion when our true analysis remained true,
and was sharpened, by appeal to general equilibrium theory? I thought
that the teacher was saying something quite different today, namely that
our commonsense notion was in fact misleading.
Teacher: Indeed, that is so.
Student A: Are you now saying that Debreu is wrong?
Teacher: No, I'm saying you don't understand Debreu.
Student B: But we've just applied Debreu's model intertemporally using
Debreu's suggestion for treatment of dated commodities.
Teacher: Be careful. Over what objects are consumer preferences and firm
productions defined?
Student B: Commodities.
Teacher: This means that consumers must have coherent preferences
among all intertemporal consumptions, and firms must have the ability to
rank, by profitability, alternative intertemporal production plans.
Student A: I agree we've introduced something new here. Firms certainly
can't value a gallon of 1993 oil with certainty.
Student B: They don't have to do so. All they need is to have a set of

current prices and a set of expected prices, one for each commodity at each date. A competitive equilibrium is, in this context, simply a set of prices for each commodity at every date such that, were all agents to optimize given those prices and expected prices, the resulting consumption and production plans would mesh in every period.

Student C: Of course future "shocks" could lead to revisions of plans.

Teacher: Very good, very good indeed. Now, how does there come to exist an actual, as opposed to an expected, price for a commodity, like 1993 oil, whose market time has not yet come? Aren't prices determined in markets?

Student C: Just as in the extension of consumer choice, we extend the concept of the market to cover future goods.

Teacher: And what is a market for a future good?

Student C: A futures market. I suppose that in this market individuals buy and sell, today, contracts for forward or future delivery of the commodity in question. The price of oil_{t+1} is thus the spot price for a one-period futures contract.

Teacher: It appears then that you need a complete array of futures markets, a market for each commodity at every future date, to ensure merely the existence of an intertemporal competitive equilibrium.

Student A: That's correct.

Teacher: Thus the price system allocates resources like oil efficiently over time when there is a complete set of futures markets for those resources.

Student B: There's something wrong here. There is no market, to my knowledge, for 1993 oil.

Teacher: No market, so no guarantee of an intertemporal equilibrium and the associated intertemporal efficient allocation. It seems that the price system might not work to allocate depletable resources efficiently.

Student C: Wait a moment. Debreu's theorem provided sufficient conditions for an equilibrium to exist, not necessary conditions. An intertemporal competitive equilibrium might exist even without a complete array of futures markets.

Teacher: How?

Student A: Long-term contracts, insurance markets, storage facilities, inventories, and so on might all mitigate the nonexistence of markets and induce equilibrating behaviors. Further, capital markets for oil-using facilities are continually revaluing the worth of those facilities and contracts.

Teacher: You see, don't you, the perspective that emerges. The strength of general equilibrium theory is to show economists what they must be assuming when they assert, for example, that the price system allocates exhaustible resources over time in an efficient manner (Hahn 1973, p. 14).

Student B: Are you saying that the price system doesn't allocate resources in an efficient manner over time?

Teacher: No, not exactly. Rather I am saying we have little support in economic theory for *any* general proposition on the issue. We should not be so quick to answer yea or nay on such an ill-posed question. That is, the central theory of prices and allocations, general equilibrium theory, doesn't force your desired conclusion. Other theories are even less robust. Our knowledge is insecure. And if we don't know, perhaps we should be, if not quiet, then quieter.

Scene: Friday. Same place.

Student A: We now have two different kinds of reasons to study general equilibrium theory. First, you argued that it was a *positive* theory, helping us to make sense out of complicated problems. Second, you suggested that it was *negative*, of some value in keeping us from claiming too much for standard economic models.

Student B: I'm bothered by what appears to be an implication of this second use of general equilibrium theory. It's almost as if Teacher is saying that the Debreu model defines the scope of economics in some fundamental way.

Teacher: That is precisely what I'm saying.

Student B: But what is the fundamental problem that the theory is supposed to address? Is it an economic problem or a methodological problem?

Student C: Let me put B's question another way. You have suggested that general equilibrium theory can aid us in both positive and negative ways in our study of economics. But I also hear an implicit message that general equilibrium theory is coextensive with economics. And this kind of claim makes me nervous.

Teacher: "There is by now a long and fairly imposing line of economists from Adam Smith to the present who have sought to show that a decentralized economy motivated by self-interest and guided by price signals would be compatible with a coherent disposition of economic resources that could be regarded, in a well-defined sense, as superior to a large class of possible alternative dispositions. Moreover, the price signals would operate in a way to establish this degree of coherence. It is important to understand how surprising this claim must be to anyone not exposed to this tradition. The immediate 'common sense' answer to the question 'What will an economy motivated by individual greed and controlled by a very large number of different agents look like?' is probably: There will be chaos. That quite a different answer has long been claimed true and has indeed permeated the economic thinking of a large number of people who are in no way economists is itself sufficient grounds for investigating it seriously" (Arrow and Hahn 1971, pp. vi–vii).

Student A: You've raised an irrelevant point. None of us has claimed that the price system is ineffectual, or inferior to central planning. None of us is even much interested in such abstruse issues.

Student B: Perhaps we're at cross purposes. You, Teacher, have been trying to show us how we, in our applied work, can be made better off by studying general equilibrium theory. We, on the other hand, believe that, although such study may occasionally pay a practical dividend, on balance our time is better spent on more concrete matters.

So let us turn the tables on you. I assume that you, yourself, don't do general equilibrium theory for the sole purpose of keeping your students from committing minor errors in their applied work. How is your life as an economist shaped by your calling yourself a general equilibrium theorist?

Teacher: I think that my credo, if I had to articulate one, would be "Let us not speak nonsense." As you may have noticed, economists are a quarrelsome lot, given to frequent, and public, disagreements over practical issues. Let me ask you a question: How do you know something? More to the point, when is your knowledge about some economic problem secure?

Student B: Epistemology has always bored me. I know what I've learned, and I see whether the facts support what I've learned.

Teacher: You're too glib. I believe that economic knowledge is associated with models, or rather sequences of models, whose assumptions are linked with assumptions and conclusions of other models. We have confidence in our knowledge when the sequence of models has conclusions that are neither falsified by empirical tests nor logically inconsistent with the conclusions of other accepted model sequences. I believe, in other words, that the growth of economic knowledge occurs, as the philosopher Imre Lakatos suggested, within the framework of scientific research programs.

Student A: But where do these sequences of models come from? What generates them?

Teacher: In general, a scientific research program is organized around a group of propositions accepted as true and irrefutable by all adherents to the program. Lakatos called these propositions the *hard core* of the program. There are various derived propositions that the hard core generates. For example, associated with the hard core of a research program are rules that generate models based on the propositions of the hard core. Propositions, or conclusions, that emerge from the models, are thus linked to the hard core.

In economics, I believe that general equilibrium theory constitutes the hard core of the most progressive research program that economists have today. I call this the neo-Walrasian Research Program. The sequence of models associated with general equilibrium analysis (which in Lakatos's language should not be called a theory) has had immense success in explaining (that is, making coherent) empirical regularities and extending economists' thinking into new areas. In other words, the neo-Walrasian program is a progressive one.

Student C: This is too abstract. Can you give us an example of what you mean?

Teacher: Of course. Until fairly recently, most questions about demographic issues (fertility, marriage, divorce, birth spacing, etcetera) were nonissues for economists. The new-home-economics literature over the past two decades has, I think you'll agree, increased our understanding, our knowledge, of these issues. How did this come about?

Student B: A new theory was created.

Teacher: Yes, but it was predictable in some sense; at least in retrospect its creation should not be surprising. The models that are used in the new home economics are variants of preexisting models. Their assumptions, like utility maximization and household production functions, say, are linked to a more basic set of propositions in general equilibrium theory. Specifically, I would argue that if there is something called the neo-Walrasian research program, the models of the new home economics are firmly in this program, the hard core of which – the organizing center – is closely connected to general equilibrium theory.

Student A: I think that you claim too much. You said that the hard core contains irrefutable propositions. You then suggested that, speaking loosely, the Debreu model is associated with the hard core. But Debreu's assumption of, say, profit maximization may not be true, in the sense that most entrepreneurs don't actually try to maximize profit.

Teacher: Careful. "Accepted as true and irrefutable by adherents of the program" does not mean logically or empirically unfalsifiable. Profit maximization is simply a hypothesis that is not up for debate in the neo-Walrasian program. Its status for researchers is that of a nonagenda item, and as a neo-Walrasian that is all I am claiming for it. Further, in my view it becomes clear *why* it *should be* a nonagenda item: As a central feature of the general equilibrium model, it should not be questioned as long as the second-order models derived from the hard core continue (1) to explain regularities, (2) to generate new predictions that are corroborated, and (3) to link up with other models in the program.

Apropos this last property, ask yourself whether you are more or less likely to discard the new home economics, *for a given degree of empirical corrobation*, if it has links to traditional capital theory via the concept of human capital.

Student C: I'm a bit disturbed at the path our discussion has taken. Instead of an extended set of reasons why general equilibrium theory is, or may be, of value to economists, we've now been led to a position in which disapproval of Debreu's book is disapproval of science, or progress, or knowledge. This makes me uneasy.

Student A: Surely there are more steps in your argument, Teacher. I've not read much philosophy of science, nor have I heard of Imre Lakatos, yet it seems that I should be allowed to make a case for or against general equilibrium theory.

Student B: I quite agree. Are there no criteria we can agree about, a grading system of some kind, that would permit us to give the theory an A, say, for elegance, a B— for usefulness, and so on?

Teacher: The issues you are raising are important ones, but they stand somewhat apart from general equilibrium analysis itself. You are facing up to the very serious issues involved in the appraisal of economic theories or of areas of economics. Such concerns are always appropriate, and of course they are appropriate in discussions of general equilibrium analysis. Perhaps we will have time later in the term to discuss these issues more fully.

CHAPTER 3

Appraisal

There are several reasons why an economist might be interested in the subject of appraisal. First, one may be methodologically inclined and self-conscious about the status of the theories and modes of argument that sustain the intellectual life of the professional economist. The economist-methodologist often has a serious interest in the writings of philosophers of science, who are professionally involved with the questions that method-ologists so frequently address. Philosophers of science have developed theories about the structure of knowledge, and the growth of knowledge, to illuminate the path of science. The economic methodologist will be familiar with the kinds of prisms that philosophers employ to analyze the light of the scientific enterprise. The methodologist understands that appraisal measures the enterprise of economics, and the products of that enterprise, on the benchmarks drawn by the philosophers of science.

Historians of economic thought also produce appraisals. Constructing a historical narrative requires choice. The historian leaves "irrelevant" material out of the story; that judgment is an act of appraisal. On the basis of some criterion either implicit or explicit, what is ignored is ignorable. The food that Malthus ate, the clothes that Keynes wore, play no role in a discussion of the theory of effective demand. That the theory of effective demand itself is worth examining reflects another choice. How was that judgment made? Why did the historian accept it? As any economist recognizes, the act of choice entails not only a chooser, but also a structure of preferences on the set of objects that can be chosen.

Beyond the selection, the historian appraises the products of the economist. "How good was Malthus's theory of effective demand?" is a question worth asking in any study of Malthus's ideas; no matter how neutral the narrative, evaluation will intrude. To tell the story of effective demand from Malthus to Keynes requires some attention to the theory itself, some evaluation or appraisal. Imagine a narrative describing how Ricardo's supply theory superseded Malthus's theory of effective demand. Will not the narrative naturally contain the author's judgment about whether the change was good for economics?

The historian's craft requires sensitivity to what makes a theory good, bad or replaceable, and many historians of economic thought have read the writings of philosophers of science, such as Karl Popper, Thomas Kuhn, and Imre Lakatos. Even if the historians do not read the philosophy journals, their interest in the subject shows us that the dividing line between history of science and philosophy of science is often blurred.

Economists who create, develop, and apply new theories are also concerned with the growth of economic knowledge. For them what philosophers of science have to say is generally of less moment than what other practitioners say and do. They nevertheless are guided by some understanding like "Of course economics is (isn't!?) a science." Their ideas may have come from an introductory chapter of an economics text in which the author sought to cloak the economics enterprise in the protective mantle of scientific respectability. Alternatively, the economist may have been influenced by one of those working economists who, in a reflective moment, sought the wellsprings of the enterprise. John Stuart Mill, John Neville Keynes, Gunnar Myrdal, Milton Friedman, Joan Robinson, and many others have written about methodology, including what economic reasoning consists of, how arguments are constructed (and how to tell a good one from a bad one), what makes a theory useful, and how models may be judged.

Even without the guidance of distinguished economists, working economists learn about appropriate behavior from their own education, conversations with colleagues, and reading books and journals. The economist, like any other professional, is socialized to the customs of the profession and adopts its habits more or less critically. On matters of appraisal, economists seem to accept the idea that theories may be evaluated, and ultimately accepted or rejected. They seem to accept a framework for appraising their own, and their colleagues', creations in which logical coherence matters, in which prediction and testing matters, and in which the better will yield to the best in the marketplace of ideas. In historical time, such a mindset is new. The idea that testing a theory is a worthwhile endeavor did not appeal to the ancient Greek philosophers; that tests are related to prediction is an idea economists accepted only within the last hundred years, following its success in the natural sciences. John Maynard Keynes wrote, in the last paragraph of his *General Theory*, that "madmen in authority" are frequently the slaves of some "defunct economist." In matters of appraisal, economists are often the slaves of some defunct philosopher of science.

It thus appears that no matter what one's route to the appraisal issue, one must accept that philosophers of science are important; the remainder of this chapter will consider some of their views.

Axel Leijonhufvud once recounted the following story:

When I was a child, the itinerant knife-grinder was still a common figure in Sweden. He would show up at the kitchen door and ask: "Want to have any knives sharpened?" Most often he was told: "No thank you, we're all right." They tended to be persistent characters. Another knock: "Bet your knives are in bad shape. I know they are. People shouldn't be allowed to use knives like that. ..." And you would say: "We are busy today. Please go away." But soon he knocks again and there he is, demonstrating: "Look, with my knives you can split hairs!" Some farmers, it was said, would set their dogs on people like that. Some philosophers of science may of course feel that, without the grindstone always in evidence, charges of vagrancy without visible means of support are inevitable [Leijonhufvud 1976, p. 66].

This chapter will sketch a miniature grindstone; it is not possible to present a century's worth of philosophical cut and thrust in a half-dozen pages. The reader should consult the original works of the various individuals and also appropriate secondary sources. (The first fifty-two pages of Mark Blaug's [1980] *The Methodology of Economics* provide an excellent introduction to these issues.)

Philosophers of science since Karl Popper have, in varying degrees, accepted a variant of positivism that Lakatos has called falsificationism. This position holds first that the origination of a theory or hypothesis is a creative act, to be studied more by the psychologist than by the philosopher. Yet a theory, once created, has certain implications. A theory makes predictions about natural phenomena. Such predictions are testable in a specific fashion; real phenomena are potential falsifiers of the predictions of the theory. In older versions of the positivist view, theories were to be corroborated. Popper (1959) showed how this notion foundered on the kind of problem that Hume identified so long ago, namely, that the truth of a proposition could not be established by the accumulation of specific instances. Popper argued that, although the truth of a hypothesis could not be demonstrated, its falsity could be established. A theory of the form "if *A*, then *B*" cannot be tested by counting instances of *B*'s that are also *A*'s; one can never be sure that, tomorrow, an *A* that is not a *B* will not turn up. Instead, Popper argued that scientific progress grew not from corroborations but from falsifications. Good theories are potentially falsifiable theories.

The theory "if *A*, then *B*" is falsified by the identification, or production, of a single *A* that is not also a *B*. The theory cannot be confirmed, but it might be falsified. Popper thus changed the rules for the analysis of scientific thought by replacing the logic of confirmation with the logic of falsification. A good theory was to be one that had many potential falsifiers. The task of the scientist, for Popper, was to proffer bold hypotheses, to formulate strong theories. This means that good theories will claim much, and rule out much. *Create bold hypotheses and weed them out ruthlessly* describes the Popperian scientist's agenda.

Popper's view is not without its own difficulties. Suppose that a theory, T, is of the form "given X, Y, Z,..., if A, then B." The X, Y, and Z can be thought of as auxiliary hypotheses related to, but secondary to, the theory T itself. A falsifying instance may not be a falsifier of T; it might indicate that X could not be assumed in the actual case (i.e., not-X was true). Given a falsifier "A and not-B," should the scientist give up T or should he keep T and search for a falsifier "X and A and not-B"? Is the main hypothesis to be rejected, or is some auxiliary hypothesis to be abandoned? In practice, of course, all theories are tested jointly with other theories. If the economic data falsify a prediction of a Keynesian macromodel, is one to reject (a) Keynesian economics, (b) a specific consumption function, (c) something else, or (d) nothing at all? Rejecting hypotheses is no simple matter. Instructing the scientist to seek such falsifications may not be very helpful.

Popper was fully aware of these issues and wrote about them extensively (Popper, 1959, 1972). His position was that deviations from the framework of falsification require explanation. Those who would maintain theories in the face of falsifying instances need to justify their actions. The burden of proof is on those who argue that science can progress in cases where refutation does not lead to hypothesis repudiation. For Popper, the growth of knowledge is associated with a process of "conjectures and refutations." Popper drew on the history of science for examples in which one theory was superseded by another and in which historians inferred a growth in knowledge. Popper, a philosopher, used the history of science to provide case studies to corroborate, falsify, and refine his theory of the growth of knowledge. For example, he told the story of Einstein's relativity theory as a series of conjectures and refutations; the history of quantum mechanics was also presented in that fashion.

Thomas Kuhn's *The Structure of Scientific Revolutions* appeared in 1962. It challenged Popper's apparent view that science did progress in the conjectures–refutations sequence. For Kuhn, a historian of science, progress is associated with revolutionary episodes in which a *paradigm* changes. That is, at each period in the history of a scientific discipline, there is a ruling view about the subject that is embodied in terms, conventions, methods, theories, and assumptions. *Normal science*, in Kuhn's view, develops the implications of the ruling paradigm; normal science uses the paradigm to solve problems or puzzles. In periods of normal science, corroboration, not falsification, is customary.

There are occasions when a paradigm is challenged by a revolutionary alternative. A crucial experiment may falsify one of two well-defined alternative theories. After a period of revolutionary ferment, one of the paradigms emerges triumphant: It may have a falsified "opponent," or it may simply have been able to predict anomalies that its predecessor chose to ignore. A falsified theory, however, does not create a revolution. A scientific revolution is a paradigm change. There are complicated shifts in both scientific thought and practice. Appraising a scientific theory, for Kuhn, thus involves more than an examination of the tests that it has survived. One must consider the place of a theory within the ruling paradigm, how the theory has been corroborated, what problems it can solve, and what anomalous instances remain to confound it. Appraisal is thus a historical task.

Kuhn had described scientific progress, but did this description mean that all good science could be so described? Must progress be defined as the alternating periods of normal science and revolutionary paradigm change? In the language of economics, was Kuhn to be read positively or normatively? Was he describing or prescribing?

Kuhn had called attention to some problems with the austere Popperian view of science. Scientists seemed to favor Kuhn, and they began using the words "paradigm" and "revolution" in their critical writings. Most scientists, while they would like to identify with the rational Popperian, in fact spend little time trying to overthrow theories. Their work involves problem solving, using and confirming theories. They do not wake up each morning saying, "Today I shall create a revolution." Kuhn's vision more nearly corresponds to their actual behavior, behavior that most agree has led to the growth of scientific knowledge.

Philosophers took Kuhn's argument seriously. In discussions that followed the book's publication in 1962, one philosopher emerged as the leading spokesman for the rationalist position. Imre Lakatos, formerly a close associate of Popper, put forward a view that he called "sophisticated methodological falsificationism" (Lakatos 1970). This theory accepted Popper's claim that the task of the scientist was to seek not corroboration but falsification. Yet Lakatos argued that the unit of analysis could not be the individual scientific theory; he defined a more complex entity, called a *scientific research program* (SRP). The program bore a family resemblance to Kuhn's paradigm.

A Lakatosian scientific research program has several elements. First, it has a *hard core* of propositions that are taken to be irrefutable by all scientists associated with that particular SRP. This is not to say that the hard core is true, only that it is to be *accepted* as true. The hard core thus functions as the set of axioms for a program. Linked to the hard core are two other sets of propositions, which Lakatos called the *positive heuristic* and the *negative heuristic*. The former contains the *metarules* that indicate how the hard core can generate falsifiable theories. The negative heuristic consists of propositions that "immunize" the hard core and protect it from criticism. It prevents attempts, within the particular SRP, to weaken or even evaluate the hard core. The final component of the program is the *protective belt*, which contains theories and auxiliary theories (constructed in accord with the positive heuristic) to be tested.

For Lakatos, one appraises a research program, not a theory in the program's belt. It is legitimate to ask whether a research program is associated with some growth of knowledge. An SRP is said to be *progressive* if successive theories (in the protective belt) represent *progressive problem shifts*. That is, if T is the successor of S, then T represents a progressive problem shift if (1) instances that corroborate S also corroborate T; (2) T has excess content, which is to say that T makes some predictions that S does not; and (3) some of T's excess content is corroborated. A program that is not progressive is said to be *degenerating*. Progress and degeneracy are thus relative terms that structure appraisals of competing research programs. A degenerating problem shift, which is identifiable within a program, calls forth different responses by the appraiser depending on whether there is no alternative program or an alternative program that is progressive.

The Lakatosian vision of scientific research programs provides an account of actual scientific practice. It is a less austere vision than Popper's. It suggests that it may be rational to maintain what appears to be a falsified theory if that "theory" is in fact a hard-core proposition. Even if a theory in the protective belt is falsified, a scientist should not abandon it unless there is some alternative. One does not give up something for nothing. The methodology of scientific research programs (MSRP) has merit. As a theory of good scientific practice, it commends itself by its rationalist virtues. As an account of actual scientific practice, it has both virtues and faults.

Lakatos's MSRP has been criticized, sometimes severely, over the past dozen years. An alternative to the rationalist MSRP position was presented by the philosopher Paul Feyerabend (1975) in his book *Against Method*. This "anarchist" critique of rationalism developed from the history of "good" science, which appears to falsify every theory of scientific progress. For Feyerabend, the successful scientist is well advised to follow the methodological dictum "anything goes." Put another way, there are an infinite number of paths to the growth of knowledge, to scientific success, and any rationalist prescription limits the quest.

As with any theory, MSRP needs to be appraised. Specifically, there should be tests of the assertion that actual progress in science conforms to the notion of a progressive problem shift. One way to test this proposition is to examine case studies of scientific practice. Does the historical record corroborate or falsify Lakatos's view? In the past dozen years there have been numerous attempts to write case studies of scientific developments using MSRP to see whether practice conforms to the MSRP model (Hands 1983). Lakatos's own view of the history of science should be noted here (Lakatos 1978a). He believed that the historian who accepted the MSRP framework needed to provide a rational reconstruction of episodes of scientific growth. The scientist, for the purposes of history, should be portrayed as an exemplar of the scientist, as one who chooses theories and experiments and tests that increase the growth of knowledge in conformity with MSRP. The history should thus be written as a series of rational choices within the MSRP framework; the real history, for Lakatos, should appear in footnotes showing how actual scientific practice did or did not deviate from the rational reconstruction of that practice.

Philosophers of science have defined many issues associated with appraisals of scientific contributions. Despite their professional disagreements, they share certain presuppositions about the growth of knowledge. Focusing on their disagreements, I myself have, at different times in the past, been convinced by each of Popper, Kuhn, Lakatos, and Feyerabend, among others. Indeed I have been convinced, disabused, and reconfirmed on several occasions. As I have grown to look for the views they share, I am left with the following working position on the issue of appraisal, a position that, although otherwise unremarkable, structures this book. Quite simply, I've come to believe in the philosophers' questions but not in their answers. That is, I am confident that any appraisal of general equilibrium analysis must address at least the following questions: Is general equilibrium analysis a theory? Is it associated with a scientific research program? Can the program be described? What is the role of empirical tests, of corroborations or falsifications? In what sense, if any, can there be said to have been progress in general equilibrium analysis? How would the answers to each of the previous questions change were they to be asked of the work in 1920? 1930? 1940? Today?

CHAPTER 4

Classroom interlude II

Setting: Another classroom, with a higher room number. It is a methodology course.

Student α: The students in your applied-economics course have shown us their class notes. Reading them over, I'm not sure that you ever confronted a deeper set of issues that can be broached in a study of the scope and role of general equilibrium analysis.

Student β: I think I can be more specific about those issues. It appears that you did an excellent selling job for the *idea* of general equilibrium. Yet I am less bothered by the idea of general equilibrium analysis than I am disturbed by its association with various mathematical techniques and tools. These issues were recognized, but not fully explored, in an essay by Koopmans.

Teacher: I know the reference. Koopmans (1957, pp. 182–3) said that "the success of a mathematical tool or theory in one field (such as physics) creates no presumption either for or against its usefulness in another field (such as economics). But each transfer of a tool between fields is attended by a risk.... The test of suitability of a tool of reasoning is whether it gives the most logical and economic expression to the basic assumptions appropriate to the field in question, and to the reasoning that establishes their implications.

"...The difficulty in economic dynamics has been that the tools have suggested the assumptions rather than the other way around."

Student α: I'm glad that you are aware of the problem; it is a real one indeed. For me, I certainly don't side with the mathematically illiterate. Those people bemoan any use of sophisticated, or even unsophisticated, mathematics in economics, which, they argue, is a "human" discipline. To the contrary, I believe in using models and in developing accessible and falsifiable chains of reasoning. Thus my quarrel is not with economists who would force economic analysis into particular frameworks with which they are comfortable. I simply don't take their views seriously. My quarrel instead is with economists like you who are technically sophisticated, reasonably free from technical prejudices, and who believe in, practice, and teach competent economic analysis.

Teacher: Just what is your point?

Student α: It's related to Koopmans's warning, but it may be phrased a bit differently. Specifically, I would like to convince you that the growing acceptance of sophisticated mathematical analysis by economists *necessarily* biases economic theorizing. As the mathematical biologist Anatol Rapoport (1980, p. 259) wrote: "Mathematically you can cook up anything. You can imagine any sort of situation and represent it by a mathematical model. The problem becomes that of finding something in the real world to fit the model.

" . . . There was a man who liked to fix things around the house, but the only tools he could use were a screwdriver and a file. When he saw a screw that wasn't tight, he tightened it with his screwdriver. Finally there were no more screws to tighten. But he saw some protruding nails. So he took his file and made grooves in the caps of the nails. Then he took his screwdriver and screwed them in. To paraphrase Marshall McLuhan's famous remark, 'The medium is the message,' the mathematician could well say, 'The tool is the theory.'"

Teacher: How does this differ from what Koopmans said?

Student α: Koopmans argued that economists must be careful about using new tools since they could introduce biases. Rapoport's point, which I agree with, is that all tools, but especially sophisticated mathematical tools, bias economic discourse.

Student β: If I understand him correctly, α is arguing that there is a tendency for the mathematics to lead the economics. For example, in your first meeting of the other class, you stated that the gross substitutability theorem was "discovered" in a chain of reasoning that began with a multimarket exchange problem. You seemed thus to suggest that there existed a prior, and recognizable, economic conundrum that could be studied only by the introduction of formal (i.e., mathematical) rigor into the analytic schema. Once the exchange problem was so embedded, the theorem was discovered. The theorem is then a link in an economic chain of reasoning. You suggested that embedding the preexisting economic problem in a general equilibrium model allowed mathematical tools to be applied, but that the economic problem preceded the mathematical analysis.

Student α: I hope we don't have a "chicken-and-egg" argument developing here. You, Teacher, presented an example to the other class that purported to show that the economics precedes the choice of the tool. We all agree that this is a desirable state of affairs.

Student γ: Speak for yourself. I find this insistence on the priority of economic reasoning deplorable, indeed intellectually stultifying.

Teacher: Are you denying even Koopmans's point that there is a danger in using inappropriate tools?

Student γ: If you are saying that inappropriate tools are inappropriate, I can hardly disagree. No, I'm disturbed instead at your shared suspicion of "sophisticated" mathematical techniques.

Student α: Come now. Surely you can't mean to defend, say, models of consumer behavior that are mere reinterpretations of physical models. You would not advocate spending valuable research time on models of economic behavior based on relativity theory, so that an economy is identified with a spacetime path and the development of that economy over time is interpreted as a growth path on a Riemannian manifold? Surely you would not want to spend time investigating the new biological models of morphogenesis – catastrophe-theory models – to explain how the form of economic structures evolves over time?

Student γ: But I do!

Student β: Tell me, γ, why do you call yourself an economist? I should think you would be more comfortable among applied mathematicians.

Teacher: I too find γ's position puzzling. He seems to be denying the idea of economics as a discipline, or at least he seems to deny that progress occurs within Lakatosian research programs.

Student γ: With all due respect to the late Imre Lakatos, your interpretation of his notion of progress is an oversimplification. Specifically, the idea that progress is identified with progressive research programs denies the fact that at any time there are competing research programs. In economics, suppose we could define the hard core of the neoclassical program. Then the negative heuristic of that program would exclude numerous lines of inquiry. Work on such lines would not represent progress.

Teacher: Is your motto to be "let a thousand research programs bloom"?

Student γ: Yes.

Student α: And these other programs are, to you, economics?

Student γ: Of course. But I am uninterested in labels. In your Lakatosian concern about the negative heuristic of the neoclassical program, you place sociology beyond the pale, and so too physics, information theory, psychology, biology, engineering, and mathematics.

Teacher: I am concerned that you would take as a methodological dictum that the role of an economist is to create revolutions in a Kuhnian sense. Surely you cannot mean to overthrow everything that is known every time you attempt to do economics.

Student β: γ is not saying that. At any rate, I am comfortable with a heuristic for generating new insights, new hypotheses if you will, that allows the use of analogy, which is the wellspring of mathematics.

Student α: What exactly do you mean?

Student β: Doesn't it seem curious that Walras's vision, which is at the heart of neoclassical economics, was based on his interpretation of classical mechanics in physics? Schumpeter wrote of Walras's engineering training and the influence on his thinking of a book on celestial mechanics. Isn't the Walrasian vision itself an attempt to treat economic agents as heavenly bodies, to write down the equations of their positions and motions?

Marshall, with his biological metaphors, was also brought to certain economic insights by his understanding of another field. Irving Fisher has a photograph of a complicated piece of hydraulic machinery as a model in his book on value theory. Keynes's *Treatise on Probability* was not irrelevant to his *General Theory*. Games of chance and strategy were the basis for the von Neumann–Morgenstern work. And don't forget Georgescu–Roegen and thermodynamics.

Student α: But what of the role of mathematics?

Student γ: Quite simply, mathematics is a metaphor machine. I believe that mathematics is a fundamentally human activity. I am convinced by some of Piaget's arguments in *Structuralism* (1971), which suggest that mathematical structure, and the fact that mathematicians are structure analysts, is a reflection of basic structures of the human mind. Put another way, I believe our brains are "hard wired" to do mathematics. You can't doubt that an understanding of the world comes from a mind's structuring the experiences of the world and making them coherent.

The physicist E. P. Wigner once wrote about "The Unreasonable Effectiveness of Mathematics in the Natural Sciences." He noted, "We are in a position similar to a man who was provided with a bunch of keys and who, having to open several doors in succession, always hit on the right key on the first or second trial. He became skeptical of the uniqueness of the coordination between keys and doors" (Wigner 1969, p. 124).

Unlike that man, I am not skeptical. I believe that mathematical structures are the best way to understand real structures because the *idea* of a real structure is meaningful only to the extent that the human brain is so wired that it searches for structures. And mathematics, the analysis of structures, is a creation of the human mind. I am not surprised at the value of mathematics. I am only surprised at resistance to its full use.

Student α: Nicely said, but as a credo, not a prescription. I am getting increasingly nervous about considering these matters without any case materials. Can we challenge γ on a matter of fact, not belief?

Student β: You started this, α. Can you find an example in economics of mathematics generating irrelevant or silly economics?

Student α: Of course. Open any issue of the *Journal of Economic Theory* and find an article about "nonatomic measure spaces of economic agents."

Teacher: Excellent. Now, γ, I offer you three choices: (1) You can defend the proposition that a study of such measure spaces of agents is *mathematically* interesting and *thus* should be explored by economists; (2) you can argue that this theory is rich in falsifiable conclusions; or (3) you can try to convince us that this theory, or class of models, is naturally suggested by the economic context.

Student β: The choices are neither exclusive nor exhaustive, of course, but each seems possible to defend. Which will *you* choose?

Student γ: The third, of course.

Student α: Oh, come now. Show me a nonatomic measure space of economic agents "out there" in the economy.

Student γ: How about any set of agents we call competitors?

Student β: Why not call them competitors, then?

Student γ: Because "perfect competition" is too sloppy a term.

Student α: I think you'd better explain yourself.

Student γ: Basic economic theory contains two related notions of competitive agents. First, they are agents who take price as given; and, second, they are agents who are very numerous. Let me ask you, Teacher, how many agents do you need in a market to have "numerous" competitors. Further, are the two notions of competitive agents consistent, one with the other?

Teacher: As Frank Knight (1921, pp. 78–79) taught us, competition is a *limiting* assumption. In your example, adding up lots of perfectly elastic individual demand curves generates a market demand curve. Demand is "smooth" if one averages over many individual agents.

Student β: How many is "many"?

Teacher: I think γ is about to tell you.

Student γ: Indeed I am. The problem is neither recent nor contrived. Edgeworth, in his *Mathematical Psychics* of 1881, argued that two traders attempting to make themselves better off through trade would stop trading when they had reached any one of a number of redistributions, or allocations, defined as the contract curve. We commemorate this insight in Edgeworth–Bowley box diagrams. If each trader is a competitor *in the sense of a price taker*, then a unique allocation on the contract curve is established. That allocation is the competitive equilibrium with respect to the given price system. Further, since allocations on the contract curve are Pareto efficient, we see immediately that the competitive equilibrium allocation is Pareto efficient. Welfare economics flows from this theorem.

Student β: What does this have to do with "nonatomic measure spaces of economic agents"?

Student γ: A great deal, but you must be patient a bit. You see, Edgeworth also conjectured that, as the number of traders increased, the contract curve would shrink. He argued that "we see that in general for any number short of the *practically infinite* (if such a term be allowed) there is a finite length of contract curve...at any point of which if the system is placed, it cannot by contract or recontract be displaced; that there are *an indefinite number of final settlements*, a quantity continually diminishing as we approach a perfect market" (Edgeworth 1881, pp. 38–9).

The result of this argument was that, *if* there were a large (i.e., "practically infinite") number of traders, the resulting contract curve would include an arbitrarily small number of allocations. In the limit, there would be a single allocation. But the role of the price system, which each trader "took as given," was to single out the competitive equilibrium. In the limit, that equilibrium allocation is obtained *without a price system*. The *role* of competitive agents, in the sense of price takers, has been *subsumed* "in the limit" by the notion of competitive agents as "very numerous."

Student β: I grant the importance of this insight; it in fact seems to have had little effect on such writers as Knight and other champions of the concept of perfect competition. But you're talking about 1881. Continue your story to its "atomic" conclusion.

Student γ: The story is very murky. Von Neumann and Morgenstern, in their theory of games circa 1944, refer to Bohm-Bawerk's marginal-pairs analysis without recognizing its similarity to Edgeworth's work, which they do not cite. As a trading "game," Edgeworth's problem certainly had more than two players, but useful solution concepts for n-person ($n \geqslant 3$) games took a number of years to develop. One solution concept, developed in the mid-1950s, was the *core*. It was a purely game-theoretic idea.

In 1959, however, Martin Shubik phrased Edgeworth's bargaining problem as an n-person game and showed that, for such "Edgeworth market games," the core *coincides* with the contract curve. Furthermore the core, which is here a set of allocations, shrinks in a well-defined way as the number of players, n, increases. In other words, Shubik provided a rigorous proof of Edgeworth's conjecture. Shubik's analysis depended on the full panoply of game-theoretic tools. Specifically, utility functions played an important role.

In 1963 Gerard Debreu and Herbert Scarf showed that this mathematical scaffolding could be removed. Their model used traditional neoclassical assumptions about agents and their preferences. Edgeworth's conjecture thus had an economic proof, in the sense that the mathematical structure used by Debreu and Scarf had been used by economists to model economic problems.

It took a mathematician to phrase the crucial question that economists, by their own training, had not thought to ask. Robert Aumann, in 1964, noted that "though writers on economic equilibrium have traditionally assumed perfect competition, they have, paradoxically, adopted a mathematical model that does not fit this assumption. Indeed, the influence of an individual participant on the economy cannot be mathematically negligible, as long as there are only finitely many participants. Thus *a mathematical model appropriate to the intuitive notion of perfect competition must contain infinitely many participants*" (Aumann 1964, p. 39).

Briefly, Aumann had assumed that there are as many agents in a market (or economy) as there are points on the closed unit interval $[0, 1]$. There are an uncountably infinite number of such points: They form a continuum.

Aumann then showed that with a continuum of agents the core (or the contract curve) *coincides* with the set of competitive equilibrium allocations. The contract curve did not approach the equilibria in the limit; it *was* the equilibrium set. Aumann also showed that the equilibrium set actually existed under standard assumptions. Consequently the *function* of competitive agents could be modeled by their large numbers, where "large" is now a well-defined number (equal to the number of points in $[0, 1]$, sometimes called χ_1). The phrase "competitive price takers" was redundant.

Student α: I never realized that Aumann was addressing such a problem. I thought he was simply generalizing a previous model to see what conclusions would still remain.

Teacher: Aumann's paper was exceptionally careful, though. It is one of the best motivated papers in mathematical economics; his "discussion of the literature" itself should alert the reader to its unusual nature.

Student γ: In any event, Aumann's model provided a new approach to the study of the role of competition. What followed in the literature was eminently logical. If we want to model monopoly, we use one trader; if competition, then χ_1 traders. What about intermediate cases: Would they model mixed markets like monopolistically competitive or oligopolistic ones? Aumann's model itself provided the framework for modeling this problem.

Ask yourself, what *is* a point, anyway? Within $[0, 1]$ it is simply an element of a set whose removal does not change the length, or volume, of that set. We say that a point has *measure zero* in an interval. Its measure is a reasonable proxy for the power of an agent vis-à-vis *all* agents in $[0, 1]$, since the set of *all* agents has measure equal to 1 (think of length).

Now if the "power" of a market is defined to be the measure of the set of agents that models the market, a duopoly problem would be modeled by assigning each of *two* traders a measure of $\frac{1}{2}$. In Aumann's terms, this would be like calling the first duopolist $[0, \frac{1}{2}]$ and the second $[\frac{1}{2}, 1]$, since each has measure $\frac{1}{2}$ and their conjunction has measure 1. But to *really* have duopolists, it must be the case that $[0, \frac{1}{2}]$, say, contains *no other agents who can affect any outcome*. The only allowable subsets (or agents) in $[0, \frac{1}{2}]$ must be modeled as having measure zero. Mathematically, any set with a concept of volume (called a measure) is termed a *measure space*. If every set of positive measure contains subsets of smaller positive measure, then that space is called a *nonatomic measure space* – like $[0, 1]$.

Student β: Thus nonatomic measure spaces are used to study competition, and I suppose it is "atomic" measure spaces that model imperfect competition.

Student γ: Precisely. An *atom* in a measure space is a set of positive measure (like $[0, \frac{1}{2}]$) that contains only subsets of zero measure. By saying that $[0, \frac{1}{2}]$ is an atom, we are saying that $[0, \frac{1}{2}]$ represents an *individual* trader – our duopolist – and hence its name "atom."

Consequently theorems about measure spaces of agents hold true for various market structures, but theorems about nonatomic measure spaces of agents are interpretable only in the language of competition.

Recent work is thus directed to the exploration of the role of perfect competition *in contrast* to the role of imperfect competition *where both terms have a precise meaning*.

Teacher: Well now, α, I think γ has provided the case study you sought. How do you respond? It would appear that you have no line of retreat into "the mathematics doesn't say anything new to economists." The results *are* new. You can't argue that the mathematics preceded the economics; in this case they did if your perspective is 1953, but they did not if you start in 1881. The mathematical model wasn't unnatural or forced, no matter what you felt when you first read Aumann's 1964 paper. What is "natural" is a habit or a result of training.

Student α: I think my defense would have to rest on the paucity of falsifiable implications of this theory, although frankly they appear to unify, to organize, various disparate theories already used. They provide an economical, albeit formal, set of models where previously there was, if not chaos, at least moderate confusion.

I appreciate γ's willingness to express these developments in such an intelligible fashion. The language of the *Journal of Economic Theory* admits no such discussion. I still find it hard to imagine, however, that all mathematical economics has as much economic content as γ described.

Student γ: Of course it doesn't.

Student β: Is this, finally, an admission of technical preciousness, or abstraction for abstraction's sake?

Student γ: Not really. It's a different point. Just as there can be sloppy, unimaginative, or nit-picking empirical studies of the demand for wheat, say, and just as there can be illogical, ill-conceived, and ill-written discussions about monetary policy or advertising, so too can mathematical economics, or economics expressed primarily in terms of mathematical structures, be unimaginative, ill-conceived, or grotesquely trivial. Mathematical economists are human, too. They long for recognition, even acclaim. They enjoy seeing their names in print. They sometimes, like others, are too lazy to tackle a large problem if they can get away with tackling a trivial one. What their papers *cannot* be, however, is sloppy or illogical. Sloppy mathematics isn't mathematics, and illogical models mean false theorems.

It is for *this* reason, I would argue, that mathematical economics is a difficult subdiscipline. One cannot complain that a journal referee has misinterpreted one's argument: The mathematics admits no such misinterpretation. It is hard to "fake it" professionally in mathematical economics, to rewrite the same paper a dozen times, to cast a hoary idea in new terms and present it as an insight. It isn't impossible, of course, for mathematical economics to be faked in this way. It's simply that it is too easily scrutinized by one's peers, too easily identified as garbage. The professional self-policing is easy to do.

Teacher: Of course, economics doesn't have to be written mathematically to possess such attributes. We all know economists whose papers, although relatively devoid of mathematics, are themselves models of intellectual integrity. It is extremely difficult to be a good economist in this sense; perhaps it is even more difficult than it is to be a good physicist. I do not know. All intellectual creations, all genuine contributions, are hard work and require discipline and integrity. Mathematical economics is no different.

CHAPTER 5

General equilibrium analysis: a survey of appraisals

I noted at the start of Chapter 3 that three groups of economists are concerned with appraising economic arguments. Methodologists, historians of economic thought, and practicing economists are represented among those who have found it useful, or necessary, to appraise what they have called "general equilibrium (GE) theory." Additionally, in recent years a number of philosophers have examined that "theory" and have used their appraisals as tests of one or another general theory of appraisal. That is, philosophers of science have recently used GE theory[1] as a test case for some philosophical theory, hoping both to develop their own critical enterprise and to evaluate work in economics.

This chapter examines various appraisals of general equilibrium theory. I shall consider some of what has been said about general equilibrium analysis and examine how those conclusions have been reached. I shall suggest the incommensurability of these appraisals one with another and note strengths and weaknesses of the various arguments. With obeisance paid to past work, the remainder of this chapter can then outline the questions that any such appraisal must ask and identify the kinds of evidence that must be adduced to resolve the problems that work in general equilibrium theory appears to pose.

Appraisals by historians

We can leave aside in this survey consideration of appraisals by practitioners, since the kind of interest that a general equilibrium theorist has in appraising general equilibrium theory will be manifest in either a historical discussion or a methodological one. Consequently, we can begin our survey by examining histories of general equilibrium analysis.

A number of studies approach the content of general equilibrium analysis from a historical perspective. The most common histories are found in the footnotes, chapter notes, or notes on the literature in papers

---

[1] Hereafter I shall drop the quotation marks around "general equilibrium theory." The phrase is, we shall see, rather misleading – its meaning changes as the appraiser changes. With this understood, hereafter its use can go unnoted.

or books that contain either new propositions in the general equilibrium literature or reformulations of the existing theory. As an example of this use of history, consider *General Competitive Analysis* by Arrow and Hahn (1971), still the best presentation of the theory of general equilibrium. In their notes to Chapter 5 Arrow and Hahn write:

> The first theorem on existence of equilibrium in a fully developed model of production and consumer choice, in which supply and demand may be multi-valued correspondences, is due to Arrow and Debreu [1954]; they were influenced by the earlier work of Wald, as well as by Nash's fundamental result on the somewhat related problem of existence of equilibrium points in *n*-person games [Arrow and Hahn 1971, p. 127].

This kind of history serves to link the present with the past in a correct fashion, although it actually obscures the historical line. It propagates the idea that there was a perceived problem, which had been partially addressed by Wald, but whose solution was somehow imperfect. Using the theorem, developed apart from the study of the particular problem of John Nash (1950), Arrow and Debreu solved the problem, and that is why we now sometimes speak of the Arrow–Debreu model. This kind of history, because it does not lead to an appraisal of general equilibrium theory (certainly Arrow and Hahn believe that that task is accomplished by the chapters, not the notes), is window dressing of a particular sort. It informs the modern reader that Wald and Nash, for instance, are associated with the development of general equilibrium theory, a fact not immediately apparent if one pays attention only to the names that the theorems carry.

There are many similar textbook treatments. In their excellent *Introduction to General Equilibrium Theory and Welfare Economics*, James Quirk and Rubin Saposnik (1968) present summaries of the literature at the conclusion of each chapter. At the close of their chapter on the existence of a competitive equilibrium (p. 94) they note that "the first actual proofs of the solvability of the system of equations describing a general equilibrium were those of Abraham Wald." They then footnote *another* set of footnotes from the (1958) monograph on linear programming by Robert Dorfman, Paul Samuelson, and Robert Solow. Subsequent paragraphs show that von Neumann, as well as Arrow and Debreu, also provided existence proofs that can be related to the proofs that Quirk and Saposnik develop in their own text. This historical material identifies the precursors, informing current students that some older economists should be identified with the general equilibrium tradition. Once again the history does not appraise general equilibrium theory. That theory is to be appraised on its merits as a theory.

As methodologists look at general equilibrium theory

Perhaps because of its central position in the intellectual structure called neoclassical economics, general equilibrium theory seems to receive more than its share of attention from methodologists. It seems that anyone who wishes to provide a methodological appraisal of current economic theory will, sooner or later, examine the theory of general equilibrium.

Critiques of general equilibrium analysis appear to be based on one of two perspectives. Either the economist detests the subject and dresses up a discomfiture with a philosophical attack on the despised, or else the economist is interested in appraising some work in economics and finds that to be fair to that work there must be *en passant* an appraisal of general equilibrium theory. In neither case, of course, is the history of the theory called forth to define a case study that can be used to make or defend an appraisal. What is actually appraised is the current state of the theory, or what the appraiser understands to be the current state of the theory. There are many examples of intellectually shoddy work in this genre, and it is well not to take such noncontributions as a standard. Instead I shall examine two pieces of work that are more judicious in tone and sensible in argument, although both are partially misguided.

In an article in *Economic Inquiry*, "The Rationale of General Equilibrium Theory," the late Alan Coddington (1975) attempted an appraisal. This paper was Coddington's response to Frank Hahn's (1973) Cambridge inaugural lecture, *On the Notion of Equilibrium in Economics*. Coddington, as a methodologist, had to respond to Hahn's claims on behalf of GE theory. He put forth an alternative evaluation; it is this evaluation that will concern me here. Coddington's argument led to the following conclusion:

> i) the GE construction does not contribute to the ease with which theories may be falsified (by evidence) but to the ease with which inconsistencies between a theory and a theoretical counter-example, within the formalism, may be established; ii) the GE construction does not contribute to the precision with which ideas may be expressed, but rather to syntactical watertightness within a semantically-uncharted sea; iii) the GE construction does not facilitate the refutation of unsound arguments by the provision of stronger counter-arguments, but rather to the detection of logical defects within unsoundly-formulated arguments.... My argument has been that the...GE construction...provides insulation of a tractable problem from a surrounding cluster of intractable ones [Coddington 1975, p. 557].

Coddington examined general equilibrium theory in a methodologically self-conscious fashion. He faced the issue of testing, and its absence in the case of GE theory, not as a defect of the theory. (Recall that nearly all views of science require that theories be, if not tested, at least testable; if GE theory is not testable, this creates a fundamental problem that any appraisal of general equilibrium analysis must face.) Coddington answered the question of GE analysis's "theoryness" by referring to the "GE construction" instead of GE theory; his points i–iii suggest that the GE construction is less a theory than a strategy for doing economic analysis – a method or an investigative logic.

Coddington reached this position with no reference to any specific work in general equilibrium theory. His paper refers neither to history nor to current analysis. One test of whether Coddington was correct in viewing GE analysis as an investigative logic would be to see whether it had indeed functioned in that fashion for a particular sequence of papers. Such an argument is absent. Instead Coddington claimed that the GE construction must be a method because (a) it is not a theory and (b) it is not even useful by itself. The claim may be reasonable; what it lacks is evidence to support it. In any event, Coddington faced the testability question directly. The integrity of his answer should not go unremarked.

A more recent methodological appraisal of general equilibrium theory was forced to pose the same question. Its answer is antithetical to that given by Coddington. Mark Blaug's (1980) *The Methodology Of Economics* developed a critique of general equilibrium theory as one portion of an extensive examination of neoclassical economics. Blaug used the first part of his book to present a logic of appraisal based in large measure on Lakatos's view that the unit of appraisal should be the scientific research program and not the individual theory. Blaug used such conceptual categories as core, heuristics, belt, and falsifiers as he examined "subprograms" of neoclassical economics, including the theory of consumer behavior, the theory of the firm, GE theory, marginal-productivity theory, the Heckscher–Ohlin theory, and human-capital theory. For each of these subprograms Blaug tried to establish whether and in what sense progress had occurred. How, for instance, had the research program in human capital led to a growth in knowledge? What new knowledge was developed in the general equilibrium research program?

The second section of Blaug's chapter on general equilibrium theory is titled "A Theory or a Framework?" suggesting that Coddington's idea had been at least partially accepted by Blaug. Yet he noted that "the GE framework would seem to lack any bridge by which to cross over from the world of theory to the world of facts" (p. 191). This remark suggests that GE theory is not an investigative logic, just as rationalism and mysticism are not investigative logics, for who would ever require them to deal with facts? There is a category mistake here. The logic or set of strategies or rules for constructing theories are not the same things as the theory itself.

This is not to say that GE theory is indeed not a theory, but rather that if Blaug is serious in his claim that GE analysis *might* be a framework or program and not a theory, then his appraisal, which requires a bridge from GE theory to the facts of experience, is curiously biased.

Blaug's last paragraph in Chapter 8 is a strong negative appraisal of general equilibrium analysis:

> There can be no question, therefore, of simply abandoning the GE framework, which is in fact deeply embedded in the received corpus of economic doctrine, being, so to speak, at the intersection of all the satellite research programs that together make up the larger neoclassical SRP. But without throwing away the GE construction, such as it is, what may be doubted is the notion that it provides a fruitful starting point from which to approach a substantive explanation of the workings of an economic system. Its leading characteristic has been the endless formalization of purely logical problems without the slightest regard for the production of falsifiable theorems about actual economic behavior, which, we insist, remains the fundamental task of economics [p. 192].

Is general equilibrium theory a theory, a research program, or something else – like mathematics, a semantical framework, or an investigative logic? I would ask one set of questions if I were appraising a theory and another set were I appraising a scientific research program in the sense of Lakatos. Blaug blurs the distinction. The failure of GE analysis to produce falsifiable theorems is a condemnation of it as a theory, for it is theories that have testable implications. "Endless formalization" is a criticism of GE analysis as a research program: It implies that (as a program) GE analysis is degenerating since successive variants of the theories in the protective belt fail to have corroborated excess empirical content. Yet Blaug also writes of "the intersection of all satellite research programs...in neoclassical" economics, which suggests that GE analysis is, if a program, a rather special program. Blaug does not identify what is common to all neoclassical subprograms; there is no evidence to test Blaug's assertion that the GE program *is* that common set of propositions. What is additionally curious about Blaug's appraisal of general equilibrium theory is its ahistoricism. Blaug, the premier historian of economic theory, appraises with scant reference to the history of the doctrines themselves. "By their fruits ye shall know them" denies testing an appraisal by how well it explains the history of a particular line of development in economics.

Coddington and Blaug provided intelligent and thoughtful methodological examinations of general equilibrium analysis. Yet of each it can be said, as Keynes said of Hayek's *Prices and Production*, "[It] seems to me to be one of the most frightful muddles I have ever read.... It is an extraordinary example of how, starting with a mistake, a remorseless logician can end up in Bedlam" (Keynes 1973, p. 252).

The Popperian influence on methodological studies in economics, and its perniciousness, will someday be documented. For the present it suffices to note that, for both Coddington and Blaug, it is the unfalsifiability of GE theory that is the fundamental problem that an appraisal of it must resolve. Coddington denied that it was a theory. Blaug treated it as a theory, and found it unsound. Are general equilibrium theorists like the Japanese dancing shrimp – dead, headless, but wriggling? Or are they instead engaged in an activity that is associated with the growth of knowledge, an activity as yet not understood? If the latter, what accounts for such stern, but inappropriate, appraisals of general equilibrium analysis?

I shall suggest in Chapter 11 that the influence of positivism, or Popper, has induced a questionable disjunction in economics between facts and theories. If facts are taken to be separate from theories, there is indeed a problem of the relationship of the two, a problem so severe that general equilibrium theory is inevitably appraised in negative terms. It is thus possible to argue, as I shall later, that economists' methodological canons are, *because* they are positivistic, too quickly mobilized to identify theories here and evidence there. As a consequence of such Manichaeism, appraisals most frequently focus on the relationship of what are perceived to be distinct entities, theories and facts.

The difficulty that even the most talented economic methodologists have in providing a framework for evaluating general equilibrium analysis, let alone an appraisal of GE analysis that, once provided, could command assent, should alert us to a singular possibility: Without agreement on a description of general equilibrium analysis as an activity, there can be no agreement on the framework appropriate to appraise it. The method of appraisal depends on the nature of the object to be appraised. The first task for appraising GE analysis must then be to state what it is. The mechanics and results of an appraisal of general equilibrium analysis will follow such an examination. They cannot precede it.

Appraisals by philosophers

Kuhn's challenge to philosophers of science, implicit in his book *The Structure of Scientific Revolutions* (Kuhn 1962), was that they should develop appraisals of science that respect actual scientific practice and explain or rationalize the best gambits of successful scientists. This challenge, to reconstruct the history of science, was taken up by both Lakatos and

Feyerabend. Lakatos's MSRP framework appeared sufficiently flexible to preserve the critical rationalism of Popper's school; Feyerabend's anarchism suggested that any rationalist model of the growth of scientific knowledge would be falsified by best scientific practice.

Leaving off the story at this point, however, would be misleading. Since this upheaval in the philosophy of science more than two decades ago, tens of thousands of pages have been written, both in English and in German, to accommodate Kuhn's insights about normal science, paradigms, and revolutions within a framework that reconstructs scientific practice as a rational process.

To an outsider such work seems to have two organizing centers. There is first a theoretically oriented literature, which develops models of the structure of scientific work. Second, there is an empirically oriented literature, which applies the new models to actual scientific practice. One of the main figures in the former tradition is J. D. Sneed, whose 1971 book, *The Logical Structure of Mathematical Physics*, has been extremely influential. Its opaqueness perhaps prompted Wolfgang Stegmüller to write *The Structure and Dynamics of Theories* (1976), an elaboration and extension of Sneed's ideas. He claimed that his book "*is entirely dedicated to reconciling* the logic-oriented proponents and the 'rebellious' opponents of the philosophy of science" (p. ix). The ideas of Sneed and Stegmüller are too complex to present in even a caricature. Suffice it to say that these philosophers have developed a view of theories in which certain identifiable elements and themes must be present in order that 'theoryness" be proclaimed. Their views also appear to allow particular theories to change in well-defined ways. In any event, their views require support from the evidence of scientific practice, and physics and chemistry are intensely mined for examples and corroborations. But, and this is of more interest to economists, general equilibrium theory is also used to examine the applicability of Sneed's model-theoretic approach to a social science. Because the required components of a scientific theory are found lacking, or denied, such analyses lead inexorably to appraisals of general equilibrium theory itself as faulty.

One group of papers flowing from the work of Sneed and Stegmüller appeared in the conference-proceedings volume *Philosophy of Economics* (Stegmüller, Balzar, and Spohn 1982). These papers were less concerned with appraising work in economics than with testing the "structuralist" or model-theoretic framework. For example, the paper by Franz Haslinger (1982) titled "Structure and Problems of Equilibrium and Disequilibrium Theory" reconstructed the Arrow–Debreu model as a Sneedian theory. On such a view, "a concept is T-theoretic if its measurement presupposes the validity of this very theory T" (p. 70). Haslinger argues:

Of course, a concrete economy, i.e. the consumer's utility functions, their initial endowments and profit shares, as well as the technologies of the producers, can be measured without any recourse to equilibrium theory. The states of an economy (i.e. the consumer's and producer's plans together with a price structure) can be ascertained in like manner independent of the validity of equilibrium theory. It is therefore claimed that the only *T*-theoretical concept of [general equilibrium theory] is the concept of equilibrium states itself [p. 70].

I have little interest in showing that Haslinger has or has not correctly applied the Sneed–Stegmüller framework. It is, however, pernicious nonsense to claim that the "plans" are independent of the "theory," since those plans themselves are only coherent if equilibrium is established. We cannot measure incoherent plans. (Indeed, we cannot measure plans at all.)

David Pearce and Michele Tucci (1982), in "A General Net Structure for Theoretical Economics," argue that "systematic enquiry...ought to commence with a detailed study of the logical and conceptual *form* of economic theories" (p. 85). They purport to demonstrate that there is a theory, called general disequilibrium theory, that is linked to almost every economic structure from Walras to Keynes, from Debreu to Sraffa. The linkages form a "theory net." The elaborate taxonomy proposed by Pearce and Tucci need not concern us here. It suffices to recognize that their approach does great violence to both historical and current practice. It is not very useful to say that Sraffa's and Lucas's models are variants of some central model unless we are given some guide to appraising those models. Saying that *X* is a subcase of *T* is finger pointing; it is not an evaluation of *X*.

More appropriate to our concerns is Rudolf Kötter's (1982) "General Equilibrium Theory: An Empirical Theory?" which opens by noting that GE theory "demonstrates very well that the formal strength of a theory is not necessarily followed by a consensus among scientists concerning its methodological status" (p. 103).

After his analysis of some elements of general equilibrium analysis, specifically utility theory, Kötter concludes:

The GE [theory] should be an analysis of the functioning of the economic system. It should not have the de facto economic actions for subject, but the de facto norms and rules, according to which economic actions have to be performed.... The GE [theory] could be understood as a germ-cell of a general theory of economic institutions which in its present state serves at the least as a pattern for theory construction within the framework of neoclassical economics [pp. 115–17].

Such an analysis is hard to understand. General equilibrium theory is, it appears from Kötter, more than a theory but less than, or a part of, "the framework of neoclassical economics." There is clear recognition that general equilibrium analysis is important; Kötter seems to view it, as did Coddington, as an investigative logic, a framework for theory construction. But how can it itself be appraised? By testing? By testing its induced theories? How has GE theory developed? Can its development be reconstructed? Kötter fails to provide evidence for his varied claims, and we are left, as before, with another exemplar of *ex cathedra* philosophizing about economics.

Not all philosophical work is so neutral on the subject of appraising or evaluating (as opposed to classifying) general equilibrium theory. Professional philosophers have on occasion provided such appraisals. To a working economist their attention is unusually hostile and disrespectful. For example, in a lengthy paper in the philosophy journal *Erkenntnis*, Ernst W. Handler (1980) examined the logical structure of "modern neoclassical static microeconomic equilibrium theory." Handler first reconstructed the theory according to the model-theoretic rules of Sneed and Stegmüller. He went further, however, and concluded by noting that, for general equilibrium theory,

> no explicit statements are made about the ontological status of the objects these theories refer to. The reader usually learns that these symbols denote quantities, those prices, and last [but] not least that the premises of the expounded theory are yet much too simple to correspond to reality. But what sort of objects do these theories refer to [Handler 1980, p. 50]?

Handler has no simple answer to this question. Other philosophers have been less cautious.

The philosopher Alexander Rosenberg has often written about economic theory. From a position that he once described as generally sympathetic to economics and economists, he has of late been edging toward a position that reflects great irritation with the stuff and substance of economics. With respect to general equilibrium theory, he wrote that GE theorists' work

> is clearly not the attempt to develop an empirically controlled theory of economic behavior; it seems much more like an exercise in mapping out the formal consequences of a set of topologically expressible axioms whose evidential basis and explanatory power [are] almost completely irrelevant to the economists' interest in them [Rosenberg 1980, p. 93].

Rosenberg's baffled observation in 1980 had yielded by 1983 to a disturbing question and a mind-boggling answer. In "If Economics Isn't Science, What Is It?" (Rosenberg, 1983) he began by citing what he regarded as its thoroughgoing predictive weakness. Microeconomics, he argued, is an extremal theory in the sense that it is to explain everything that comes under its domain. Such theories are thus insulated from falsification, and they function as the core of research programs. All this is to the good if there is any predictive success to boast of, but Rosenberg claimed that for economics there has been none, at least in the sense of predicting a novel fact or explaining an anomalous phenomenon: "I have come to think that the failure of economics is not methodological, or conceptual, but very broadly empirical.... This formalism does not any longer have the aims, nor does it make the claims, of an unequivocally empirical theory" (Rosenberg 1983, p. 304). For Rosenberg, economics continually falls back on the claim that it is a science because of its ability to predict. Yet to that observer from philosophy its history is a series of failures in prediction. "Occasionally, qualitative predictions are borne out, and even more frequently, retrospective economic explanations of events that were unexpected, like a 15% reduction in the consumption of gasoline, can be given" (p. 304). Yet this is a far cry from the notion of prediction that is used by physicists or philosophers of science. Indeed, given the falsity of the assumptions of economic theory, and its predictive failures, economics is to be compared with, not Newtonian mechanics, but something else: "Thus economics and phlogiston theory are not methodologically defective. They are simply false" (p. 305).

Rosenberg argued that falsity was not necessarily an evil, for Euclidean geometry was false, too. But relativity showed exactly how that geometry was false. "There is no such theory that enables us to improve on the applicability of economic theory" (p. 307). Economists seem to have no interest in developing such other theories. Economists, "not really much interested in questions of empirical applicability at all, ... [have ignored] some of the attractive non-intentional and/or non-extremal approaches to economic behavior (p. 308)," [where he includes those of H. Simon and S. Winter].

Rosenberg's answer to the question posed by his title is worth quoting at length:

> Much of the mystery surrounding the actual development of economic theory – its shifts in formalism, its insulation from empirical assessment, its interest in proving purely formal, abstract possibilities, its unchanged character over a period of centuries, the controversies about its cognitive status – can be comprehended and properly appreciated if we give up the notion that economics any longer has the aims or makes the claims of an empirical science of human behavior. Rather we should view it as a branch of mathematics, one devoted to examining the formal properties of a set of assumptions about the transitivity of abstract relations: axioms that implicitly define a technical notion of "rationality," just as geometry

examines the formal properties of abstract points and lines.... [Consequently,] we cannot demand that it provide the reliable guide to the behavior of economic agents and the performance of economies as a whole for which the formulation of public policy looks to economics. We should neither attach much confidence to predictions made on its basis nor condemn it severely when these predictions fail [pp. 311–312].

What can we respond if respond we must? The outline of a response may be given in two parts: We first deny that Rosenberg has correctly understood the historical development of what he terms the formal theory; second, we argue that he misinterprets applications of the theory in actual cases. This latter argument is well made in an unpublished rejoinder to Rosenberg by Hands (1984), who correctly cites evidence that the market pays for the predictions of economists in ways that Rosenberg does not appreciate. Nor does Rosenberg's attack take cognizance of actual predictions on matters as diverse as the demand for electricity, the funding of social security, the deregulation of ethical drugs, and the design of reenlistment pay schedules for the armed forces.[2] Rosenberg has a curious blindness about prediction: He identifies prediction with the prediction of macroeconomic variables, but the theory he identifies as the formal theory of economics is general equilibrium theory. This confused conjunction makes his argument, which in places has considerable merit, finally fail. What is needed to rescue its strengths is a fuller treatment of just what general equilibrium analysis consists of and how exactly it developed. The lessons of that story can then be applied to evaluate Rosenberg's broader claims.

---

[2] It is not easy to see how Rosenberg would answer the question were he to analyze the following situation: Until the mid-1970s, the Utilities Commission of the State of North Carolina relied on engineering forecasts of growth in demand for electricity in the various service regions. After the early 1970s "oil shocks," those predictions consistently overestimated demand growth. By the late 1970s the public staff of the commission developed a large econometric model, based on demand theory, that forecast demand. This forecast generated a supply response, which led to prices that earned the utilities a reasonable return, which led back to the prices that were taken as parameters by the various consumers (imitating a fixed-point argument for a general equilibrium model).

Because the price of electricity, with a nonzero demand elasticity, was the only restraining influence on demand growth, ignoring the economic analysis, and thus general equilibrium analysis, had created horribly inaccurate forecasts. The result of the public staff's quite accurate model analysis has been to rein in growth in system capacity, which has led to the abandonment of several nuclear generating plants under construction. More importantly perhaps, the models themselves suggested how, for example, conservation and load-management programs would affect load growth and construction schedules.

My own view is that this kind of applied general equilibrium analysis has saved rate payers billions of American dollars. One who claims that general equilibrium analysis leads to no empirical work, or only to retrospective qualitative predictions, makes a serious error (see Public Staff of the North Carolina Utilities Commission 1979, 1981; see also ICF 1981; Miedema et al. 1981).

What the history of general equilibrium analysis can teach

The usual way, of course, to learn what GE analysis is is by studying its substance directly from books and articles. This might mean examining books like that of Arrow and Hahn (1971), or it might mean reading the current journal literature with some attention to the structure and method of the analysis. This approach will indeed provide insight into the nature and scope of the GE program. We have seen, however, that such study did not produce agreement as to whether GE analysis is a theory, to be appraised according to one set of guidelines; a program, to be appraised according to Lakatosian rules; or an investigative logic, to be evaluated according to some other criteria.

At present the actual practitioners do not share a common understanding of what their creations are or what they are meant to accomplish. Some theorists believe that the GE framework is a descriptive theory; others believe that although it is not now descriptive, it should someday become so. Some defend the view that it is a mathematical subdiscipline, and so the rules for evaluating it are those that guide appraisals of mathematical creations. Still other analysts argue that GE economics produces falsifiable propositions; they point to Leontief models and computable equilibrium models like those of Scarf and of Shoven and Whalley. This disparity of viewpoints suggests that the individuals who do GE analysis, while not the last to ask, cannot provide final guidance in appraising the GE enterprise. I doubt that there *is* any final guidance.

We have also noted that the history of the subject rarely proceeds beyond the contributions of Walras and Pareto. Such historical materials as exist are not very helpful for the methodologist, being primarily notes or footnotes on precursors of current lines of enquiry. One of the rare attempts to approach GE analysis from an historical perspective was that of Harvey Gram and Vivian Walsh (1980). Their book *Classical and Neoclassical Theories of General Equilibrium* promised much with its subtitle, "Historical Origins and Mathematical Structure." The first part of this excellent book presents the history of the classical models from the physiocrats through Smith, Ricardo, and Marx; the mode of comparison is a two-sector model of general equilibrium. When Gram and Walsh get to neoclassical authors like Menger, Walras, Pareto, and Edgeworth, the narrative is carried forward by use of a variant of the classical model to show that the classical and neoclassical GE models, while different, do share a number of common elements. The historical reconstruction disappears, however, when Gram and Walsh discuss the modern (post-1930) versions of GE theory. In their appraisal of these works, Gram and Walsh examine the structure of a set of models associated with the original

Arrow–Debreu model. There is no history here, no recognition that the period from 1930 to the 1954 Arrow–Debreu–McKenzie model includes much that could influence one's appraisal of the theory. Moreover, the period from that model to the present covers another thirty years. The ahistorical character of the Gram and Walsh treatment of the twentieth century is unfortunate; yet they used the best histories that they could find. The fault, if such can be said to be present, lies with the historians of economic thought, who have not developed the appropriate materials.

We noted that to appraise GE theory we first need to say whether it is a theory, a research program, or something else entirely. This knowledge cannot be elicited from current work alone. We need historical case studies to appraise this body of work. Unlike for Keynesian theory, the other twentieth-century structure of importance, the historical materials are scanty. This is a real bother.

The only solution is to provide such a history. Yet I am not a historian, and to do the entire job would require a booklength treatment. As a consequence I have chosen to focus on but one set of materials, that pertaining to the development of the proofs of the existence of a competitive equilibrium. Although this focus appears to be a narrow one, it does encompass the development of the now standard basic general equilibrium model of Arrow, Debreu, and McKenzie. It leaves out questions related to the stability of the competitive equilibrium.

In an earlier book (Weintraub 1979) I tried to show that the stability literature was linked to the development and articulation of the Keynesian research program. My treatment, while historical in form, was close to the notes-on-the-literature approach. Indeed, that entire book was an exercise in appraisal of the literature on the "microfoundations of macroeconomics." I argued that the literature could best be understood as an attempt to link two scientific research programs, which I identified as the Keynesian program and the neo-Walrasian program. The present work attempts to see whether, and in what sense, neo-Walrasian economics is good economics.

Part II

The five chapters of Part I have raised a number of questions. The three chapters of Part II attempt to answer some of them. Chapter 6 is a case study of one group of papers in general equilibrium analysis. It develops some evidence that will illuminate the subsequent appraisal. The history is interesting, apart from the issue of appraisal, because its narrative compass touches several points infrequently noted. For example, although there are many studies of the effect on physics of the intellectual migration from central Europe in the 1930s, little has been written about the effects of that migration on the economics profession.

From the case study, Chapter 7 draws several inferences about general equilibrium analysis. I attempt there to give answers to the questions "What is general equilibrium theory?" and "How can it be appraised?"

Chapter 8, a classroom interlude, informally introduces a number of issues associated with the appraisal.

Part II

CHAPTER 6

The existence of a competitive equilibrium: 1930–1954

Although the general equilibrium story begins with Walras, for my purposes the state of knowledge of general equilibrium analysis in 1930 can be defined by Gustav Cassel's (1932) *The Theory of Social Economy*,[1] the first edition of which appeared in German in 1918. (An English translation of the first edition appeared in 1923.) In the early pages of this part treatise, part textbook, Cassel clearly set out the divisions between the consumers and producers, and integrated the market outcomes in product and factor markets. As in his earlier (1899) "Grundriss einer elementaren Preislehre," Cassel argued strongly against marginal utility and "value." Instead Cassel placed *prices* at the center of his allocation theory and used demand itself as a primitive concept. His verbal treatment of production, the relationship of inputs to outputs, recognized substitution possibilities in a way that his mathematical analysis did not.

After the introduction of his laws, or market principles, Cassel set out a formal system in Chapter IV, Section 16 (Cassel 1932), "Arithmetical Treatment of the Problem of Equilibrium." Although there are no references in his book to Walras (a fact noted by Wicksell and Schumpeter), Cassel presented a Walrasian system *without utility* and organized its components in a way that would later suggest an approach to the existence question.

His production system considered r factors of production with "R_1, $R_2, \ldots, R_r$, the quantities of them which are available in a given period" (Cassel 1932, p. 142). There are n goods produced with a technology given by the technical coefficients a_{ij}, where "to produce the unit quantity of commodity 1, the quantities $a_{11}, \ldots, a_{1r}$ of the factors of production may be necessary." With factor prices $q_1, q_2, \ldots, q_r$ and product prices $p_1, p_2, \ldots, p_n$, we have Cassel's equations

---

This chapter originally appeared, in a slightly different form, in *The Journal of Economic Literature* (March 1983), pp. 1–39. It is reprinted here with permission.

[1] I do not mean to suggest by this that Cassel's book was as important as Walras's *Elements*. Rather, the literature I shall examine is based on Cassel's treatment. In that sense *The Theory of Social Economy* is the natural overture to the acts that followed.

(3) $a_{11}q_1 + a_{12}q_2 + \cdots + a_{1r}q_r = p_1,$

$a_{21}q_1 + a_{22}q_2 + \cdots + a_{2r}q_r = p_2,$

$$\vdots$$

$a_{n1}q_1 + a_{n2}q_2 + \cdots + a_{nr}q_r = p_n,$

so factor prices, and unit costs, determine product prices.[2]

Cassel went on to state that, once prices are known, demands for each commodity "can be calculated by means of the following series of equations" (p. 143):

(4) $D_1 = F_1(p_1,\ldots,p_n),$
$D_2 = F_2(p_1,\ldots,p_n),$

$$\vdots$$

$D_n = F_n(p_1,\ldots,p_n).$

Cassel's "principle of scarcity," akin to a tendency to market clearing, was then invoked by asserting that "when prices are in equilibrium every demand must be satisfied by the supply,"

(5) $D_1 = S_1, \qquad D_2 = S_2, \qquad \ldots, \qquad D_n = S_n,$

"where $S_1, S_2, \ldots, S_n$ are the quantities of each of the different commodities produced within a unit period" (p. 144).

Cassel, without explicitly defining a symbol for factor demands, next argued that knowing the quantities S_i "we can calculate the demands which are made upon the factors of production" (p. 144) as

(6)   the quantity $a_{11}S_1 + a_{21}S_2 + \cdots + a_{n1}S_n$ of factor of production 1,

the quantity $a_{12}S_1 + a_{22}S_2 + \cdots + a_{n2}S_n$ of factor of production 2,

$$\vdots$$

the quantity $a_{1r}S_1 + a_{2r}S_2 + \cdots + a_{nr}S_n$ of factor of production r.

Because available factor supplies are denoted R_i, equilibrium (Cassel's "scarcity") requires (p. 144)

---

[2] To preserve the integrity of quoted passages that refer to equations, I shall in this chapter identify those equations by the equation numbers that appear in the source.

$$(7) \qquad R_1 = a_{11}S_1 + a_{21}S_2 + \cdots + a_{n1}S_n,$$

$$R_2 = a_{12}S_1 + a_{22}S_2 + \cdots + a_{n2}S_n,$$

$$\vdots$$

$$R_r = a_{1r}S_1 + a_{2r}S_2 + \cdots + a_{nr}S_n.$$

Cassel then argued that his system reached equilibrium by suggesting that, given a set of factor prices, product prices are determined by (3). This yields demands from (4) and thus supplies from (5). Supplies determine factor demands from (6), and "the coincidence of these requirements with the available quantity of factors of production is guaranteed by equations (7)" (p. 145).

There are two points to notice. First, Cassel specifically restricted his argument to goods and factors that are "scarce," and therefore he necessarily thought of factors as having positive factor prices, so that, because $a_{ij} > 0$, all product prices are nonnegative. Second, although he *argued* for the existence of a solution by an iterative or causal chain (he indeed had as many equations as unknowns), he did *not* argue that a solution exists *because* of this equality. Indeed, he did not count equations at all. (Later in the section he argued that the functions F_i are, in effect, homogeneous of degree zero in prices and income, so that simple equation counting would produce the wrong answer for the existence of a relative price equilibrium.)

It is not usually recognized that Cassel's discussion of this system, on pp. 152–5, was then extended to "the society which is progressing at a uniform rate. In it, the quantities of the factors of production which are available in any period, that is our $R_1, \ldots, R_r$, are subject to a uniform increase. We shall represent by c the fixed rate of this increase, and of the uniform progress of the society generally" (p. 152). The result is that, for his given system, (3) and (7) must be modified, for "as production is now assumed to increase uniformly, there must be substituted, for these unit quantities, other quantities which steadily increase in the percentage c. . . . [If] a series of successive unit periods are considered, they must be multiplied by ascending powers of a constant factor, which is clearly determined by c" (p. 153). For this dynamic, albeit uniformly growing, society, Cassel again turned from his equations to a less-formal argument for the existence of equilibrium, one that now involved a new relationship: "The ratio between the two parts [the reproduction sector and the real increase of capital] determines the degree of saving and the rate of progress c" (p. 154). A rate of interest had appeared.

It is not necessary to refocus Cassel's argument. What is important is to recognize that Cassel's statement of the pricing problem, or the determination of prices by a system involving interrelated supply and demand in product and factor markets, was textbook knowledge prior to 1930, especially in those European countries where written German could be understood. S. L. Barron of the London School of Economics (LSE) prepared an English translation from the fifth German edition, and that translation appeared in the United States in 1932. I do not claim, nor do I believe it to be true, that Cassel's book represented an analytical improvement on Walras or Pareto. Rather, the significance of *The Theory of Social Economy* was as a text, as a book that, like Marshall's *Principles* could, and was, used by teachers and students. As we shall see, it was Cassel's formulation that spurred developments in the 1930s. We may thus begin the real narrative by assuming that Cassel's presentation of the Walrasian general equilibrium system, modified by the exclusion of utility considerations, was available for study by any interested economist immediately before the early 1930s.

Menger's Vienna colloquium

Wittgenstein's Vienna (Janik and Toulmin 1973) is a charming, detailed, and well-argued intellectual and cultural history of Vienna before the First World War. In this book the authors identify the social, political, and philosophical milieu that formed the backdrop for Ludwig Wittgenstein's philosophical contributions. I am not aware, however, of a similar full-length history of Vienna in the late 1920s and 1930s, a period of intense activity in mathematics, philosophy, and economics.[3]

A. J. Ayer's (1977) autobiography, *Part of My Life*, notes the impact of Vienna of this time on a young English philosopher who had letters of introduction to Moritz Schlick and thus to the center of philosophical activity. The group of philosophers, mathematicians, and scientists "had come into being in the late 1920s. Its manifesto: Wissenschaftliche Weltauffassung: Der Wiener Kreis – the Scientific View of the World: The Vienna Circle – was published in 1929" (Ayer 1977, p. 129). The tradition of Ernst Mach was carried on by Schlick, Otto Neurath, Rudoph Carnap, Friedrich Waismann, together with the mathematicians "Menge [sic] and Hahn" (p.133) and Kurt Gödel. The Polish logicians, particularly A. Tarski, and the Berlin philosophers Hans Reinchenbach, Richard Von Mises, and Carl Hempel, maintained close relations to the Circle. Ayer and W. V. O. Quine were the most distinguished overseas visitors.

As Ayer notes, "one of the principal aims of the Vienna Circle was to

---

[3] George Clare's recent autobiographical memoir, *Last Waltz in Vienna* (1982), does, however, recreate the mood of the city in the period from 1900 to the Anschluss.

rebuild the bridge between philosophy and science which had been largely broken by the romantic movement and the accompanying rise of idealist metaphysics at the beginning of the nineteenth century" (p. 129). The related view that science is central to philosophy and that mathematics must play the premier role in philosophy (and science) can be said to have infused the intellectual life of all who participated, and specifically Karl Menger.[4]

Menger was, at that time, a professor of mathematics at the University of Vienna. The son of the distinguished economist Carl Menger, he played an important role in Central European mathematics, since there were few professorial positions, and Vienna was an intellectual magnet for the generation of gifted mathematicians of the time. As S. M. Ulam (1976), in his own autobiography, *Adventures of a Mathematician*, wrote, "My plans were to go west (go west, young man!); first I wanted to spend a few weeks in Vienna to see Karl Menger, a famous geometer and topologist, whom I had met in Poland through Kuratowski" (p. 56).

As Ulam stresses repeatedly, there was a burgeoning of mathematical activity in Central Europe in the period from the mid-1920s to the mid-1930s. The Poles included Banach, Kuratowski, Schauder, Borsuk, Mazur, Tarski, Steinhaus, Kac, Lomnicki, and, of course, Ulam. The Hungarians included John von Neumann and the physicists E. P. Wigner and Edward Teller. Vienna attracted them all.

As Menger later recalled, "In the fall of 1927 a man of 25 called at the Mathematical Institute of the University of Vienna. Since he expressed a predilection for geometry he was referred to me. He introduced himself as Abraham Wald" (Menger 1952, p. 14). As a Jew in Cluj, Rumania, "Wald was not admitted to the local gymnasium.... He studied by himself and was admitted to the University of Cluj" (Wolfowitz 1952, p. 1). Upon graduation, Wald came to Vienna.

"Wald enrolled in the university, but during the next two years Vienna did not see much of him" (Menger 1952, p. 14) because of the lack of formal course restrictions, the freedom to learn on one's own, and, for Wald, service in the Rumanian army. "It was not until February 1930 that he and I again had extended conversations. Then he came unexpectedly to hand me a manuscript which purported to contain the solution of a famous problem." There was a serious error in the paper, but Wald

---

[4] Dr. Earlene Craver Leijonhufvud has recently opened up the history and structure of Austrian economics, in this period, by extensive oral histories taken from surviving participants. An early version of her work, "The Emigration of the Austrian Economists," was presented at the seventeenth national colloquium of the Oral History Association (October 8, 1982, San Antonio, Texas). For a more complete version, see *History of Political Economy* (1985).

persevered, asking for other problems and topics to explore. He had some success.

> "It seemed to me that Wald had exactly the spirit which prevailed among the young mathematicians who gathered together about every other week [alternating weeks with the Wiener Kreis?] in what we called our Mathematical Colloquium, so I at once invited him to present his results there. Gödel and Nöbeling, Alt and Beer... [were regulars, and] Cěch, Knaster, and Tarski were frequent guests,... [together with] students and visitors... from abroad, especially the United States and Japan. It was in this stimulating atmosphere that Wald spent his formative years" [p. 15].

Writing after Wald's death, Menger recalled (and understated) his own act of great personal decency:

> [Wald] received his Ph.D. in 1931. At that time of economic and incipient political unrest, it was out of the question to secure for him a position at the University of Vienna, although such a connection would certainly have been as profitable for that institution as for himself. Outside of the Colloquium, my friend Hahn was the only mathematician who knew Wald personally.... Wald, with his characteristic modesty, told me that he would be perfectly satisfied with any small private position which would enable him to continue his work in our Mathematical Colloquium. I remembered that my friend Karl Schlesinger, a well-to-do banker and economist, wished to broaden his knowledge of higher mathematics, so I recommended Wald to him [p. 18].

Karl Schlesinger, who was born in Budapest in 1889, moved to Vienna after Bela Kun's communist revolution in 1919. He was the real link between Walras, the progenitor of general equilibrium analysis, and the nascent developments. As Oskar Morgenstern has remarked, "Schlesinger's *Theorie der Geld- und Kreditwirtschaft* (1914) made him the only immediate follower of Walras, other than Wicksell, to advance Walras's theory of money" (Morgenstern 1968; 1976, p. 509). In addition to developing a theory of the indirect utility of money, "Schlesinger derived an excess demand equation for money that is virtually identical with the one commonly ascribed to Keynes. He was also probably the first to develop the notion of the equilibrium rate of interest."

Although Don Patinkin (1965, pp. 576–8) gives Schlesinger appropriate recognition for his contributions to monetary economics, few others have appreciated his work, leading Schumpeter (1954, p. 1082n) to write that Schlesinger's book is a "striking [instance] of the fact that in our field first-class performance is neither a necessary nor a sufficient condition for success."

Morgenstern notes that "in his 1914 book Schlesinger made extensive use of some simple mathematics, uncommon at that time in German economic writing.... A wealthy financier and a member of many industrial and financial boards,...he never held an academic post but was an active and highly respected member of the Vienna Economic Society" (Morgenstern 1968; 1976a, p. 509). Indeed, the 1934 volume of *Econometrica* lists Schlesinger as a member of the fledgling Econometric Society, whose Viennese business may have been conducted "frequently at odd hours in coffee houses" (p. 510).

It is quite clear that the association between Schlesinger and Wald was educational on both sides, and it is likely that the banker used Cassel's newly revised *Theory of Social Economy* as a touchstone for the mathematical discussions. We can surmise that Menger kept track of the pair's progress because he reports that perhaps in 1931, "I asked Schlesinger to present his formulation of the equations [of economic production] to the Colloquium" (Menger 1952, p. 18). Menger goes on to refer to "Schlesinger's modification of the original equations of Walras and Cassel."

It was probably an early version of Schlesinger's (1933) paper "Über die Produktionsgleichungen der ökonomischen Wertlehre" ("On the Production Equations of Economic Value Theory") that formed the colloquium presentation; the final paper appeared in the 1933–4 edition of the proceedings of that colloquium.

Recalling Cassel's notation, let r_i denote "available...units of input R_i." Assume m inputs and n outputs S_i, where s_i is the amount of S_i produced. Schlesinger defined input prices to be ρ_i and output prices σ_i. He thus produced the equations (Schlesinger 1933, pp. 278–9):

$$r_1 = a_{11}s_1 + a_{12}s_2 + \cdots + a_{1n}s_n,$$

$$r_2 = a_{21}s_1 + a_{22}s_2 + \cdots + a_{2n}s_n,$$

$$\vdots$$

$$r_m = a_{m1}s_1 + a_{m2}s_2 + \cdots + a_{mn}s_n,$$

$$\sigma_1 = a_{11}\rho_1 + a_{21}\rho_2 + \cdots + a_{m1}\rho_m,$$

$$\sigma_2 = a_{12}\rho_1 + a_{22}\rho_2 + \cdots + a_{m2}\rho_m,$$

$$\vdots$$

$$\sigma_n = a_{1n}\rho_1 + a_{2n}\rho_2 + \cdots + a_{mn}\rho_m,$$

$$\sigma_1 = f_1(s_1, s_2, \ldots, s_n),$$

$$\sigma_2 = f_2(s_1, s_2, \ldots, s_n),$$

$$\vdots$$

$$\sigma_n = f_n(s_1, s_2, \ldots, s_n).$$

Schlesinger noted that both Heinrich von Stackelberg (1933) and Hans Neisser (1932) had "observed that these equations do not necessarily possess a solution, and above all, do not necessarily possess a solution whose values are positive (as is required for it to represent the values of ρ_i, σ_j, and s_j)" (Schlesinger 1933, p. 279). The problem he identified was that Walras and Cassel used the R_i to refer only to scarce inputs. Yet scarcity is not exogenous, being "in turn dependent on demand curves, technical production possibilities, etc."

The short paper then argued that for scarce inputs

$$r_i = a_{i1}s_1 + a_{i2}s_2 + \cdots + a_{in}s_n \qquad \text{and} \qquad \rho_i > 0,$$

whereas for free inputs,

$$r_j \geq a_{j1}s_1 + a_{j2}s_2 + \cdots + a_{jn}s_n \qquad \text{and} \qquad \rho_j = 0.$$

Thus the first m equations must be replaced by

$$r_i = a_{i1}s_1 + a_{i2}s_2 + \cdots + a_{in}s_n + u_i$$

(for $i = 1, 2, \ldots, m$), where $u_i \geq 0$; and if $u_i > 0$, then $\rho_i = 0$ (for $i = 1, 2, \ldots, m$).[5]

In effect, the $m + 2n$ Casselian equations are replaced by "$m + 2n$ equations and m side conditions in $2m + 2n$ unknowns, u_i, σ_j, s_j, r_i ($i = 1, \ldots, m; j = 1, \ldots, n$)" (p. 279).

There are two important points here. First, equilibrium has been characterized by inequalities and equations, so arguments based on "as many unknowns as equations" break down. The existence of equilibrium is problematical. Second, the complementary slackness conditions of the later programming literature are fully defined.[6] It is not stretching the imagination to attribute the conciseness, and elegance, of this note to the help of the Menger colloquium and Wald, although the idea is certainly Schlesinger's. (But see p. 279n, citing a similar argument by F. Zeuthen.)

[There is, however, a conundrum. Cassel wrote the demand relationship $D_i = F_i(p_1, \ldots, p_n)$. Schlesinger writes it $\sigma_i = f_i(s_1, \ldots, s_n)$. The former expresses demand quantities as functions of prices; the latter gives demand prices as functions of quantities. I have no hypothesis about the reasons for this change from a Walrasian to a Marshallian demand

---

[5] u_i is a *slack* variable. It measures the discrepancy between the two sides of an inequality.
[6] Such conditions entail that if a certain inequality is nonbinding, a related variable is zero.

relationship. Mathematically, if the Jacobian $(\partial f_i/\partial s_j)$ is everywhere invertible, then the inverse function theorem could produce a simple local translation from one system to the other. Alternatively, Schlesinger's formulation allows the analyst to solve for the σ_i unknowns at an early stage of the conceptual argument, but there seems to be an information loss in this procedure. In any event, it was this system, using inverse Walrasian demand functions, that formed the basis for Wald's subsequent analysis of the existence of equilibrium.[7]]

It is hard to escape the feeling that Menger foresaw this analysis since non-negativity, as Morgenstern (1951; 1976a, p. 494) wrote, "was only part of a wider interest, felt especially by Menger, namely, that the practice of the mere counting of equations and unknowns, which had satisfied economists up to that time, had to be overcome by the actual demonstration of whether or not such systems have a solution." Yet Menger, by later admission, was on his own approaching the problem incorrectly:

> I had frequently discussed the problem with members of the Mathematical Colloquium,...but I must confess I was on the wrong track. I believed imputing the price of a product to its factors to be somewhat analogous to finding the distribution of the weight of a horizontal plate over its various points of support. In statics this problem is insoluble if the plate is supported at more than three points, since statics supplies only three linear equations.... In constructing bridges and the like... the support is not rigid and by supplementing the static considerations with the theory of elasticity one indeed obtains a unique solution of the (non-linear) problem. I asked myself whether there was perhaps an economic analogue of the elasticity considerations [Menger 1973, p. 47].

Yet it was the economist Schlesinger who, by recasting the Walras–Cassel system with complementary slackness conditions, led the way to the existence theorem that Wald developed. A little thought suggests that, if a solution to the Schlesinger system can be obtained, its character must be rooted in the non-negativity conditions and the restrictions on the functions f_i. "The great achievement of Wald was the proof...of the unique solution...provided that the functions...connecting the prices of the products with the quantities produced satisfy certain conditions implied by the Principle of Marginal Utility" (Menger 1973, p. 51). We can speculate on the pleasure this approach must have provided to the son of Carl Menger.

Wald actually wrote four papers on the subject of the existence of an

---

[7] See E. C. Leijonhufvud (1984), however, for a possible explanation of this use of quantities as functional arguments.

equilibrium for the (modified) Walras–Cassel system. The first appeared in print in the *Ergebnisse* (the Menger colloquium's proceedings) of March 1934, as "Über die eindeutige positive Lösbarkeit der neuen Produktionsgleichungen (I)" ("On the Unique Non-negative Solvability of the New Production Equations, Part I"; Wald 1934). The paper is completely formal, beginning with the following theorem (Baumol and Goldfeld 1968, p. 281): "Theorem: The equation system (Sch) [Schlesinger]

$$r_i = \sum_{j=1}^{n} a_{ij}s_j + u_i \qquad (i = 1,\ldots m),$$

$$\sigma_j = \sum_{i=1}^{m} a_{ij}\rho_i, \quad \sigma_j = f_j(s_j) \qquad (j = 1,\ldots,n)$$

in which the r_i and a_{ij} are given quantities, the f_j are known functions, the u_i, ρ_i, s_j, σ_j are unknown quantities, possesses a single valued solution set in the values u_i, s_j, σ_j when the following conditions hold:

1. $r_i \geqslant 0 \quad (i = 1,\ldots,m)$.
2. $a_{ij} \geqslant 0 \quad (i = 1,\ldots,m; \quad j = 1,\ldots,n)$.
3. For each j $(j = 1,\ldots,n)$ there is at least one i $(i = 1,\ldots,m)$ for which $a_{ij} \neq 0$.
4. For each of the values $j = 1,\ldots,n$, the function $f_j(s_j)$ is defined for every positive value of s_j, its value is non-negative, continuous, and strictly monotone decreasing, i.e. $s_j' < s_j$ implies $f_j(s_j') > f_j(s_j)$, and in addition $\lim_{s_j=0} f_j(s_j) = \infty$, provided that the following side conditions also hold:
   (a) $s_j \geqslant 0 \quad (j = 1,\ldots,n)$,
   (b) $\sigma_j \geqslant 0 \quad (j = 1,\ldots,n)$,
   (c) $\rho_i \geqslant 0 \quad (i = 1,\ldots,m)$,
   (d) $u_i \geqslant 0 \quad (i = 1,\ldots,m)$,
   (e) If $u_i > 0$ then $\rho_i = 0 \quad (i = 1,\ldots,m)$."

The fundamental feature (and limitation) of the theorem[8] is the simplification introduced by assuming that the demand price for good j is a function only of the quantity of good j. All other goods quantities have no effect on good j's price, and good j has a downward-sloping demand curve. The proof itself is tedious; it proceeds by mathematical induction on n, the number of goods, and involves a trial solution of the r_i, which from the linear equalities and side conditions generate sequences of r_i, ρ's, u's, and σ's; then delicate continuity arguments develop into a proof by

---

[8] Conditions 1 and 2 are non-negativity constraints, as are conditions 4(a)–4(c). Conditions 4(d) and 4(e) are the complementary slackness restrictions.

contradiction. The inductive step is even more tedious,[9] although Wald makes clever use of the concept, later explicitly introduced by Hicks, of a composite commodity.

This paper is an excellent example of what one of Wald's later collaborators noted about Wald's lecture notes. "They are rigorous, accurate, and clear, but some of the proofs are clumsy, and the organization... could be improved.... Wald seldom bothered to rework his writings for mathematical elegance or clarity – only new results interested him.... He seldom gave an intuitive justification of the theorems, probably because he himself needed it so little" (Wolfowitz 1952, p. 3).

The paper, as it appeared, was followed by comments by Schams, who noted that Wald had introduced a value-theoretic premise into Cassel's equations, and by Menger, whose closing remark was prophetic:

> In any event I wish to remark in conclusion that with Wald's work we bring to a close the period in which economists simply *formulated* equations, without concern for the existence or uniqueness of their solutions, or at best, made sure that the number of equations and unknowns be equal (something that is neither necessary nor sufficient for solvability and uniqueness). In the future as the economists formulate equations and concern themselves with their solution (as the physicists have long done) they will have to deal explicitly with the deep mathematical questions of existence and uniqueness [Wald 1935; Baumol and Goldfeld 1968, p. 288].

In November 1934 Wald published "Über die Produktionsgleichungen der ökonomischen Wertlehre (II)" ("On the Production Equations of Economic Value Theory II"; Wald 1935), which replaced the demand functions of the March paper with the Schlesinger functions $\sigma_j = f_j(s_1, s_2, \ldots, s_n)$ $(j = 1, 2, \ldots, n)$.[10]

This paper replaced assumption 4 concerning the monotonicity of $f_j(s_j)$ with the following assumption:

> (6) Let $\Delta s_1, \ldots, \Delta s_n$ be n numbers among which at least one is <0, and let $\sum_{j=1}^{n} \sigma_j' \Delta s_j \leqslant 0$, then we must have $\sum_{j=1}^{n} \sigma_j' \Delta s_j < 0$ where $\sigma_j' = f_j(s_1 + \Delta s_1, \ldots, s_n + \Delta s_n)$ $(j=1,2,\ldots n)$ [Baumol and Goldfeld 1968, p. 290].

The proof is a simple generalization of the earlier proof. Most significant, however, are the remarks on assumption (6). Wald states:

---

[9] In an argument by mathematical induction one first proves the proposition for $n = 1$; then, from the assumption that the proposition is true for $n = k$, one proves its truth for $n = k + 1$. This establishes the result for all n. An existence proof by contradiction, moreover, provides no hint of *how* the assumptions guarantee existence.

[10] It is worth remembering that Wald's demand functions refer to the market demand, not individual demands.

Let w be any number of the economy who, when prices are $\sigma_1,\ldots,\sigma_n$ demands s_{w1} of $S_1,\ldots$, and s_{wn} units of S_n. The amount s_j – the number of units of S_j produced [in equilibrium] – is the sum of the amounts s_{wj} for all members of the economy, $W.\ldots$ [Now suppose]

(6w) if at prices $\sigma_1,\ldots,\sigma_n$ individual w demands $s_{w1},\ldots,s_{wn}$, and with prices $\sigma_1',\ldots\sigma_n'$ he demands $s_{w1} + \Delta s_{w1},\ldots,s_{wn} + \Delta s_{wn}$ where at least one of the $\Delta s_{wj} < 0$ and where [if] $\Sigma_{j=1}^n \sigma_j \Delta s_{wj} < 0$ then $\Sigma_{j=1}^n \sigma_j' \Delta s_{wj} < 0$ [p. 292].

Wald then remarks that, although (6w) holds for every individual, it may happen that (6) is not true. It is clear that (6w) is the weak axiom of revealed preference refined by Samuelson a decade or so later. Wald requires, however, (6) or (6w) to hold in the aggregate. It may not. The weak axiom of revealed preference is an extremely strong assumption.[11]

Even more interesting, however, is Wald's final remark, in which he states that (6w) in the aggregate can be derived from the assumption that, if ϕ denotes marginal utility, "for every j the number $\partial\phi_{wj}/\partial s_{wi}$ is negative and...is large in comparison with the number $\partial\phi_{wj}/\partial s_{wk}$ for $k \neq j$" (p. 293). This is similar to the restrictions that appear in a version of the dominant-diagonal theorem discovered over two decades later in the literature on the stability of equilibrium. The effect of that theorem is that multimarket interaction can be conceptually identified with partial equilibrium, in which neither uniqueness nor stability is of great moment.[12] The power of Wald's intuition is thus evident, for strong forms of the uniqueness of equilibrium theorems of the 1950s and 1960s required the assumption of aggregate revealed preference.

One cannot leave the discussion of this paper without citing Kurt Gödel: "In reality the demand of each individual depends also on his income, and this in turn depends on the prices of the factors of production. One might formulate an equation system which takes this into account and investigate the existence of a solution" (Baumol and Goldfeld 1968, p. 293).[13]

---

[11] If p is a price vector, $E(p)$ is an n-market set of excess demand functions, and $p = p^*$ is equilibrium, then the derivative of the Liapunov function $V = \Sigma_i (p_i - p_i^*)^2$ is $2 \Sigma \dot{p}_i(p_i - p_i^*)$. If the tatonnement is given by $\dot{p}_i = E_i(p)$, then $\dot{V} = 2 \Sigma p_i E_i(p) - 2 \Sigma p_i^* E_i(p)$. The first term is zero by Walras Law. If the weak axiom holds in the aggregate, the second summation is positive, so $\dot{V} < 0$ and thus equilibrium is stable. This is the strongest stability theorem extant, and it follows immediately from the unreasonable strength of the aggregate weak axioms.

[12] Conceptually, the dominant-diagonal theorem reduces the multimarket interaction problem $\dot{p} = Ap$ to the problem $\dot{p} = (\text{diag } B)\, p$ where the $n \times n$ matrix A is reduced to the diagonal matrix B. For the latter problem, the price *change* for good i depends only on the price of good i, *not* on the price of other goods. The multimarket linkages are effectively broken, and therefore partial equilibrium analysis gives acceptable results.

[13] This suggested generalization of Wald's system is not feasible. In a comment to me on an

Wald wrote two other papers on this subject of equilibrium. One, on equilibrium in an exchange economy, was mentioned by title only in the final issue of the *Ergebnisse*, that of 1935–6 (p. 84). Chipman, in his classic "Survey of the Theory of International Trade, Part 2," quotes a letter from Morgenstern that states, in part, "The paper...was written but is lost. Probably Wald himself lost it when coming to this country and never bothered to rewrite it" (Baumol and Goldfeld 1968, p. 270).[14]

On the fourth and final paper, Morgenstern recalled in 1951 that "in view of the significance [of the three papers] I persuaded Wald to write an expository article" [Morgenstern 1976a, p. 494). This paper, titled "Über einige Gleichungssysteme der mathematischen Ökonomie" (Wald 1936) appeared in the *Zeitschrift für Nationalökonomie* and was translated by Otto Eckstein in 1951 for *Econometrica* as "On Some Systems of Equations of Mathematical Economics."

This monumental, and clear, survey paper reviewed the theorems (but not the proofs) of the two published papers and took great care to develop the ideas and intuition behind the various assumptions. There is a full discussion, for example, of the "revealed-preference" argument. This initial section of the paper ends with a passage that has not, I believe, been previously noted:

> It is assumed that nothing is saved, and hence the problem of capital formation and of the rate of interest is not treated at all;...second, it is assumed that the production of a unit of S_j is technically possible by one method only.... In a later note the author will treat a corresponding dynamic system of equations in which capital formation and the interest rate will be considered, and in which the technical coefficients will be assumed to be variable. The solvability of this system will then be examined [Wald 1951, p. 379].

earlier version of this section, Lionel McKenzie (personal communication) noted that "Walras had written his demand functions with factor prices as well as goods prices as arguments. How these could be turned into Wald's inverse demand functions is far from obvious. Somehow income would have to be specified, even for outputs which are not producible. The only way to make sense of Wald's demand functions is to fix income at unity, say, and invert the ordinary demand functions $x_i = d_i(p_1,...,p_n,1)$. However, this does not work if there is more than one consumer, since it does not reflect changes in income distribution which will accompany price changes. In other words, to make sense of the demand functions it seems necessary to anticipate the solution of the whole system, or else to suppose there is only one consumer."

[14] Arrow (personal communication) notes that "there is an historical puzzle here, which may not be solvable with our data. The results on the equilibrium in an exchange economy do not seem provable with the methods Wald used earlier. In the *Zeitschrift* paper, [Wald] refers to these results and states that they require modern results in mathematics. This hints at the possibility that he did use a fixed point theorem. Gerard Debreu and I will try to consider this problem further. However, since the manuscript is lost, we shall probably never know."

Section II of this paper dealt with the "equations of exchange." Wald supposes that indifference curves are given by differential equations; the first-order conditions and budget equations appear, and Walras's Law is used to reduce the number of independent equations by one. The assumptions that no individual holds negative stocks, that there are positive stocks of each good, that each individual has a positive endowment, and that diminishing marginal utility prevails are claimed by Wald to ensure a competitive exchange equilibrium as long as the marginal utility of a good is independent of the amount held of other goods; substitutes *and* complements are excluded. These demand restrictions are very strong. Wald takes Walras to task by presenting Walras's own discussion and interjecting (p. 384) "a rather vague argument!" It is indeed a tragedy that the proofs of the theorems in this paper never appeared because of the forced closing of the *Ergebnisse*.

The final substantive section of this 1936 paper concerned the "Existence and Stability of Equilibrium in Cournot's Duopoly" and contained, aside from some very uninteresting specific reaction functions, an early and correct use of the equilibrium–stability distinction. Wald wrote:

> We define an equilibrium point D to be stable if, with a sufficiently small, but otherwise arbitrary, departure of the supplies of the two producers from the equilibrium point D, *the reaction mechanism* again leads to the equilibrium point D [Wald 1951, p. 392, italics added].

Morgenstern's advice to Wald to do an expository survey had not been gratuitous. In 1933, shortly after Wald had done his two initial papers, Menger introduced Wald to "Oskar Morgenstern, who was then director of the Institut für Konjunkturforschung. Morgenstern appreciated Wald's talents and increasingly employed Wald in his institute" (Wolfowitz 1952, p. 2). As Morgenstern recalled in 1951, "[Out] of an arrangement made at first only for convenience – he getting a modest subsidy from the Institute for advising on a variety of minor statistical difficulties such as were to be expected in an economic research unit – I developed a strong desire to interest him genuinely and more fully in economics and statistics" (Morgenstern 1976, p. 493). Morgenstern was persuasive. In 1936 Wald published a book on the analysis of seasonal variations of time series, *Berechnung und Ausschaltung von Saisonschwankungen* (Beiträge zur Konjunkturforschung, Volume 9), and thus developed the interest in statistical theory that increasingly drew him away from mathematical economic theory. Wald continued, however, to attend the Menger colloquium and indeed was a coeditor with Gödel and Menger of Volume 7 of the *Ergebnisse*; he had three mathematical pieces in the final issue, Volume 8 (1937), which contained the remarkable paper by John von Neumann, "Über ein

Ökonomisches Gleichungssystem und eine Verallgemeinerung des Brouwerschen Fixpunktsatzes" (von Neumann 1936).

The von Neumann connection

John von Neumann was born in 1903 in Budapest to a well-to-do family. Privately educated before entering gymnasium, he showed early mathematical talent, received private tutoring, and "was already recognized as a professional mathematician" (Ulam 1958, p. 2) before his matriculation at the University of Budapest. Although enrolled there as a mathematics student, he instead took courses at the Eidgenössische Technische Hochschule in Zurich in chemistry, returning to Budapest only to take exams at the end of each semester. "He received his doctorate in mathematics in Budapest at about the same time as his chemistry degree in Zurich."

In 1927 he became a Privat Dozent at the University of Berlin, a position he held for three years. "[During] that time [he] became well-known to the mathematicians of the world through his publications in set theory, algebra, and quantum mechanics."

It was a paper submitted to *Mathematische Annalen* in July 1927 (von Neumann 1928), titled "Zur Theorie der Gesellschaftsspiele" ("The Theory of Games"), that initiates an economist's interest in von Neumann. That paper contains an articulation of games with finitely many strategies, as well as the first proof of the minimax theorem. The proof used a fixed-point argument to establish the existence of a saddle point for a function

$$h(\xi,\eta) = \sum_{p=1}^{M+1} \sum_{q=1}^{N+1} \alpha_{pq} \xi_p \eta_q,$$

where the α_{pq} are constants and ξ_p and η_q are vertices of simplexes of appropriate dimension[15] (von Neumann 1963, p. 13). (We shall return to this paper later when discussing the theory of games.) For the present, it suffices to note that the minimax theorem has, as a context, certain dual systems of inequalities with explicit non-negativity constraints on the ξ_p and η_q (somewhat masked by their interpretation as weights on the vertices of a simplex). It can be assumed that this paper of von Neumann's was known to mathematicians by 1930.

In that year von Neumann accepted a visiting professorship at Prince-

---

[15] A simplex in R is the point 1. In R^2 it is the line formed by joining $(0,1)$ and $(1,0)$. In R^n it is the set of points $\{x : x_i \varepsilon [0,1]$ and $\Sigma_{i=1}^n x_i = 1\}$. A simplex in R^n is thus an R^{n-1}-dimensional object.

ton, a position made permanent in 1931. In 1933 he accepted an invitation to join the Institute for Advanced Study, where he remained through his mathematical career, as a professor. During summers through the 1930s von Neumann traveled to Europe to seminars, conferences, and mathematical meetings. It is certain that he passed through Vienna and visited Menger's seminar. [It is also certain, however, that he and Morgenstern did not meet until 1939 (Morgenstern 1976b, p. 807).]

Von Neumann apparently presented a talk to a Princeton mathematics seminar in the winter of 1932 on equilibrium in a dynamic economy.[16] A final version of this paper (von Neumann 1936) appeared in 1937 as the last paper of the last *Ergebnisse* issue; it was also presented to the Menger colloquium in 1937 (Morgenstern 1976b, p. 807) and Wald, a coeditor of the issue, may have played a role in its polishing. In any event this paper, "Über ein ökonomisches Gleichungssystem und eine Verallgemeinerung des Brouwerschen Fixpunktsatzes" ("On an Economic Equation System and a Generalization of the Brouwer Fixed-Point Theorem")[17] compels our attention.

Von Neumann's paper is, in my view, the single most important article in mathematical economics. As Tjalling Koopmans noted, "The paper contains the first explicit statement...of what has been subsequently called the activity analysis model of production.... [Further, its main purpose was to] exhibit a model of competitive equilibrium,...[and] the

---

[16] I have recently been told the following story by Axel and Earlene Leijonhufvud who, in the course of their oral history project on emigré economists, had been told it by the late Jacob Marschak.

During the late 1920s (approximately 1928) Leo Szilard organized several mathematicians and physicists in Berlin into an informal study group to hear lectures on the role of mathematics in other disciplines. Marschak was asked to give such a lecture about economics. He talked about the Walrasian (Cassellian?) equations of general equilibrium and apparently noted some problems about free goods. One of the mathematicians became extremely agitated and began a stream of interruptions, arguing that the equilibrium relationships should be described by inequalities instead of equations. That mathematician was von Neumann.

This story, told by Marschak, suggests that the genesis of von Neumann's *Ergebnisse* paper was quite specific and roughly contemporary with von Neumann's paper on game theory. The min–max idea, the duality ideas, and the strategy of proof to be used later for the fixed-point theorem are found in each paper. The papers appear, then, to be naturally related not only by content, but also by place of origin.

[17] This article was translated for the *Review of Economic Studies* in 1945–6 by George Morgenstern (who later changed his last name to Morton) as "A Model of General Economic Equilibrium." The printing was terrible. The *Ergebnisse* date is wrong. The translator changed the name of the economy from W to E, making the second reference to the "splitting" of W a total mystery. It is in this form that the paper is reprinted in both von Neumann's *Collected Works*, and in Peter Newman's *Readings in Mathematical Economics*. Although Baumol and Goldfeld, in *Precursors in Mathematical Economics*, reprint with the corrections for the *Ergebnisse* date, the mysterious W continues to plague even an attentive reader.

paper contains the first rigorous, formal, and fully explicit model in non-aggregative capital theory" (Koopmans 1964, p. 356). Yet Koopmans claims too little. The paper also contains the first use in economics of certain now common tools: explicit duality arguments, explicit fixed-point techniques for an existence proof, and convexity arguments.

The paper assumes n goods $G_1, \ldots, G_n$ and m processes $P_1, \ldots, P_m$, so, if the processes are linear,

$$P_i: \sum_{j=1}^{n} a_{ij} G_j \longrightarrow \sum_{j=1}^{n} b_{ij} G_j,$$

where a_{ij} is "used up" and b_{ij} is "produced."[18] If x_i is the intensity of the ith process y_j is the price of good j, the economy expands at a rate α, and β is the interest factor, then the equations of the economy are (using von Neumann's numbering scheme)

(3) $x_i \geq 0;$

(4) $y_j \geq 0;$

(5) $\sum_{i=1}^{m} x_i > 0;$

(6) $\sum_{j=1}^{n} y_j > 0;$

(7) $\alpha \sum_{i=1}^{m} a_{ij} x_i \leq \sum_{i=1}^{m} b_{ij} x_i,$

(7')   where, if $<$, then $y_i = 0;$

(8) $\beta \sum_{j=1}^{n} a_{ij} y_i \geq \sum_{j=1}^{n} b_{ij} y_j,$

(8')   where, if $>$, $x_i = 0.$

Von Neumann's model[19] thus assumes "that there are constant returns (to scale); . . . that the natural factors of production, including labour, can be expanded in unlimited quantities, . . . [and] consumption of goods takes place only through the processes of production which include the necessities of life consumed by workers and employees. In other words

---

[18] Thus the process P_i maps, or transforms, the first sum to the second sum. a_{ij} is thus the amount of good G_j used up in process P_i operating at unit intensity, while b_{ij} is the amount of good G_j produced by that same process. Modern usage suppresses the letters P and G.

[19] Thus the intensities x_i and prices y_j are dual variables. Assumptions (3) and (4) are non-negativity restrictions, and (5) and (6) are viability assumptions; (7), (7') and (8), (8') are complementary slackness conditions for the dual inequality systems.

we assume that all income in excess of necessities of life will be reinvested" (von Neumann 1936, p. 2). Von Neumann also assumes that $a_{ij} + b_{ij} > 0$ to prevent the breakup of the economy into subeconomies.

The proof that there exist x's and y's satisfying $(3)-(8')$ is instructive. First replace (3) and (5) by $(3')$ and $(5')$, respectively, where x' replaces x, and replace (4) and (6) by $(4')$ and $(6')$, respectively, with y' replacing y. Now define

$$\phi(X',Y') = \frac{\displaystyle\sum_{i=1}^{m}\sum_{j=1}^{n} b_{ij}x'_i y'_j}{\displaystyle\sum_{i=1}^{m}\sum_{j=1}^{n} a_{ij}x'_i y'_j},$$

where x'_i and y'_j are variables. Von Neumann shows (p. 5) that a solution to the original system exists if, and only if, for X a vector of x's and Y a vector of y's,

(7**) $\phi(X,Y')$ assumes its minimum value for Y' if $Y' = Y$;

(8**) $\phi(X'Y)$ assumes its maximum value for X' if $X' = X$.

Thus the existence of an equilibrium is equivalent to the existence of a saddle point of $\phi(X',Y')$ and, at an equilibrium (saddle point), $\alpha = \beta = \phi(X,Y)$.

Homogeneity in X and Y allows the x_i and y_i to be elements of m- and n-dimensional simplexes; the vector $(X,Y) = (x_1,\ldots,x_m; y_1,\ldots,y_n)$ lives in R^{m+n}. The problem is really to show that the x's that solve (8**) for given y's can be used to generate y's that solve (7**) for given x's. Thus if "$V =$ the set of all $(X,Y) = (x_1,\ldots,x_m;y_1,\ldots,y_n)$ fulfilling [(7)**, and]$\ldots W =$ the set of all $(X,Y) = (x_1,\ldots,x_m;y_1,\ldots,y_n)$ fulfilling [(8)**]" then if V and W have a point in common, that point is the equilibrium (p. 6).

Von Neumann demonstrated this by establishing a much more general result. Notice first that homogeneity in X and Y enables one to use the facts that X is essentially a simplex in R^m and Y is almost a simplex of R^n. The problem is thus set up as one of establishing a fixed point of a mapping whose domain is (almost) a simplex in R^{m+n}. The Brouwer fixed-point theorem applies to continuous mappings of simplexes to themselves. Von Neumann established a more general result than Brouwer's concerning fixed points of continuous mappings. This enabled him to show that indeed V and W do have a point in common: A set of points that solve (7**) can generate a set of points that solve (8**), and there is at least one point that each such set has in common.

The narrow focus of our narrative, on equilibrium, rules out noting more than the fact that von Neumann had actually solved the problem, initially posed by Cassel and further defined by Wald, of establishing an equilibrium in a uniformly expanding economy. Indeed, von Neumann established that, for an economy in such an equilibrium, the rate of interest equals the rate of growth. Such a result, however, paid explicit attention to the price–quantity duality, the complementary slackness conditions induced by the non-negativity constraints, and the convexity of the production and price sets induced by returns to scale and homogeneity. (In some ways, one of the most interesting and curious ironies of this history is that the very general fixed-point theorem developed in the von Neumann paper was not necessary to obtain his result on the existence of an equilibrium growth path. A decade later several authors, starting with Loomis in 1946, were able to demonstrate this fact.[20])

As a matter of history, it is unclear just how von Neumann's 1932 seminar paper at Princeton, certainly done independently of Wald and the Menger colloquium, was refined by contact with Menger (or Wald) into the version that was published in 1937. In his 1936 survey Wald had indicated that *he* intended to examine equilibrium in a growing economy, which suggests that when that paper was written, probably in 1935, he was not aware of von Neumann's work. In any event Wald did not write such a paper; perhaps in helping edit the von Neumann paper for the final volume of the *Ergebnisse* he saw results stronger than those of his own projected paper. It is also true, of course, that Wald's own models had a different flavor from von Neumann's. Wald had emphasized factor use and supply and the problem of allocating scarce resources. Von Neumann emphasized the choice of activities, and his complementary-slackness relations involved factor prices, activity levels, and profit inequalities.

It is worth noting another element of the story here. Morgenstern, well trained as an economist, had had a continuing interest in the interaction of events and predictions, especially the interaction of agents when their predictions and foresight link their behaviors in the marketplace. In "Vollkommone Voraussicht und Wirtshaftliches Gleichgewicht" Morgenstern (1935) presented the now famous Sherlock Holmes–Moriarty "I think – he thinks..." problem, with its "strategic" reasoning. Morgenstern was invited by Schlick to present these ideas to the Vienna Circle; he later recalled that "I repeated this talk, at Menger's request, in his Colloquium and after the meeting broke up, a mathematician named Edward Čech came up to me and said that the questions I had raised were identical with those dealt with by John von Neumann" in his 1928 paper (Morgenstern 1976b, pp. 806–7).

---

[20] I am grateful to Gerard Debreu (personal communication) for alerting me to this point.

The westward movement

Von Neumann obtained a permanent position in the United States in 1931. Other European scientists, no less conscious of what Churchill called "the gathering storm," had likewise begun to consider emigrating by the mid-1930s. There was a lengthy period in which "the political situation in Austria deteriorated from month to month. The *Ergebnisse* was criticized [in 1937] (with specific reference to Wald) for its large number of Jewish contributions" (Menger 1952, p. 19). Schlick had been assassinated.

The Nazis entered Vienna March 11, 1938. "Schlesinger, who occupied a rather prominent position, chose death that same day" (Menger 1952, p. 19).[21] As Morgenstern recalled, "I was dismissed as 'politically unbearable' from the University as well as from my Institute, which I had left [while on a trip to the United States] in the hands of my deputy who emerged as a Nazi" (Morgenstern 1976b, p. 807). "Wald himself continued for a few weeks after Hitler's arrival in Vienna. He was dismissed by Morgenstern's successor but not otherwise molested. But I was greatly worried about his future as long as he remained in Austria, and with other friends, I tried to get him to the United States" (Menger 1952, p. 19).

That effort had been proceeding even before March 1938. On Morgenstern's initiative (and also that of Ragnar Frisch) Alfred Cowles had extended an invitation, in 1937, to Wald to become a staff member of the

---

[21] There is a terrible irony in Schlesinger's suicide, since he was instrumental in arranging the mechanism by which many German academics were relocated in England. Leo Szilard's (1969) "Reminiscences" tells the following story, which is worth recounting here. Szilard wrote that "while I was in Vienna [in April 1933] the first people were dismissed from German universities, just two or three; it was however quite clear what would happen. I met, by pure chance, walking in the street a colleague of mine, Dr. Jacob Marschak, who was an economist at Heidelberg and who is now [1968] a professor at Yale. He also was rather sensitive; not being a German, but coming from Russia he had seen revolutions and upheavals, and he went to Vienna where he had relatives because he wanted to see what was going to happen in Germany. I told him that I thought since we were out here we may as well make up our minds what needed to be done and take up this lot of scholars and scientists who will have to leave Germany and the German universities. He said that he knew a rather wealthy economist in Vienna who might have some advice to give. His name was Schlesinger and he had a very beautiful apartment in the Liechtensteinpalais. We went to see him and he said, 'Yes, it is quite possible that there will be wholesale dismissals from German universities; why don't we go and discuss this with Professor Jastrow.' Professor Jastrow was an economist mainly interested in the history of prices, and we went to see him – the three of us now – and Jastrow said, 'Yes, yes, this is something one should seriously consider,' and then he said, 'You know, Sir William Beveridge is at present in Vienna. He came here to work with me on the history of prices, and perhaps we ought to talk to him.' So I said, 'Where is he staying?' and he said, 'He's staying at the Hotel Regina.' It so happened that I was staying at the Hotel Regina, so I volunteered to look up Sir William Beveridge and try to get him interested in this.

Cowles Commission in Colorado Springs. He had apparently decided to accept the offer even before the Nazi takeover, yet as a Rumanian citizen Wald had to exit from that country, and "he had great difficulty getting back to Rumania, from where he went to the United States" (Morgenstern 1951; 1976a, p. 493), apparently by way of Cuba (Wallis, personal communication).

Menger had also gone to the United States in 1937, taking an appointment first at Notre Dame and eventually settling at the Illinois Institute of Technology in Chicago. Morgenstern, with half of his salary paid for three years by the Rockefeller Foundation (which had supported the Vienna Institute), secured a position at Princeton. Gerhard Tintner, also associated with the group of Vienna economists at Morgenstern's Institute, came to the Cowles Commission in 1936 and began teaching at Colorado College. In 1937 he left for a distinguished career at Iowa State University. It is reasonable to believe that Tintner, as well as Frisch, was the link between Cowles and Wald.

Wald's reputation had preceded him. Volume 5 of *Econometrica* (1937, p. 188) contains the first reference in English that I have been able to locate to Wald's work.[22] A report on the December 28–30, 1936, meeting of the Econometric Society in Chicago notes:

> [Tintner] also referred to the remarkable work of a young Viennese mathematician, A. Wald, who has shown the conditions under which the

---

"I saw Beveridge and he immediately said that at the London School of Economics he had already heard about dismissals, and he was already taking steps to take on one of those dismissed, and that he was all in favor of doing something in England to receive those who have to leave German universities. So I phoned Schlesinger and suggested that he invite Beveridge to dinner. Schlesinger said no, he wouldn't invite him to dinner because Englishmen, if you invite them to dinner, get very conceited. However, he would invite him to tea. So we had tea, and in this brief get-together, Schlesinger and Marschak and Beveridge, it was agreed that Beveridge, when he got back to England, and when he got the most important things he had on the docket out of the way, would try to form a committee which would set itself the task of finding places for those who have to leave German universities. He suggested that I come to London and that I occasionally prod him on this, and that if I were to prod him long enough and frequently enough, he thought he would do it. Soon thereafter he left, and soon after he left, I left and went to London.

"When I came to London I phoned Beveridge. Beveridge said that his schedule had changed and that he found that he was free and that he could take up this job at once, and this is the history of the birth of the so-called Academic Assistance Council in England." [From "Reminiscences" by Leo Szilard, edited by Gertrud Weiss Szilard and Kathleen R. Winsor, in *The Intellectual Migration*, edited by Donald Fleming and Bernard Bailyn (Cambridge: Harvard University Press, 1969), pp. 97–8. Copyright 1968 by Gertrud Weiss Szilard.]

[22] There was an additional reference to Wald's survey paper in 1938 in the *Zeitschrift für Nationalökonomie*. A paper by Alexander Bilimovic (1938), "Einige Bermerkungen zur Theorie der Planwirtschaft," refers (on p. 151) to Wald's allocation equilibrium results with reference to planning.

Walrasian equations have one and only one solution. His proof (published in *Ergebnisse eines Mathematischen Kolloquiums*, edited by Karl Menger, 1935 and 1936) assumes, however, that the utilities derived from different commodities are independent. There is not yet a solution of the general case.

(The same *Econometrica* volume, p. 91, also notes that both Schlesinger and Wald attended the Econometric Society's meetings in France on September 11–15, 1937.)

Wald had arrived in the United States as a mathematician familiar with the problems associated with statistical time series of interest to economists; such work was related to the interests of the Cowles Commission at that time. He was known, and his work on equilibrium was known, at least to Morgenstern at Princeton and to Tintner at Cowles and then Iowa State. The work had been noted at the Econometric Society meetings in 1936 and referred to in *Econometrica* in 1937. His paper in the *Zeitschrift für Nationalökonomie*, a major economics journal, placed the analysis of equilibrium in general equilibrium systems before the public; although written in German, it was available to those interested.

Wald's work had crossed the Atlantic before its author. He himself owed his life to that work, which had helped to gain him a U.S. visa. "His parents and his sisters were murdered in the gas chambers of Ossoviec (Auschwitz); his brother Martin, the engineer, perished as a slave laborer in Western Germany" (Menger 1952, p. 19). Eight members of his immediate family had been murdered. After the war, "he succeeded in bringing the sole survivor, his brother Hermann, to this country, and he took great comfort in his company" (Morgenstern 1951; 1976a, p. 497).

The United States: the 1930s[23]

As early as 1912, while [Irving] Fisher was vice-president of the American Association for the Advancement of Science, he had attempted to organize a society to promote research in quantitative and mathematical economics. Wesley C. Mitchell, Henry L. Moore, and a few others had been interested but they were too few, and for the time being nothing came of their vision [Christ 1952, p. 5].

It was not until 1928, when Frisch enlisted the support of Charles F. Roos and Irving Fisher, that this threesome took the steps to organize the Econometric Society. The members formally constituted themselves as an international society in December 1930 in Cleveland, and in September

---

[23] Much of the material for this section is drawn from *Economic Theory and Measurement: A Twenty Year Research Report, 1932–1952*, written by Carl Christ in 1952 for the Cowles Commission. This report is the most useful source on the topic of this section.

1931 in Lausanne, Switzerland. Activities of the society at first were limited to meetings, usually held in conjunction with the American Economic Association and the American Association for the Advancement of Science.

At about this time Alfred Cowles, discouraged by the poor performance of stock-market and business forecasters, was persuaded to foster his own interests by subsidizing the fledgling Econometric Society and a journal, to be called *Econometrica*. To this end, in September 1932 the state of Colorado, Cowles's home base, chartered the Cowles Commission for Research in Economics, a group whose purpose was "to educate and benefit its members and mankind, and to advance the scientific study and development...of economic theory in its relation to mathematics and statistics" (Christ 1952, p. 11).

In organization, the Econometric Society sponsored the Cowles Commission and guided it through an advisory committee whose initial members included Fisher, Frisch, A. L. Bowley of LSE, Mitchell of the National Bureau of Economic Research (NBER), and Carl Snyder of the New York Federal Reserve bank. The first issue of *Econometrica* appeared in January 1933.

It would be fair to characterize the American members of the Econometric Society as more guided by statistical interests than by theoretical ones. Despite the renown of Fisher, much of the economics profession had a bias against mathematical theory, a bias that did not extend as much to statistical work. Although there were individual exceptions, it was not uncommon for an economist to eschew completely any training in mathematics. (My colleague Martin Bronfenbrenner, a graduate student at Chicago beginning in the mid-1930s, took some calculus courses while a graduate student and recalls that such training was not required.)

It is not that formal theory, or even general equilibrium economics, was unknown in the United States. Cassel's *The Theory of Social Economy* was used as a textbook for an economic-theory course in the University of Chicago Business School in the mid-1930s. Henry Schultz was developing a research tradition in quantitative economics at Chicago. Harold Hotelling, at Columbia, was cited and well regarded. The NBER was fully involved in careful measurement and analysis of economic time series.

Yet the times were hostile to mathematical economics. The central problems of economic science were focused by the depression and mass unemployment. Many young economists shaped the policy experiments of the New Deal. Theoretical work followed such events. And the theoretical explosion associated with Keynes's *General Theory of Employment, Interest, and Money* in 1936 consumed the passion and interest of economists with a taste for theory. There were not that many professional economists, many fewer still with interests in theory, and for these the intellectual action was in the emerging Keynesian program.

It is thus not too far off the mark to identify the Cowles Commission with mathematical economic theory in the United States.[24] The summer conferences in Colorado in 1935 and 1936 included Harold T. Davis, Hotelling, August Loesch, Isadore Lubin, Snyder, Fisher, R. A. Fisher, Corrado Gini, E. J. Working, and others with interests in the relationship between economics, mathematics, and statistics.

The Cowles staff was forming too; Tintner joined in 1936. The position of director was hard to fill on Roos's departure in 1937. The distinguished director sought could not be induced to move to Colorado Springs; neither Frisch, Jacob Marschak, nor Theodore Yntema would move west. The summer conferences in 1937–9 saw such visitors as R. G. D. Allen, Mordechai Ezekiel, Trygve Haavelmo, Abba Lerner, Horst Mendershausen, Renè Roy, Schultz, and, in 1938, Wald, who was appointed a fellow of the commission for 1938–9.

In 1939 the Cowles Commission left Colorado for Chicago and an affiliation with the University of Chicago. Schultz's tragic death in November 1938 had led that university to consider "the possibility of adopting a group such as the Cowles Commission" (Christ 1952, p. 20) to replace Schultz. Yntema became director of research for the commission, and Chicago staff members Oscar Lange, Jacob Mosak, and H. Gregg Lewis became part-time staff of the commission. Wald did not move from Colorado to Chicago; instead he accepted a position proferred by Hotelling (on a grant from a Carnegie Foundation) as Hotelling's assistant at Columbia, and a temporary faculty position in mathematics at Queens College.

Lange left Chicago in 1942 to visit Columbia and resigned from Chicago in 1945. During 1942–5 Yntema resigned as research director for Cowles, and Marschak accepted a professorship on the Chicago faculty and the directorship of the Cowles Commission. He brought Koopmans first and then Lawrence R. Klein to the commission in 1944; Haavelmo came shortly after, and Kenneth Arrow, Herman Chernoff, and Herbert Simon came in 1947.

> The reorientation which Marschak and his new staff wrought in the Cowles Commission's research program is sketched in the following passage from the Annual Report for 1943: "The method of the studies . . . is conditioned by the following four characteristics of economic data and economic theory: a) the theory is a system of simultaneous equations, not a single equation; b) some or all of these equations include 'random'

---

[24] The major exception was to be Paul Samuelson, who was later joined by Robert Solow.

terms;...c) many data are given in the form of time series;...d) many published data refer to aggregates.... To develop and improve suitable methods seems, at the present state of our knowledge, at least as important as to obtain immediate results. Accordingly, the Commission has planned the publication of studies on the general theory of economic measurements.... It is planned to continue these methodological studies systematically" [Christ 1952, pp. 30–1].

With such a program adumbrated by 1943, there was clear recognition of the centrality of general equilibrium analysis in the development of economic theories sufficiently rich to provide a basis for empirical work. As an exemplar, consider the book *Studies in Mathematical Economics and Econometrics in Memory of Henry Schultz*, published in 1942. This volume, edited by Lange, Francis McIntyre, and Yntema, drew its contributions primarily from those associated with the Cowles Commission, Schultz's "successor" at Chicago.

For our purpose, it suffices to note William Jaffe's article on Walras, Lange's on Say's Law in a general equilibrium system, and Mosak's on the Slutsky equation (an article that thanks Wald for a crucial proof in an optimization argument). Tintner had a piece on "nonstatic" production theory that cites the Wald and von Neumann *Ergebnisse* papers in the course of an argument for the existence of equilibrium. The paper by Allen Wallis and Milton Friedman on indifference functions cited an immensely important 1940 paper by Wald on indifference surfaces and Engel curves. General equilibrium theory was in the air, but it was not the Menger colloquium that had cast it aloft. The primary reference was John R. Hicks's (1939) *Value and Capital*.

In an earlier book (Weintraub 1979) I attempted to indicate how Hicks's volume effected one of its primary objectives, stated in the book's introduction, of allowing economists "to see just why it is that Mr. Keynes reached different results from earlier economists on crucial matters of social policy" (Hicks 1939, p. 4). Nonetheless, Hicks's work had a more concrete genesis: "Our present task [in this book] may therefore be expressed in historical terms as follows. We have to reconsider the value theory of Pareto [and Walras] and then to apply this improved value theory to those dynamic problems of capital which Wicksell could not reach with the tools at his command" (p. 3).

Hicks's book was not unique in its concern to revive Walras and Pareto, or at least to bring the Lausanne tradition to bear on the concerns of English-speaking economists. Students at LSE in 1939–40 did not find *Value and Capital* surprising: They had been encouraged to think along those lines by various teachers. (Sidney Weintraub, at LSE at that time, recalled having *gone* there with a portion of Pareto's *Manual* translated.)

Nevertheless, Hicks's book developed the classical general equilibrium theory from the theory of the household and the theory of the firm in modern, neoclassical language. He then provided an equilibrium and stability analysis, the former by equation counting, the latter by static characteristics of the equilibrium relationships. The properties of equilibrium were well treated; the possibility of equilibrium was not recognized as a technically serious issue. Nonetheless Hicks's *Value and Capital* was a signal event for economists. The general equilibrium approach was developed in English; the most modern results in value theory – indifference curves and production functions – were integrated in the analysis, and the properties of the enriched system were explored in the clear prose of an Oxford-trained economist. The formal mathematical underpinnings were confined, as in Marshall, to mathematical appendices. It was there that mathematically sophisticated readers could appreciate the design. The macroeconomic orientation of Hicks's argument linked the concerns of the Keynesian literature, a macroeconomic literature, to an intellectual framework, general equilibrium theory, in which the microeconomics was fully articulated. The result was that microtheorists and Keynesians, mathematical sophisticates and "innumerates," could study *Value and Capital* together and see in its analysis a unity where before there appeared chaos.

The book had an immediate impact. It suffices to note in this vein the April 1941 *Econometrica* article by Paul A. Samuelson, "The Stability of Equilibrium: Comparative Statics and Dynamics," which set out and explored the mathematical definitions of stability and equilibrium (but recall Wald's 1936 *Zeitschrift* paper). Comparative static analysis was formally defined; both stability analysis and comparative statics were applied to the problem of multiple markets. Samuelson contrasted his approach with that of Hicks and further explored the problem by analyzing the IS–LM Keynesian model as a system of simultaneous equations that deserved an explicit analysis of equilibrium. However, Samuelson assumed the existence of equilibrium. He simply noted that the behavior of variables x_i in a set of n functional equations of the general form

$$F^i(x_1{}_{-\infty}^{\,t}(\tau),\ x_2{}_{-\infty}^{\,t}(\tau),\ldots,x_n{}_{-\infty}^{\,t}(\tau)) = 0, \qquad i = 1,2,\ldots n,$$

is "determined once certain initial conditions are specified" (Samuelson 1941).

Further he stated (pp. 137–8), following Frisch, that "stationary or equilibrium values of the variables are given by the set of constants $(x_1^0,\ldots,x_n^0)$ which satisfy these equations identically, or $F^i[x_1{}_{-\infty}^{\,t_o},x_2{}_{-\infty}^{\,t_o},\ldots,$ $x_2{}_{-\infty}^{\,t_o}] = 0$, $i = 1,2\ldots n$." He had, however, a footnote to this sentence:

Of course, such a set need not exist. Thus, the simple system $dx/dt = e^x - x$ has no stationary equilibrium values since $e^x - x$ has no real roots. Similarly, $dx/dt = 1$ defines no stationary equilibrium position.

Samuelson's techniques, including those present in his later *Foundations of Economic Analysis* (Samuelson 1947), avoided existence problems for general equilibrium systems. Samuelson generally linearized the functions $f_i(x_1, \ldots, x_n)$ that appear in a system like $x_i = f_i(x_1, \ldots, x_n)$, where the Taylor series is taken at an "equilibrium" x^*. Then nonvanishing of a Jacobian suffices for independence of the equations, and thus the assumed equilibrium is not inconsistent with the equations. This procedure, however begs all existence of equilibrium questions for nontrivial equation systems.[25]

Lest it be said that all economists followed Hicks in his approach to the analysis of general equilibrium systems, consider the June 1941 appearance, in the *Journal of Political Economy*, of the article "Professor Hicks on Value and Capital" by Oskar Morgenstern. This twenty-nine-page review article was a polemic. One object of Morgenstern's assault was Hicks's method of counting equations to establish the existence of an equilibrium for a general equilibrium system. Morgenstern wrote:

> Hicks' assertion is incorrect even from the point of view of history of doctrine. Moreover it is systematically incorrect because the determinateness of a system of equations does not necessarily depend only upon the equality of the number of unknowns with the number of equations.... We have as yet such [existence] proofs only for two systems of equations, those of von Neumann and of Wald [Morgenstern 1976a, pp. 370–1].

Morgenstern's basic point was that difficulties, truly serious difficulties in the mathematical-logical analysis of economic systems, cannot simply be assumed away by cheerful prose and appeals to common sense. Morgenstern later recalled von Neumann's comment on Hicks and on mathematical economics in the Hicksian tradition:

> "You know, Oskar, if those books are unearthed sometime a few hundred years hence, people will not believe they were written in our time. Rather they will think that they are about contemporary with Newton, so primitive is their mathematics. Economics is simply still a million miles away from the state in which an advanced science is, such as physics" [Morgenstern 1976b, p. 810].

---

[25] Put another way, the Taylor series–Jacobian technique defined the conditions under which equation counting provides necessary and sufficient conditions for the existence of a *local* equilibrium. However, because the Taylor series technique usually involves an expansion *around* the equilibrium point, the entire procedure was more directed toward exploring the properties of a putative equilibrium than toward demonstrating the possibility that such an equilibrium exists.

Morgenstern wrote his blast at Hicks, recalling von Neumann's comments on such writings, while he and von Neumann were fully engaged in the collaboration that resulted in the *Theory of Games and Economic Behavior* (von Neumann and Morgenstern 1947). It was this work, and the development of activity analysis and programming, that led to the articulation of the general equilibrium model and to the analysis of equilibrium in the early 1950s by Arrow, Debreu, and McKenzie.

The theory of games

Cěch's comment to Morgenstern that von Neumann had a similar interest in strategic behavior led to Morgenstern's first conversation with von Neumann, in February 1939 in Princeton during an afternoon tea with Niels Bohr. "Von Neumann told me that he had done no work on game theory since 1928 or on the expanding economy model. He may have thought one way or the other about it, but never in any systematic way, nor had he put down anything on paper" (Morgenstern 1976b, p. 808).

Morgenstern's conversations with von Neumann led to the economist's decision to "write a paper showing economists the essence and significance of game theory as it then existed." An early draft of the paper was read by von Neumann, who suggested a collaboration. This delighted Morgenstern, who later referred to this event, which took place in the fall of 1940, by saying " 'Er war mir ein Geschenk des Himmels!' [He] was my gift from Heaven" (Morgenstern 1976b, p. 808).

The collaboration was intense, and the paper expanded first to two papers, then to a small pamphlet, and ultimately to a very large book. The substantive Chapter II, defining and axiomatizing the mathematical concept of a game, was entirely new. (The 1928 paper had rather taken "game" to be as it is understood in ordinary language; the paper then proceeded to an analysis of the choice, or strategy, structure for two- and three-person zero-sum games, with extensions of the zero-sum idea to games with more than three players.) The fundamental existence theorem for two-person zero-sum games appeared in Section 17 of the book, with references to von Neumann's 1928 paper.[26] A footnote states that the min−max problem that is related to the game appears in a more general setting in certain economic models, such as those presented in von Neumann's *Ergebnisse* paper.[27] The authors there note that

---

[26] The theorem states that any two-person zero-sum game has an equilibrium solution in mixed strategies.

[27] Recall that the function ϕ, introduced in von Neumann's *Ergebnisse* paper, has a minimax solution at the "equilibrium" of the activity levels and prices.

it seems worth remarking that two widely different problems related to mathematical economics – although discussed by entirely different methods – lead to the same mathematical problem – and at that to one of a rather uncommon type: The "Min–Max type." There may be some deeper formal connections here [with the *Ergebnisse* paper].... The subject should be clarified further [von Neumann and Morgenstern 1947, p. 154n].

The footnote continues, pointing out that the original proof used Brouwer's fixed-point theorem and the *Ergebnisse* paper a generalization of that result that had itself been simplified by Kakutani (1941). Kakutani's paper, "A Generalization of Brouwer's Fixed Point Theorem," appeared in the *Duke Mathematical Journal*, which received it in January 1941 while Kakutani was at the Institute for Advanced Study, von Neumann's base. Kakutani had, however, begun corresponding with the editor of that journal in 1939, from Japan, so it would appear that the article, although perhaps polished near von Neumann, was conceived independently. The anonymous referee of the paper ("Referee's Report on Kakutani Paper" 1941) was willing to accept it for printing primarily because it was short and, unlike other fixed-point theorems, written in English, not German. (Kakutani thanked A. D. Wallace, the topologist, for help in discussing the problem.) The fixed-point theorem itself stated that "If $x \rightarrow \phi(x)$ is an upper semicontinuous point-to-set mapping of an r-dimensional closed simplex S into $A(S)$ [the set of closed convex subsets of S], then there exists an $x_0 \varepsilon S$ such that $\phi(x_0) \varepsilon A(S)$." A corollary showed that S could be any compact convex subset of a Euclidean space.[28] Using the theorem, Kakutani proved the von Neumann minimax theory in seven lines.

There was, however, a simpler way to prove the minimax theorem. As von Neumann and Morgenstern state in the footnote already cited, Jean Ville (1938) had likewise provided a proof of the minimax theorem, using elementary (nontopological) techniques, in his paper "Sur la Théorie Générale des Jeux où Intervient l'Habileté des Joueurs." This proof is based on convexity arguments, and the supporting hyperplane theorem.[29]

---

[28] Intuitively, the Brouwer theorem says that if a continuous function f maps a compact–convex set $S \subset R^n$ to itself as $f : S \rightarrow S$, then there is at least one point $\hat{x} \varepsilon S$ such that $f(\hat{x}) = \hat{x}$. The Kakutani theorem generalizes this result (or simplifies von Neumann's generalization of Brouwer) in two ways. First, f is a correspondence that maps points of $x \varepsilon S$ to *subsets* $S_x \subset S$. Continuity of the function is then weakened to upper semicontinuity of the correspondence. If S is compact and convex, and S_x is convex, then the conclusion of the Kakutani theorem states that there is some $\hat{x}$ such that $\hat{x} \varepsilon f(\hat{x}) = S_{\hat{x}}$.

[29] This theorem is now recognized as a corollary to the Hahn–Banach theorem of functional analysis. One version used by economists, the separating hyperplane theorem, states that, given a convex set and a point outside that set, there is a plane through the point that does not intersect the interior of the convex set.

[Morgenstern's discovery of the Ville paper is discussed in his 1976 article (Morgenstern 1976b).]

The importance of this proof, originally due to Ville but much improved by von Neumann and Morgenstern, should not be understated. Section 16 of the *Theory of Games and Economic Behavior* contains the tools used in the proof of the fundamental minimax theorem of Section 17. In particular, Section 16 contains a clear and comprehensive discussion of the geometry of R^n, vector operations, hyperplanes and half-spaces, convex sets in R^n, and the supporting hyperplane theorem. This discussion leads to the theorem of the alternative for matrices, which generates the fundamental duality results for the dual systems of linear inequalities crucial to minimax, and the later programming, arguments. This section presaged an entirely new approach to the structure of economic optimization theory, an approach that led to a global characterization of objective functions and constraint sets through convexity arguments. (Local characterization, using partial derivatives or marginal conditions, had been the standard approach since the "marginal revolution" of the latter part of the nineteenth century.)

The manuscript went to the printer in 1943 and appeared in September 1944. Von Neumann indicated to Morgenstern that "he did not expect a rapid acceptance [of the book's ideas;] rather we would have to wait for another generation. This view was shared by some of our friends, especially by Wolfgang Pauli and Hermann Weyl" (Morgenstern 1976b, p. 813).

In a magnificent understatement, Morgenstern reflected, "matters turned out in some ways quite differently." Leonid Hurwicz and Marschak wrote lengthy notices of the theory in 1945 and 1946, as did Wald in 1947, and Wald "in 1945 had already laid a new theory of the foundations of statistical estimation based on the theory of the zero-sum two-person game."[30]

The basic payoffs in the games von Neumann and Morgenstern considered were not money sums, or arbitrary "stuff." Early in the collaboration Morgenstern had argued against von Neumann's money-payoff idea. "I was not very happy about this, knowing the importance of the utility concept, and I insisted we do more" (p. 809). Their thinking about the possibility of a numerical representation of utility led to an axiomatiza-

---

[30] Lest this connection go unremarked, we refer to Wallis's excellent history (1980a, b) "The Statistical Research Group, 1942–1945": "Wald's work on decision theory [based on the minimax idea] had begun before his association [in 1943] with SRG [The Statistical Research Group]. When Savage first joined SRG, I introduced him to Wald at lunch one day. Wald discussed some of his ideas on decision theory and Savage, who was a former research assistant of von Neumann's, remarked that he knew a rather obscure paper that would interest Wald, namely, von Neumann's 1928 paper on games. Wald laughed, and said that some of his ideas were based on that paper. It is a highly technical and academic paper" (Wallis 1980b, p. 334).

tion of choices in risky situations; this allowed the inference of the existence of a real continuous function as an order-preserving representation of utility. Now called the von Neumann–Morgenstern utility indicator, it is unique up to linear transformations and is interpretable as "expected utility." The first edition, of 1944, contained the axiomatization and the indicator, but no proof. The book's success, and the need for a second edition in 1947, allowed the drafting of "a substantial appendix, giving the proof that our system of axioms for a numerical utility, set forth in the first edition, indeed gave the desired result" (Morgenstern 1976b, p. 814).

This line of analysis may be carried ahead to the early 1950s, when it had an indirect relationship to the papers to be examined later on the existence of equilibrium. In an April 1950 paper in *Econometrica*, titled "Rational Behavior, Uncertain Prospects, and Measurable Utility," Marschak, formerly of the Cowles Commission, provided a simpler set of axioms for a finite set of sure prospects. Herman Rubin, a former Cowles research associate and research consultant, generalized the Marschak paper to an infinite number of sure prospects. Then I. N. Herstein, a Chicago mathematician and Cowles research associate in 1951, and John Milnor, similarly a distinguished mathematician, then at Princeton and associated with the RAND Corporation, worked separately to "clean up" the axiomatization. The subsequent Herstein–Milnor collaboration yielded a Cowles paper (number 65) late in 1952, which appeared in *Econometrica* as "An Axiomatic Approach to Measurable Utility" (Herstein and Milnor 1953).

Such work on the von Neumann–Morgenstern axiom system was very hot at the Cowles Commission in that period. The French mathematical economist Gerard Debreu, recently arrived in the United States thanks to a Rockefeller Fellowship, became a Cowles research associate in June 1950. He proved that the numerical representation (by utility) of preferences was not restricted to the case of risky prospects. His results, developed in an April 1952 Cowles discussion paper (number 2040), appeared with the title "Representation of a Preference Ordering by a Numerical Function" (Debreu 1954) as Chapter XI in the book *Decision Processes*, edited by Thrall, Coombs, and Davis.

There is one further development worth identifying at this point, for it provides a direct bridge between the papers on the theory of games and those on the existence of equilibrium. In what is certainly the shortest article (less than one page of type) of major importance to economists, John Nash, a Princeton mathematician, generalized the von Neumann–Morgenstern equilibrium for two-person zero-sum games to n-person games. His paper, submitted in late 1949 to *The Proceedings of the National*

Academy of Sciences, was called "Equilibrium Points in *N*-Person Games." Nash defined an equilibrium of an *n*-person game as an *n*-tuple of strategies (one for each player) such that the strategy of any player is optimal (yields the highest payoff) against the equilibrium $(n - 1)$-tuple defined by the remaining players (their own equilibrium strategies being determined analogously). The proof used the Kakutani fixed-point theorem to show that all *n*-person zero-sum games possess such an equilibrium (now called a Nash equilibrium); Nash noted that "in the two-person zero-sum case the 'main theorem' [of von Neumann and Morgenstern] and the existence of an equilibrium point are equivalent" (Nash 1950, p. 49). As von Neumann's *Ergebnisse* paper on economics generalized the basic equilibrium of two-person game theory presented in 1928, so the Debreu paper, and the later Arrow and Debreu papers, on economic systems would generalize the *n*-person equilibrium idea of Nash. The pace of new results had quickened; the list of contributors to this literature was growing rapidly.

There remains, however, one other distinct line of work to examine before we can again concentrate our attention on the existence-of-equilibrium literature. Simultaneously with, and related to, the burgeoning work on the theory of games, a literature was growing on "activity analysis," "linear models," or "programming." This work was to have a direct bearing on the existence-of-equilibrium literature.

Activity analysis

In late June 1949 the Cowles Commission hosted a Chicago conference on linear programming. The participants formed a virtual "Who's Who" of mathematical economics, from Arrow, George Dantzig, and David Gale to Koopmans, Samuelson, and Marshall Wood, from Arman Alchian to Tibor Scitovsky. In addition to economists, there were mathematicians, statisticians, administrators, and military planners. The subject matter, which represented the confluence of distinct lines of inquiry, was focused and developed by the papers of that conference. The proceedings formed the book *Activity Analysis of Production and Allocation*; its editor was Koopmans (1951a).

Koopmans had received his doctorate from Leiden, The Netherlands, in 1936. From 1938 to 1940 he did research at the League of Nations, in Geneva, on business cycles. In 1940 he came to the United States, and from 1942 to 1944 was a statistician at the Combined Shipping Adjustment Board in Washington. In 1944, he joined the Cowles staff, where he was appointed research director, following Marschak, in 1948.

In his introduction to the 1951 volume Koopmans identified four lines of research that had jointly created the subject matter of linear programming or activity analysis. "A specific historical origin of the work in this volume is found in discussions among Austrian and German economists in the thirties on generalizations of the Walrasian equation systems of mathematical economics" (Koopmans 1951a, p. 1). The ensuing paragraphs (p. 2) explicitly recognize the work of Wald and von Neumann: "We have dwelt on these discussions in some detail because even among mathematical economists their value seems to have been insufficiently realized."

The second line of influence was the "new" welfare economics, which from Barone through Lange and Abba Lerner had "the underlying idea ...that the comparison of the benefits from the alternative uses of each good, where not secured by competitive market situations, can be built into the administrative processes that decide the allocation of that good" (p. 3).

The third stream was "the work on interindustry relationships, initiated, developed, and stimulated largely by Leontief...and given statistical expression by measurements and tabulations provided by the Bureau of Labor Statistics." Thus the welfare economics idea of how a planner or decision maker could develop efficient allocation schemes was linked to Leontief's input–output tableaus, with their explicit linear structure.

The final stream of ideas was based on the work by Dantzig and Wood for the U.S. Department of the Air Force and on related work at the RAND Corporation (in conjunction with the Air Force) on the organization of defense, the conduct of the war, and other specifically war-related allocation problems. Koopmans's own work at the Shipping Board, for instance, had dealt with the efficient routing of cargo ships. As Koopmans (1951a) noted, "It does seem that governmental agencies, for whatever reason, have so far provided a better environment and more sympathetic support for the systematic study, abstract and applied, of principles and methods of allocation of resources than private industry." Similarly appreciative sentiments, of course, were also being voiced by physicists, chemists, and engineers in the period of the Manhattan Project.

The papers themselves, presented or abstracted in June 1949, provide a useful overview of the concerns and research directions of mathematical economists in the late 1940s. They are thus worth examining for the light they cast on the early 1950s. The general methodology was developed in the papers by Wood and Dantzig and by Koopmans. The former pair provided a revision of their 1948 paper, called in the 1951 book "The Programming of Interdependent Activities: General Discussion." The authors defined "programming, or program planning...as the construction of a schedule of actions by means of which an economy, organization, or other complex of activities may move from one defined state to another" (Wood and Dantzig 1951, p. 15). They cited von Neumann's 1937 paper as a progenitor of such an approach, which can take two forms. "In the first formulation, the quantities of each of several activities contributing directly to objectives (or 'final demand') are specified for each time period.... In the second...we seek to determine that program which will, in some sense, most nearly accomplish objectives without exceeding stated resource limitations" (pp. 16–17).

The Koopmans paper, "Analysis of Production As An Efficient Combination of Activities" (Koopmans 1951b), was the central paper of the collection. Koopmans himself has noted "that when I came to read [the *Ergebnisse* papers] I was more interested in von Neumann's...work. I brought [the *Ergebnisse*] paper by von Neumann to Dantzig's attention, who then went to explain his work to von Neumann, who in turn introduced George [Dantzig] to duality ideas" (Koopmans, personal communication).

The 1951 version of the Koopmans paper had been read, in an earlier version, at the Madison meeting of the Econometric Society in September 1948. Koopmans credited Dantzig with interesting him in a more general context than his own initial analysis of transportation problems. The idea of the paper was to go behind the given technique that economists used in their production function analysis. "The 'technique' employed in production is itself the result of managerial choice (going beyond the discarding of unwanted factor quantities). Managers choose between, or employ efficient combinations of, several processes to obtain in some sense best results" (Koopmans 1951b, p. 34). The paper axiomatized production through activity analysis, in a fashion analogous to the contemporaneous axiomatization of utility and consumer choice.

The model was developed by defining the scalar y_n, $n = 1,2,\ldots,N$, as the total *net* output of the nth commodity. The kth activity is a set of coefficients a_{nk} $(n = 1,2,\ldots,N)$ "indicating the rate of flow per unit of time of each of the N commodities involved in the unit amount of that activity" (p. 36). Nonnegative scalars x_k indicate the amount or level of the kth activity, whose corresponding flow is $x_k a_{nk}$ $(n = 1,2,\ldots,N)$.

This notation leads to the following definition:[31]

> A point y in the commodity space $[R^n]$ is called possible in a technology A $[(a_{nk})]$ if there exists a point x [in R^K] in the activity space satisfying $y = Ax$, $x \geqslant 0$ [p. 47].

---

[31] If x is an n vector, $x \geqq 0$ means that $x_i > 0$ for all i. $x \geqslant 0$ means that $x_i \geqq 0$ for all i and, for some j, $x_j > 0$. $x \geqq 0$ means $x_i \geqq 0$ for all i.

The technology A is structured by several postulates. The first states that there is no x satisfying $y = Ax = 0$, $x \geq 0$. This rules out reversible modes of production, or the production of inputs from outputs. Second, there is no vector x satisfying $y = Ax \geq 0$, $x \geq 0$; one cannot produce something from nothing.

It should be clear that the activity levels defined by x take the form of restrictions defined by the intersection of half-planes. Production analysis thus can be formally developed from the properties of cones in R^n or, alternatively, by special kinds of convex sets. Hence by defining cones to satisfy certain properties one has a formal model for the production analysis, and the production results can be interpreted in the algebraic structure of the model conclusions. Specifically, the role of prices – actually shadow prices – develops from certain orthogonality arguments related to supporting hyperplanes.

Other papers in the conference volume attest to the worth of this approach to choice under constraint. The Leontief model was explored by Harlan Smith, Samuelson, Koopmans, Arrow, and Nicholas Georgescu-Roegen. There were applications of linear programming to crop rotation, by Clifford Hildreth and Stanley Reiter; to program planning (for the military), by Wood and Murray Geisler; to the aircraft industry, by Wood; to transportation, by Koopmans; and to technical change, by Simon. Gale and Murray Gerstenhaber explored the mathematics of convex cones. The relationship between linear programming and game theory, following the von Neumann and Morgenstern conjecture (noted in the previous section), was delineated by Dantzig and by Gale, Harold Kuhn, and Albert Tucker. Finally, Dantzig, Robert Dorfman, and Koopmans defined and analyzed the computation of efficient solutions, using Dantzig's simplex method.

The conference was important. Many of the mathematical economists in the United States participated and shared their understandings. They developed a coherent framework for the programming approach, one that emphasized convexity and the allied properties of general topology and algebra:

> The belief may here be expressed that the theory of points sets in general, and of convex sets in particular, will be an increasingly important tool in economics. In many economic problems a preference ranking of alternatives representable by points in a space is confronted with an opportunity set. Often both the opportunity set and the set of points preferred-or-indifferent to any given point can be assumed convex. In such cases the use of convexity properties readily permits the study of optimizing choice from all available alternatives. On the other hand, the methods of calculus, more familiar to economists, permit at best a comparison of the

chosen alternative with alternatives in its neighborhood, and that only if the required number of derivatives exist [Koopmans 1951a, p. 10].

Thus by mid-1949, and certainly by 1950, mathematical economists had (1) some knowledge of attempts, and successes, in establishing the existence of equilibrium in sensibly specified economic models; (2) a basic understanding of useful ways to model interrelated constrained-choice systems; and (3) fixed-point-theorem techniques for demonstrating the compatibility of strategies or independent choices. The problem of showing the existence of a competitive equilibrium was accessible; the work remained to be done.

Properties of the competitive equilibrium

Koopmans's forecast that convexity and point-set-topology ideas would characterize new approaches to modeling was prescient. Simultaneously on the east and west coasts in August 1950, Gerard Debreu and Kenneth J. Arrow presented models of a competitive economy. They proved that competitive equilibria for these models are Pareto efficient and that Pareto-efficient allocations can be realized by a price system such that the allocation is also a competitive equilibrium.

Gerard Debreu had studied at the Ecole Normale Supérieure from 1941 to 1944, followed by service in the French army from 1944 to 1945. From 1946 to 1948 he was a research associate at the Centre National de la Recherche Scientifique (CNRS) and taught a course on business cycles at the Ecole d'Application de l'Institut National de la Statistique et des Etudes Economiques. He gained a Rockefeller Fellowship to study in the United States beginning in December 1949, spending the first six months at Harvard, the summer at Berkeley, and part of the fall at the Cowles Commission. He was appointed to the Cowles staff in June 1950 and held that appointment for more than ten years.

His first Cowles paper of June 1950 (new series, number 45) formed the basis of the paper he presented at the Harvard meeting of the Econometric Society; that paper was published in *Econometrica* as "The Coefficient of Resource Utilization" (Debreu 1951). The paper provided "a non-calculus proof of the intrinsic existence of price systems associated with the optimal complexes of physical resources – the basic theorem of the new welfare economics.... This proof is based on convexity properties" (Debreu 1951, p. 274).

The paper defines individual consumption vectors x_i and the now usual ordering (which Debreu notes need not entail the existence of a utility function) on consumption vectors. Production is treated by total-input vectors y whose components are negative for outputs, positive for inputs.

[Debreu cites Koopmans (1951b), although Debreu was not present at that Cowles conference on activity analysis.] With set summation, $x = \Sigma x_i$, where x is the total consumption vector. Thus $z = x + y$ is the *total* net consumption, and if z^0 is "the utilizable physical resources vector,... [the] constraints imposed by the economic system are [where Y is the set of technologically possible production vectors] $y \varepsilon Y$ [and] $z \leqslant z^0$" (Debreu 1951, p. 278). The problem is to characterize an optimal list of production vectors y_j^0 and consumption vectors x_i^0 by means of a price vector $p > 0$ such that, first, $p \cdot (x_i - x_i^0) \geqslant 0$ for all i and every x_i preferred or indifferent to x_i^0 and, second, $p \cdot (y_j - y_j^0) \geqslant 0$ for every j and every feasible y_j. Debreu thus exploited the set-theoretic structure of both the consumption and production spaces to obtain the *definition* of a competitive equilibrium and a characterization of that equilibrium as Pareto efficient.

Debreu noted (p. 282) that a paper by Arrow also "contains a non-calculus proof of the basic theorem. Unfortunately, I had his manuscript in my hands for too short a time to appraise it fully here." Recently Debreu has expanded on that note, recalling that

> in 1950–51, The Cowles Commission had an internal refereeing process and it is in this connection that I was shown the manuscript of K. J. Arrow's paper by William B. Simpson, then Assistant Director of Research of The Cowles Commission. As I recall, W. B. Simpson asked me whether Arrow's contribution should be included in The Cowles Commission Reprint Series, and also to comment on the substance of the paper. Little time was available, presumably because of a deadline imposed by the editor of the [volume] in which Arrow's paper was to appear. Since this was before the age of the Xerox machines, I had a copy of his paper in my hands only for a brief period. My comments must have been superficial and only Arrow's kindness can have led him to describe them [in his paper] as "helpful" [Debreu, personal communication].

Arrow was graduated as a mathematics major from the City University of New York in 1940. He became a graduate student in mathematics at Columbia in that year, intending to study mathematical statistics. "I found when I got there that mathematical statistics was not taught in the Mathematics Department but only by Harold Hotelling, who was a full Professor of Economics, and by an assistant, financed not by the University but by a grant to Hotelling from the Carnegie Corporation. The assistant was named Abraham Wald. Out of curiosity I took Hotelling's course in mathematical economics and immediately became hooked" (Arrow, personal communication).

Arrow's reading in this period, 1940–2, was designed to move him from mathematics to economics. He recalls that of course Hicks's *Value and Capital* made the biggest impression on me. Somewhere during this year (or possibly the next, when I was actually enrolled in the Economics Department), I realized, probably with some guidance from someone, that the existence of a solution to the equations of general equilibrium was an open question. I also learned, probably from Hotelling, of Wald's papers in the *Ergebnisse*. . . . I am pretty sure that I did not hear about Wald's papers from [Wald]; but I do remember asking him about them and about possible generalizations (particularly with regard to the production assumptions). He felt the field was very difficult and did not encourage further work. . . . I did read the papers at the time, but in retrospect I feel my understanding was most imperfect. My German was. . .not very good, but I think it was the complexity of the argument that really put me off. I did not believe I was the one capable of really improving on the results [Arrow, personal communication].

Arrow served in the weather division of the Army Air Force from 1942 to 1946, returned briefly to Columbia upon his military discharge, and joined the Cowles Commission in April 1947. He remained at Chicago until July 1949, when he accepted an appointment at Stanford. (His Ph.D. from Columbia was conferred in 1951.) In this period, from the Cowles years through the early 1950s, Arrow was immensely active.

Arrow's paper, referred to above by Debreu, was presented at Berkeley in August 1950. It appeared in print in *The Proceedings of the Second Berkeley Symposium on Mathematical Statistics and Probability*, edited by Jerzy Neyman. Titled "An Extension of the Basic Theorems of Classical Welfare Economics" (Arrow 1951) it indeed acknowledged "helpful comments" from Gerard Debreu. (It was reprinted as Cowles Commission paper, new series, number 54.) The paper's summary states that

> The classical theorem of welfare economics on the relation between the price system and the achievement of optimal economic welfare is reviewed from the viewpoint of convex set theory. It is found that the theorem can be extended to cover the cases where the social optima are of the nature of corner maxima, and also where there are points of saturation in the preference fields of the members of society [Arrow 1951, p. 507].

Arrow began by reviewing the marginal-analysis treatment of equilibrium and Pareto efficiency, pointing out the difficulties with ensuring, in a calculus treatment, non-negative prices and the necessary production of *every* product by every firm. The alternative approach, using convex sets, appeared in Section 3, with appropriate references to von Neumann, Koopmans, Wood, and Dantzig. Arrow worked with *distributions* X_{ij}, where this number represents the amount of commodity i to be given to individual j; X is a social distribution, an $m \times n$ array. For a given X, the numbers $X_{1j}, X_{2j}, \ldots, X_{nj}$ define the bundle X_j. Arrow assumed that the quantities consumed are non-negative, individuals' preferences are "selfish," and preferences are strictly convex. Suppose the social bundle ($\Sigma_{i=1}^{m} X_j$) is obtained by aggregating goods; it is thus a "bundle whose ith component is the sum of the ith components of the bundles $X_1, \ldots, X_m$"; then ΣX_j must lie in a set T known as the transformation set (p. 511). Arrow assumed T to be non-null, compact, and convex and, if $x \in T$, $x_i \geqq 0$ for every component x_i of x. Since preferences are defined over the X_j, optimality is easy to define given T. Using the separating hyperplane theorem for convex sets, Arrow demonstrated that equilibrium outcomes are optimal and that optimal distributions generate price vectors (which are defined by hyperplanes known to support the appropriate convex sets) that equate supply and demand, and are thus competitive equilibria. The paper by Arrow, like that of Debreu, indicates how consumers and producers, their respective choices, and competitive equilibria may be defined using the language of convex sets and supporting hyperplanes. The model of a competitive economy had appeared in its modern form. The welfare properties of a competitive equilibrium for this model were settled by 1951. What remained was the demonstration that there could indeed be a competitive equilibrium for the model.

Lionel McKenzie's international trade models

Lionel McKenzie was a graduate student in economics at Princeton from 1939 to 1941. His background was certainly less mathematical than that of either Arrow or Debreu, yet in 1940–1 he attended a course given by Morgenstern that examined Hicks's *Value and Capital*. He recalls (McKenzie, personal communication) that Morgenstern "cited the deep results arrived at on this subject [of solvability] by Abraham Wald and John von Neumann." (This obviously was at the time Morgenstern was writing his review of Hicks for the *Journal of Political Economy*.) McKenzie also recalls that "I was present when von Neumann presented his growth model to the Princeton graduate economics seminar.... However as Morgenstern [later noted in 1976b] the paper was not understood by anyone present, and so far as I am concerned, he is right."

There was another major influence on McKenzie at Princeton, the distinguished international trade theorist Frank Graham. In his 1974 conference paper, "Why Compute Economic Equilibria?" McKenzie noted:

> When I was a student of Frank Graham in the academic year 1939–40, he gave us a simple general equilibrium model of world trade as an exercise for his course. This model involved several countries and several

commodities, and we knew no algorithm for solving it. We used trial and error [McKenzie 1974, p. 1].

McKenzie, in that 1974 paper, quotes from a footnote in *The Theory of International Values* (Graham 1948, p. 95) on this subject. Graham had written:

> It has been suggested that a mathematical formula should be developed which would provide the solution instanter. This would, surely, be desirable, but mathematicians of great repute, to whom I have submitted the problem, have been unable to furnish any such formula (perhaps because they were not sufficiently interested to devote to it the necessary time).

McKenzie (1974, p. 5) commented on Graham's remark by noting that "tradition at Princeton was that the mathematician of [Graham's] footnote was John von Neumann.... It was also part of graduate student lore that a famous colleague [Morgenstern?] chided Graham for having no existence proof of uniqueness of equilibrium."

In any event, McKenzie's student work was interrupted by the war; he saw military service in Panama. Upon demobilization McKenzie studied economics at Oxford, recalling that "[although] I read Wilson's *Advanced Calculus* one summer [at Princeton,]...I was also reading philosophy and did not pursue the mathematical approach to economics" (McKenzie, personal communication). McKenzie's Oxford thesis, done under Hicks's supervision, was on "cost–benefit type analysis à la Harberger"; it was judged by Roy Harrod and Hubert Henderson to be in need of revision. McKenzie refused and so settled for a B.Litt degree, which in any event was no obstacle to his employment at Duke University in 1947.

While at Duke, in 1949, McKenzie noticed an abstract of the Koopmans paper given at the Econometric Society (Cowles) meeting on activity analysis. He recalls:

> I decided that this was just the type of theory I needed[32] so I wrote to Jacob Marschak at the Cowles Commission in Chicago about the possibility of visiting. This led to my stay at Chicago for one full year (12 months) in 1949–50, where I attended the seminars of Koopmans and Marschak and had the company of John Chipman, Edmond Malinvaud, Gerard Debreu, Martin Beckmann, et alia, taking the equivalent of a master's program in math. In Koopmans's class I wrote a term paper on "Specialization in Graham's Model of World Trade" [McKenzie, personal communication].

---

[32] "The need for further mathematical economics had been brought to my attention when I was writing my paper (1949) [see McKenzie 1951] on 'Ideal Output'" (McKenzie, personal communication). He notes further that the footnotes on pp. 794, 795, and 797 of that paper point to the directions he was to take.

That term paper, revised after McKenzie's return to Duke, appeared in the *Review of Economic Studies* as "Specialization and Efficiency in World Production" (McKenzie 1953–4).

It began by noting that

> the system of Walras, Cassel, and Leontiev assumes a given set of productive processes which are always in use. There is one field of traditional economics, however, where explicit discrimination between processes to be used and processes to be suppressed has always been the fundamental object of analysis. The problem of specialization in international trade according to comparative advantage is precisely the problem of selecting a group of productive processes to be used in the interest of maximum world output.... Although the classical economists would no doubt expect these points [of competitive equilibrium] to be points of maximum world output, they did not fully expose the relation of maximum output to the possibility of competitive equilibrium [McKenzie 1953–4, p. 165].

The paper is well structured. First, Graham's general equilibrium international trade model is "reduced" to a model of competition such that countries play the role of firms, and intermediate goods are ignored to permit concentration on trade in final goods produced from a linear technology. The trade model is thus formally equivalent to the Koopmans activity-analysis model. One finds the pattern of trade by using techniques introduced by Koopmans and Reiter (1951) in the Cowles conference volume. In outline, the Koopmans analysis was used to show that, for the Graham–McKenzie trade model, maximum world output is an "efficient equilibrium" in the sense of activity analysis. For a specific model of m countries, with n final goods able to be produced in each, McKenzie's first result was that sensible trade-model restrictions ensure specialization (and thus comparative advantage theorems) for each country at positive world prices. The emergent equilibrium *pattern* of trade resembles a network problem and is therefore solvable using algorithms developed for the ship-routing problem in the nascent programming literature.

While still at the Cowles Commission, McKenzie had begun thinking about the question of existence of an equilibrium for the competitive model, especially in the context of general equilibrium for international trade. "I recall walking back from Koopmans's class with Koopmans, Beckmann, and Chipman on one occasion after he had discussed the relation between activity analysis and competitive equilibrium.... [I asked] Koopmans about the existence question. He replied that it was a very deep question which had not been answered to that time" (McKenzie, personal communication).

Yet it was not until McKenzie's return to Duke, and his examination of the just-published volume on *Activity Analysis of Production and Allocation*, that he found references to the Wald and von Neumann papers, which he located in the Duke mathematics library. Thus in 1951, while writing up the paper on specialization, he "somehow...got the idea for the mapping of social demand from the origin on the world production possibility frontier [as a technique] for proving existence" of a competitive equilibrium in the Graham model. He recalls that

> I first worked this out with a smoothing of the frontier and the use of Brouwer's theorem. Then I recalled a Cowles Commission paper I had brought back with me from Chicago by Morton Slater on Kakutani's fixed point theorem and I saw that this was just what was needed for an elegant proof of the theorem.... Of course von Neumann had used essentially this theorem...in his paper [of 1937].... I had also acquired while at Chicago a set of notes [written by P. T. Bateman?] from a seminar on convex sets given by Marston Morse at the Institute for Advanced Study in Princeton in 1949–50.... They were useful to me in establishing the continuity properties of the support function of a convex set and my projection on the production possibility frontier, but also in helping me to understand the problem in a geometrical way [McKenzie, personal communication].

Except for McKenzie's remark that the idea of a cone technology did not play a real role in early versions of his existence proof, the paper, "On Equilibrium in Graham's Model of World Trade and Other Competitive Systems" (McKenzie 1954), which appeared in *Econometrica* refines his 1951–2 analysis of the existence of a competitive equilibrium. Given the length of the story to this point, some attention to this paper, and to those of Debreu and Arrow and Debreu seems appropriate. (The next section considers the related papers by Debreu and by Arrow and Debreu.)

McKenzie's paper began by discussing the Wald papers and Graham's model. He noted that, although Graham's demand functions satisfy the Wald restrictions (the weak axiom of revealed preference in the aggregate), Graham's production sector does not meet Wald's conditions; Graham used equalities not inequalities. McKenzie then stated that "it is my purpose to develop a more general existence proof where the demand functions are not confined so narrowly."

The model contained primary goods that are the labor supplies of n various countries; there are k final goods. The world technology is represented in a linear activities model by a partitioned matrix

$$A = \begin{bmatrix} A_{\text{fin}} \\ A_{\text{pri}} \end{bmatrix},$$

where $A^j_{\text{pri}} = (-1,\ldots,-1)$, so

$$
A = \begin{bmatrix} A^1_{\text{fin}} & \cdots & A^n_{\text{fin}} \\ A^1_{\text{pri}} & & 0 \\ & \vdots & \\ 0 & & A^n_{\text{pri}} \end{bmatrix},
$$

when *pri* and *fin* denote primary and final goods, respectively.

If x denotes a column n vector of activity levels, η denotes labor supplies, y_{fin} is a final−output vector, y_{pri} is a labor-input vector, w's refer to labor quantities, and p's are prices, then the model becomes as follows, using McKenzie's numbering scheme (McKenzie 1954, p. 149):

Production system:

$$(2.4) \qquad \begin{bmatrix} A_{\text{fin}} \\ A_{\text{pri}} \end{bmatrix} x = \begin{bmatrix} y_{\text{fin}} \\ y_{\text{pri}} \end{bmatrix},$$

$$(2.5) \qquad x \geqq 0,$$

$$(2.6) \qquad y_{\text{pri}} \geqq -\eta < 0.$$

Demand functions:

$$(2.7) \qquad w_{j\text{pri}} = -\eta_j, \quad p_{j\text{pri}} > 0 \qquad (j = 1,2,\ldots,n);$$

$$(2.8) \qquad w_{i\text{fin}} = b_i \frac{r}{p_{i\text{fin}}} \qquad (b_i > 0, \ \Sigma\, b_i = 1, \ i = 1,\ldots,k);$$

$$(2.9) \qquad r = p_{\text{fin}}\, y_{\text{fin}}, \quad p_{i\text{fin}} > 0.$$

It is also assumed that $a^j_i > 0$, so each submatrix A^i_{fin} of A_{fin} in (2.4) is nonzero. r is, of course, world income, and b_i is the proportion of world income devoted to the ith final good.

For this model McKenzie established directly that if X is the set of activity levels x satisfying (2.4)−(2.6), then X is compact and convex. Since feasible vectors y are such that $y = A_{\text{fin}}x$, the set of feasible y, denoted Y, is also compact and convex. McKenzie then showed that "$z \varepsilon Y$ is efficient" when $z \varepsilon Y$ and $\alpha z \notin Y$ for $\alpha > 1$. Such z are called extreme outputs, and they include the efficient points.

The economy's income is $p_{\text{fin}} \cdot y_{\text{fin}}$. "We shall then regard an equilibrium position as a price vector p and an attainable input−output vector y which (1) satisfy the demand functions and (2) leave producers with no opportunity for increasing profits" (McKenzie 1954, p. 152).

The profit condition is clearly equivalent to

$$(4.1) \qquad p \cdot A_i^j \leqq 0 \quad \text{and} \quad p \cdot A_i^j = 0 \qquad \text{if} \quad x_i^j > 0.$$

(Here all goods are final goods.)

McKenzie proceeded to characterize equilibrium: "We may now state that (p, y) is a competitive equilibrium in the Graham model if and only if

(4.2) (a) y_{fin} is attainable according to (2.4), (2.5), and (2.6).

           (b) The profit condition (4.1) is met.

           (c) p and y satisfy the demand functions (2.7), (2.8) with (2.9) and $w = y$."

The strategy of establishing existence of a competitive equilibrium thus involved producing p's and y's that satisfy (4.2a–4.2c). (Hereafter the subscript "fin" is dropped.) The proof was given in Sections 5 and 6 of the paper.

Section 5 showed that, *if* an equilibrium output exists, it is unique. The working assumption of this demonstration was the weak axiom of revealed preference, which McKenzie noted was "Samuelson's fundamental postulate for the theory of demand for a single consumer... [and which] Wald believed... probably held also for the body of consumers [in the aggregate]" (p. 154). The argument was straightforward, using Y's convexity, equilibrium, and the weak axiom.

The existence proof of Section 6 did *not* use the axiom, but it did postulate that the demand functions for final goods are homogeneous, nonnegative, and continuous for positive prices. Also, for fixed income there is no satiation of demand for a good as its price goes to zero. The economics of the proof was explained simply (p. 155): "We shall consider all social budget planes which touch the production transformation surface. Then we assume that total purchases, when the goods are available, will always lie on the budget plane.... Finally, we will prove that there is a budget plane for which the chosen point lies in the section of the plane which touches the production transformation surface, assuming the demand functions to be continuous functions of the prices of final goods."

Normalizing prices, McKenzie took p in the closed unit simplex S (a compact, convex set). Every $p \varepsilon S$ is normal (perpendicular) to some $y \varepsilon Y$, where Y is also compact and convex. Now, $r(p) = \max p \cdot z$ for $z \varepsilon Y$ is continuous, and so is $h(w) = \alpha w$, $\alpha < 1$, $\alpha w \varepsilon Y$, $k w \notin Y$ for $k > \alpha$. [$h(w)$ is the intersection of the ray from the origin containing w, a noninterior point of Y, with the set of extreme outputs of Y.]

If y is in the set of extreme outputs, define "$g(y) = K_y$ where K_y is the intersection of the set of normals to y [which include p's] with S" (p. 157). McKenzie then established that g is upper semicontinuous. However, the domain of g is a compact convex set, and K_y is a convex set, so the composition mapping $F = g \circ h \circ f^*$ [where f^* is the demand function suitably restricted by using $r(p)$] involves an upper semicontinuous map composed with two continuous ones. F is thus upper semicontinuous. Further, the domain of F is S, and its range is K_y, a compact convex subset of S. The Kakutani theorem immediately yields that F has a fixed point, "so there is a p which is contained in the set K_y into which it maps" by F (p. 158).

If p^* is the fixed point, define $y^* = h(f(p^*))$. Then this (p^*, y^*) is easily shown to be the competitive equilibrium, demonstrating (p. 158) "Theorem 2: Any Graham model has a competitive equilibrium."

The final sections of the paper generalized the results using a free-disposal assumption, variable labor supplies, and many primary goods under the assumption that consumers always have income. An appendix demonstrated the continuity of $r(p)$ and $h(w)$.

McKenzie presented his results one and one-half years after he left Cowles. He notes:

> My paper and the paper of Arrow–Debreu, which were developed completely independently, were presented to the (December) 1952 Chicago meetings of the Econometric Society. I recall that Koopmans, Debreu, Beckmann, and Chipman were at my session. The Arrow–Debreu paper had been given the day before and I had stayed away. However, Debreu rose in the discussion period to suggest that their paper implied my result. I replied that no doubt my paper also implied their result. As it happens, we were both wrong. Debreu [has told me] he spoke up after asking Koopmans's advice before the session. Later in his office, Debreu gave me a private exposition of their results [McKenzie, personal communication].

The Arrow–Debreu model

Debreu had not attended the 1949 Cowles Commission conference on linear programming; he joined the Cowles staff in June 1950. His paper on "The Coefficient of Resource Utilization," published in July 1951 and certainly written prior to June 1950, had gone part way to an analysis of the existence of a competitive equilibrium. Debreu recalls that

> it was when [the Koopmans monograph] was published that I learned of the existence of A. Wald's papers on general economic equilibrium, and only when the English translation appeared in *Econometrica* [see Wald 1936], October 1951 [as a memorial to Wald who, with his wife, had died in a plane crash in India], did I get acquainted with its contents. At that time, in the Fall of 1951, I was already at work on the problem of existence of a general economic equilibrium.... The influences to which I responded in 1951 were the tradition of the Lausanne School

and, in particular, the writings of Divisia, Hicks, and Allais; the theory of games and, in particular, the article of J. Nash; the [paper on fixed points by] Kakutani and the [1937] article of von Neumann...[as well as] the linear economic models of the Cowles Commission monograph [Debreu, personal communication].

The analysis that Debreu was doing paralleled the thinking of Kenneth Arrow, who had gone from the Cowles Commission to Stanford in 1949. Arrow notes:

> According to my recollection, someone at RAND prepared an English translation of the [Wald] *Ergebnisse* papers to be used by Samuelson and Solow in their projected book (sponsored by RAND), which emerged years later in collaboration with Dorfman. I read the translations and somehow derived the conviction that Wald was giving a disguised fixed-point argument (this was after seeing Nash's papers). In the Fall of 1951 I thought about this combination of ideas and quickly saw that a competitive equilibrium could be described as the equilibrium point of a suitably defined game by adding some artificial players who chose prices and others who chose marginal utilities of income for the individuals. The Koopmans paper then played an essential role in showing that convexity and compactness conditions could be assumed with no loss of generality, so that the Nash theorem could be applied.
>
> Some correspondence revealed that Debreu in Chicago...was working on very similar lines, though he introduced generalized games (in which the strategy domain of one player is affected by the strategies chosen by other players). We then combined forces and produced our joint paper [Arrow, personal communication].

This collaboration led to two papers, the first by Debreu, the second by Arrow and Debreu. They should be read as a pair. The former (Debreu 1952) was communicated to the *Proceedings of the National Academy of Sciences* on August 1, 1952, and appeared in Volume 38 of those *Proceedings*. The second paper (Arrow and Debreu 1954) was read on December 27, 1952, at the same Chicago meeting of the Econometric Society that heard McKenzie's paper on December 28. It was published in *Econometrica* as "Existence of an Equilibrium for a Competitive Economy."

The Debreu paper is the heart of the existence proof provided by Arrow and Debreu. Debreu began by noting that "the existence theorem presented here gives general conditions under which there is for [a certain type of] social system an equilibrium, i.e. a situation where the action of every agent belongs to his restricting subset [of actions constrained by choices made by other agents] and no agent has an incentive to choose another action. This theorem has been used by Arrow and Debreu to prove the existence of equilibrium for a classical competitive economic system" (Debreu 1952, p. 887). The initial paragraphs introduce the necessary material on convex sets, agents, and their actions, and define equilibrium in the sense of Nash, but in a more general form. The basic idea of the paper is to restrict the choice set of the agent in such a fashion that, if the objectives can be summarized by a function defined on the choice set with suitable continuity properties, there is an equilibrium for the generalized game. To appreciate the Debreu paper it is important to see how it was used by Arrow and Debreu. Their paper began by introducing the notion, and meaning, of a competitive equilibrium. Next, Section 1 introduced the notation for vector bundles and used the Koopmans production schema. For each of the n production units j, y_j is a production plan (an l vector) in a set Y_j. Let the aggregate production be specified by $Y = \Sigma Y_j$ and let Ω be the non-negative orthant of R^l. Then Arrow and Debreu [1954, p. 267] assume

> I.a. Y_j is a closed convex subset of R^l containing 0 $(j = 1,\ldots,n)$.
> I.b. $Y \cap \Omega = 0$.
> I.c. $Y \cap (-Y) = 0$.

With the technology so described, if p is an l vector of prices, then (p^*, y^*) is a competitive equilibrium only when "1. y_j^* maximizes $p^* \cdot y_j$ over the set Y_j, for each j."

Consumption behavior is treated (pp. 268–9) in

> II.   The set of consumption X_i available to individual i $(i = 1,\ldots,m)$ is a closed convex subset of R^l which is bounded from below...[and, if u_i is a utility indicator for individual i,]
> III.a $u_i(x_i)$ is a continuous function on X_i.
> III.b For any $x_i \varepsilon X_i$, there is an $X_i^1 \varepsilon X_i$ such that $u_i(x_i^1) > u_i(x_i)$.
> III.c If $u_i(x_i) > u_i(x_i^1)$ and $0 < t < 1$, then $u_i[tx_i + (1 - t)x_i^1] > u_i(x_i^1)$.

The system is closed by supposing that individuals have initial resource holdings (e.g., labor to be supplied) and they own the various production units (p. 270):

> The ith consumption unit is endowed with a vector ξ_i of initial holdings of the different types of commodities available and a contractual claim to the share α_{ij} of the profit of the jth production unit for each j.
> IV.a $\xi_i \varepsilon R^l$; for some $x_i \varepsilon X_i$, $x_i < \xi_i$;
> IV.b for all i,j, $\alpha_{ij} \geqslant 0$; for all j, $\Sigma_{i=1}^m \alpha_{ij} = 1$.

At an equilibrium x_i^* for the ith consumer, it must be true that consumers are at an optimum, as statement 1 said that producers are at an optimum. More formally (p. 271),

> 2. x_i^* maximizes $u_i(x_i)$ over the set $\{x_i \mid x_i \varepsilon X_i, \ p_i^* \cdot x_i \leqslant p^* \cdot \xi_i + \Sigma_j \alpha_{ij} p^* \cdot y_j^* \}$.

Prices are normalized to P, the unit l-simplex, so

3. $p^* \varepsilon P = \{p \mid p\varepsilon R^l, \ p \geq 0, \ \Sigma p_i = 1\}$ [and] if $x = \Sigma_i x_i, \ y = \Sigma_j y_j$,
$\xi = \Sigma_i \xi_i, z = x - y - \xi$, [then market equilibrium is described by]
4. $z^* \leq 0, \ p^* \cdot z^* = 0$.

Thus a competitive equilibrium is described by conditions 1–4. The result Arrow and Debreu sought to establish (p. 272) was "Theorem I: For any economic system satisfying Assumptions I–IV, there is a competitive equilibrium" defined by conditions 1–4.

Section 2 of the paper presents the Debreu result on equilibrium in an abstract economy. Section 3 reshapes the competitive economy into an abstract $(m + n + 1)$-person (Debreu) game in an imaginative fashion. Let $A_i(\bar{x}_i)$ be the set of generally feasible consumption bundles for consumer i. Then

> each of the first m participants, the consumption units, chooses a vector x_i from X_i subject to the restriction that $x_i \varepsilon A_i(\bar{x}_i)$, and receives a payoff $u_i(x_i)$; the jth out of the next n participants, the production units, chooses a vector y_j from Y_j (unrestricted by the actions of other participants) and receives a payoff of $p \cdot y_j$; and the last agent, the market participant, chooses p from P. . .and receives $p \cdot z$ [p. 274].

The proof by Arrow and Debreu then proceeded in two major steps. First, it was shown that, *if* an equilibrium exists (in the Debreu-game sense) for this economic system, then that equilibrium is a competitive equilibrium as defined by conditions 1–4.

The second step requires a demonstration that the sets from which the participants choose are appropriately compact and convex. This was the delicate part of the proof; it required adjustment of the choice sets and then analysis to show that the adjustments do not affect the argument. The final step required a demonstration that the payoff functions of the various participants are appropriately continuous. This argument too has some delicate steps but, on completion of the demonstration, the hypotheses of the Debreu theorem were established, and an equilibrium point was inferred. The theorem was thus proved.

Sections 4 and 5 weaken the assumption "that a consumption unit has initially a positive amount of every commodity available for trading" (pp. 279–80). The final section, Section 6, provided a short historical note discussing the arguments and models of Cassel, Neisser, Stackelberg, Schlesinger, and Wald. Arrow and Debreu remarked (p. 289), with respect to Wald, that their own paper is "much more general since Wald assumes fixed proportions among the inputs and a single output of every process. On the demand side, he makes assumptions concerning the demand functions instead of deriving them, as we do, from a utility maximization assumption. It is on this point that no direct comparison is possible," although the effect of Wald's use of "Samuelson's postulate" leads to the conclusion that in effect "he assumes a single consumption unit."

Arrow has commented upon this 1951 discussion of Wald:

> I may add that my reading of Wald in 1951 under the influence of having read Nash was wrong. I first realized this when I read a draft of McKenzie's [1977] Presidential Address to the Econometric Society [see McKenzie 1981], which asserted that his paper and that of Debreu and myself were fundamentally different from and more general than Wald's in the treatment of consumers.... This is not the way I had read Wald, and I wrote to McKenzie to contradict him; but then I reread Wald's original papers (with the hindsight of all the work I had done, the task was no longer so formidable) and found that McKenzie was 100% right. The Weak Axiom enormously simplified the problem. Hence, my generalization in that direction was taken without awareness that I was generalizing Wald! [Arrow, personal communication].

One final point is worth noting. The Debreu part of the proof of existence for the Arrow–Debreu model was communicated to the *Proceedings of the National Academy of Sciences* by a member of the academy. That member was von Neumann.

CHAPTER 7

Appraising general equilibrium analysis

Several questions organize any appraisal of general equilibrium analysis. Philosophers of science, economic methodologists, and historians of economic thought ask these questions as they evaluate work in economics. Is general equilibrium analysis a theory, a program, or a set of interrelated theories? Is it not a proper theory at all, but rather a branch of applied mathematics? Is it a formal structure like logic, or is it a language like English? Is it a metatheory – a set of rules for constructing economic theories? Has general equilibrium analysis led to, or been associated with, a growth in knowledge, or has it wasted professional resources? Is it connected to other economic theories, or does it stand apart from concerns of applied economists?

An appraisal of general equilibrium analysis must answer these questions. It must, however, do even more. A rational reconstruction of general equilibrium analysis must make the history of the analysis coherent. That is, any appraisal of the structure of general equilibrium analysis must explain the development of that structure. A full explanation of relativistic mechanics must explain not only the theory but also its development as a response to earlier theories. De Broglie's contribution to quantum mechanics is only partially comprehensive without an appreciation of the earlier models of Rutherford and Bohr. Thus I shall show that the case study of Chapter 6, which concerns the development of an existence-of-equilibrium theorem, has a clear interpretation within the framework of my appraisal. The case, as evidence for my hypothesis, is not anomalous; it will corroborate the appraisal I shall present.

The neo-Walrasian research program

Since the days of Walras and Pareto the analysis of interrelated markets has been associated with the "Lausanne tradition." Cassel's *Theory of Social Economy*, which initiated one line of papers, was discussed in the previous chapter. In the late 1930s Hicks's *Value and Capital* promised to reinvigorate the "school" of Walras and Pareto and to blend with their work the capital-theoretic insights of Knut Wicksell. The resulting structure was designed by Hicks to integrate the theory of Keynes, particularly his monetary theory, with the older tradition in value theory that had its best articulation in the writings of the Lausanne economists. Hicks's book was well received. Oscar Lange, Don Patinkin, and others in the 1940s refined and developed the Hicksian integration of Keynesian monetary theory with the Lausanne value theory. The result was to be called the neoclassical synthesis.

As noted in Chapter 5, *Microfoundations* (Weintraub 1979) characterized the microfoundations literature as an attempt to link two scientific research programs, the Keynesian program and the neo-Walrasian program. For present purposes it is necessary to define the neo-Walrasian progam with more care.

Without claiming novelty or a definitive statement of the program's character, I assert that the neo-Walrasian research program is characterized by its hard core, its heuristics, and its protective belts. The program is organized around the following hard core propositions:

HC1. There exist economic agents.
HC2. Agents have preferences over outcomes.
HC3. Agents independently optimize subject to constraints.
HC4. Choices are made in interrelated markets.
HC5. Agents have full relevant knowledge.
HC6. Observable economic outcomes are coordinated, so they must be discussed with reference to equilibrium states.

The positive and negative heuristics of the program consist of propositions like the following:

PH1. Go forth and construct theories in which economic agents optimize.
PH2. Construct theories that make predictions about changes in equilibrium states.
NH1. Do not construct theories in which irrational behavior plays any role.
NH2. Do not construct theories in which equilibrium has no meaning.
NH3. Do not test the hard core propositions.

If these propositions define the program, practitioners will be puzzled and disturbed by those who ask whether agents do, in fact, optimize. They will be confused by the question of whether agents do in fact have full knowledge. It is not that these assumptions are incidental, that the neo-Walrasian analyst merely likes their convenience. They are tenets, overriding assumptions, that by the definition of the program command assent. The hard-core propositions are questioned only by "outsiders." A neo-Walrasian may be in sympathy with the questioner, but the question itself is meaningless within the program; to ask such a question is to place oneself outside the program.

Asserting that there is a neo-Walrasian research program in the sense of Lakatos is easy. Defending this point of view requires a willingness to "try it out," to see whether the argument can address the issues of nonfalsifiability and excessive formalization. Can it resolve as well questions concerning the independence of the Arrow–Debreu–McKenzie model from applied economics and the existence of insufficient links between the general equilibrium approach and applied economic analysis? Can the idea of the neo-Walrasian program aid in an appraisal of work in general equilibrium analysis? Can it make sense of lines of development in economic analysis?

Such questions will focus the rest of this chapter. As an indication of how the argument will proceed, of how a Lakatosian perspective addresses real issues, consider how one would appraise recent work in economic demography.

Recall that the notion of a program can be used to reconstruct a line of theorizing and generate a sequence of problem shifts. Now, suppose one were interested in explaining the number of children that families have. Suppose that one is a neo-Walrasian. First, one would assume that the number of children is an outcome or state that results from choice. One would assume that the agents are well-defined household units called families and that those families have preferences as to number of children. The families are constrained by income, time, and other factors. The optimizing choice of number of children is made together with the family's other optimizing choices. These choices are reflected in coordinated market outcomes. Research topics thus include examining how the number of children varies as the mother's income varies, as the father's number of hours worked varies, as the cost of housing varies, as race varies, and so on. The resulting sequence of models has an organic unity because the models are all constructed according to rules, heuristics, that show how the hard core of the program may be developed into potentially falsifiable theories. Appraising work in this area thus requires that one identify the sequence M of models or theories and show how each M_t, compared to its predecessor M_{t-1}, does or does not predict a novel fact. Compared with M_{t-1}, does M_t have excess empirical content, some of which is corroborated? Are M_{t-1} and M_t linked by shared features drawn from the hard core of the program? Assessing progress, or its absence, is a well-defined exercise from the Lakatosian perspective. Appraising theories of the quantity of children is an activity in which the rules are clear and the results are visible for all to see. There is nothing hidden in an appraisal developed along Lakatosian lines. An individual may believe that an appraisal of this type ignores much that is important to evaluating a theory. In the example, one may argue that it is not progress to treat children like heads of lettuce purchased by rational economic agents. Such criticisms are not, however, criticisms of the theory, of the models in the sequence; they are fundamentally criticisms of the entire neo-Walrasian program. It would indeed be intellectual progress if such criticisms were directed to the program, especially the hard core, and not to its instantiation in a theory, or sequence of theories, in the protective belt.

This example suggests some strengths of the Lakatosian approach, but since my argument is based on the idea of a scientific research program, it is well to recall some general objections to its use. First, it is not clear from Lakatos's work whether programs are "big" or "small." That is, with reference to Blaug's *Methodology of Economics*, is there a neoclassical program and a separate program in consumer behavior? Or is the latter a theory in the belt of the former? Or is it a subprogram? Remanyi's (1979) work on cores and demicores suggests one way around these questions. For my purposes, they require no answer; *if* there are any Lakatosian programs in economics, the neo-Walrasian program must be present on the list.

A second objection to the methodology of scientific research programs concerns the limited role played by falsifiability in programmatic reconstructions of scientific practice. Falsification as an activity is occasionally associated with the belts, but so is empirical work concerned with corroborating the excess content of successor theories or models. Programs are not falsified. They may degenerate, they may be subsumed by other programs or replaced by them, but they are not falsified in the sense that a critical experiment leads one to say that a program is moribund. Programs rely for their growth less on falsifications than the Popperians would have it. For economists imbued with the Popperian *Zeitgeist*, Lakatosian appraisals permit too much activity to be appraised favorably, that is, as contributing to progress or the growth of knowledge.

A third objection to Lakatosian appraisals differs from the Popperian objection. It argues instead that the methodology of scientific research programs is a brand of critical rationalism and as such cannot attend to actual scientific practice. As Feyerabend would argue, the best gambits of successful scientists show that progress is too complex to be understood as a manifestation of any single methodological canon. In good science, anything goes. Indeed, appraisals based on Lakatosian programs leave out much that can facilitate an understanding of the scientific history. In his "History of Science and Its Rational Reconstruction" Lakatos (1978a) argued that the MSRP approach represents an intellectual history of science that ignores its social history. There is no doubt that a full understanding of a line of work in economics requires a relevant social history. Yet the intellectual history, the programmatic reconstruction, allows an "internalist" test. It may permit a judgment on the strength or weakness of a line of enquiry independent of people, their beliefs, their social groupings, and their personal weaknesses. The Lakatosian approach to the appraisal of work in economics is a starting place, not a final destination.

Hardening the hard core

The best way to see how the idea of a neo-Walrasian program can aid in an appraisal of general equilibrium analysis is to put it to work. Consider the sequence of papers on the existence of equilibrium presented as a case study in the previous chapter. Is it an interesting but sterile sequence of mathematical theorems, or is it good economics? How can the idea of a neo-Walrasian program help to answer such questions?

In "Falsification and the Methodology of Scientific Research Program" Lakatos (1970, p. 48) notes that the " 'core' is 'irrefutable' by the methodological decision of its proponents: anomalies must lead to changes only in the 'protective' belt of auxiliary, 'observational' hypotheses and initial conditions." Lakatos has a footnote to this sentence which reads: "The actual hard core of a programme does not actually emerge fully armed like Athene from the head of Zeus. It develops slowly, by a long, preliminary process of trial and error. In this paper this process is not discussed."

In "Schools, 'Revolutions,' and Research Programs," in a collection (Latsis 1976) of essays on the application of Lakatosian methods to economics, Leijonhufvud (1976, p. 79) made the following remark: " 'Hard cores' do not always spring fully armed from the brow of some venerated Thunderer. Surely, they usually take a considerable time to 'harden.' Yet, Lakatos tells us little about this 'hardening process.' We probably need a theoretical account of it and criteria for recognizing it (before it is completed), for the process whereby a hard core hardens is apt, I believe, to bear at least some superficial resemblances to the activities mentioned by Lakatos as characterizing a 'degenerating' research programme."

It is my contention that the sequence beginning with the Schlesinger paper and continuing through those of Wald, von Neumann, Koopmans, Arrow, Debreu, and McKenzie should be recognized as a hardening of the hard core of the neo-Walrasian research program. This hypothesis makes sense of the historical record in a way no other explanation offered so far does.

The hard core of the program, as outlined here, contains a number of propositions. Numbering the statements of this hard core suggests that the core, *in that form*, was present from the outset, that it indeed organized the sequence of models and theoretical analyses as early as 1930. This perception is inaccurate. *The hard core as presented can be said to have existed only as early as the early 1950s. The recognition that Arrow, Debreu, and McKenzie had accomplished a major feat was precisely the recognition that the hard core of the neo-Walrasian program was, by their work, no longer problematic.* This is a strong claim. What evidence supports it?

Consider the several propositions HC1–HC6. In a different form, each of these could have been framed by Walras. That is, he would not have had difficulty providing an interpretation of each term so that every term would have been "true," or acceptable as an analytic basis or working hypothesis. Yet Walras's producer had few choices to make within a fixed-coefficient technology, utility functions and not preferences were basic, and the knowledge assumptions (e.g., perfect information) were implicit. The core proposition that equilibrium states exist was assumed by Cassel. Certainly there were attempts by Walras and Edgeworth to argue that this proposition was consistent with the other propositions. They thought it desirable to show that an equilibrium could exist and that such an equilibrium could be derived in models in which the other hard-core propositions were assumed to be true.

Look at the positive heuristic of the program and recognize that it, in Lakatos's view, "consists of a partially articulated set of suggestions or hints on how to change, develop the 'refutable variants' of the research programme, how to modify, sophisticate, the 'refutable protective belt'" (Lakatos 1978b, p. 50). In the neo-Walrasian program this leads the analyst to construct theories based on optimizing choice and equilibrium outcomes and to explore the effect of giving different interpretations, in different models, to undefined terms like "agent," "outcome," "knowledge," or "market." If such a research strategy is to produce any result at all (where results, recall, consist of propositions about equilibrium states), it is certainly required that the analysis not lead necessarily and in every case to nonsense. That is, *it must at least be logically possible that the propositions about optimizing agents be consistent with the proposition about equilibrium.* If they are not, then the positive heuristic's rallying cry, to go forth and construct models with equilibrium outcomes, leads to a quest for a mathematical economic unicorn.

The situation which is quite similar to one that comes up in any formal system, is recognizable to anyone who has studied geometry. Consider a set of axioms about lines and points that define Euclidean geometry. These axioms, of course, contain words or phrases that initially have only commonsense interpretation. Formally, "line" is simply a word that is used in a certain way. Now drop the Euclidean line-intersection postulate and replace it with the axiom that two nonparallel lines meet in exactly two points. The geometer is charged to go out and prove theorems about this system of axioms. Can any be proved? If the axioms are inconsistent, then his efforts will produce nonsense. A test of consistency is well known: Does there exist a model of the axioms? That is, does there exist a set of interpretations of the terms of the system such that the axioms are in fact, under that interpretation, true? For the geometry just presented, one can interpret "point" as a point on the surface of a sphere and "line" as a great circle passing through two diametrically opposite points on the surface. The intersection postulate is then true, even though the perfect sphere does not exist in the world of our senses.

The situation is the same for the hard core because the hard core functions like the axioms for a program; one must accept the Euclidean parallel postulate if one is doing Euclidean geometry. The question then arises, Are the hard-core propositions of the neo-Walrasian research program consistent? A demonstration of consistency requires a model for the propositions in the sense that the terms of the propositions are interpreted in that model and, for the model, the propositions are actually true. This requires the following: Given a set of propositions like HC1–HC6, the theorist must create a model in which terms like "agent," "preference," "optimize," "constraint," and "equilibrium" have a well-defined meaning. Analysis must then show that the propositions are true. For the neo-Walrasian program this requires that HC1–HC5 are taken to be true and that HC6 is true when they are. In other words, a consistency check requires the production of a model in which a competitive equilibrium exists. The papers that culminated in those of McKenzie and of Arrow and Debreu are exactly of this form.

A rational reconstruction of the history may help to convince the reader that my claim has merit.

A logical reconstruction

By around 1930, work in general equilibrium analysis had produced the following situation: There was a model of two classes of agents and their actions in the sense that there was a partial model of factor demands and supplies, there was a partial model of the supply and demand for final goods and services, and these two sectors were at least partially integrated. Choices of agents were optimizing choices, and the notion of equilibrium was understood as a balancing of forces. Equilibrium was not taken to be something that had to be proved, however. Instead, it was a feature of the situation that was believed to be consistent with the various assumptions. Asserting that there was a balance of forces did not appear to violate any of the other assumptions of the model.

The appearance was not the reality. The papers by von Stackelberg (1933) and Zeuthen (1933) showed that the equilibrium notion violated the coordination assumption in the sense that negative prices, which cannot coordinate any market outcome, could not be ruled out as solutions to the Cassel model. Schlesinger was then able to show how the assumptions of the model could be rephrased to allow agent choice, at least in a primitive production model, to be based on an optimization framework. His choice structure precluded the possibility of negative prices. The Schlesinger model also extended the idea of markets and goods to allow free goods to result from market choices and equilibrium outcomes. His model analysis did not include a demonstration that equilibrium exists; it simply presented assumptions about the agents, their choices, the markets, and the equilibrium. In other words his model interpreted the assumptions in a new way that made those assumptions mutually coherent.

It was necessary for this model to show that the agent, market, and optimization assumptions entailed the existence of a competitive equilibrium. The proof was contained in the first Wald paper (Wald 1934) under the restrictive assumption that cross-commodity interrelationships were not present in the final demand for goods. The second Wald paper (Wald 1935) removed this restriction. The third Wald paper (Wald 1936), on exchange, apparently made more coherent assumptions about the market structure: It detailed the exchange context of the optimizing choices. This paper was not published, however, and only the result, not the proof, was ever reported.

Simultaneously, von Neumann (1936) presented a different model, one based on a different tradition but that nonetheless made assumptions about agent choice, optimization, markets, and equilibrium. The von Neumann model was a disaggregated growth model, yet the issues were identical to those already identified. Von Neumann proved that there exists an equilibrium; the assumptions he made were not only coherent but mutually consistent. By the mid-1930s there were thus two general equilibrium models, models arising, perhaps, out of different traditions but nonetheless similar: Each interpreted the components of the hard core of the neo-Walrasian program, and each provided interpretations of the loosely interpreted terms of the hard core.

Yet the interpretations of the basic terms were very restrictive. They did not allow "goods," for example, to have the properties required for an analysis of the butter market, say, or the retail housing market. Very few theorems could thus be created in the protective belt. Hicks's (1939) model expanded the set of permissible interpretations with more explicit concepts of agent, optimizing choice (especially the choices of the households), commodities (by allowing time and capital goods and a form of money), and an equilibrium notion that respected the interpretations of the other hard-core terms. Hicks did not prove that the resulting set of propositions were mutually consistent. Neither did Lange (1944) or Samuelson (1941), who themselves further extended the interpretations of the basic terms. Their work permitted the hard core to generate theories in the protective belt of the neo-Walrasian program in such a way that those theories could be compared with the theories in the belt of the Keynesian program. Patinkin's work in the 1940s (Patinkin 1949) established this tradition. His interpretation of the hard core extended its monetary theoretic reach. Patinkin was aware that a full-scale existence proof was desirable and referred the reader to the proofs of Wald and von Neumann. The difficulty was that their proofs of existence were for much less complex models.

The work of the late 1940s modified the interpretations of Hicks and Patinkin. Although the models that were developed had a very rich conceptual framework of agents, their choices, and the markets in which those choices were manifest, there were components of the models that had inadequate interpretations. For example, production was not based on optimizing decisions. Koopmans's (1951a, b) production model was developed at this time and was quickly incorporated into the standard general equilibrium model. That is, the emerging standard model used Hicks's households with preferences and optimizing choices, Koopmans's production choice theory, Patinkin's rich framework of market interrelationships, and the idea of equilibrium as the potential prereconciliation of plans, a notion probably derived from Samuelson. Those assumptions, interpretations of the hard-core propositions really, led to a family of consistent models. Within a short period of time Arrow and Debreu presented a proof as did McKenzie independently, of the existence of a competitive equilibrium in such canonical models. Those models, now demonstrated to be consistent, have been the basis for further work up to the present. Recent studies have extended the interpretations of such terms as "money," "knowledge," and "market," allowing the theories in the protective belt to be directed to new sets of questions. For example, one cannot construct theories about inflation or persistent unemployment in the neo-Walrasian program unless the commodity concept subsumes a rich concept of money. One has to prove the existence of equilibrium for a model so interpreted; if no such equilibrium can be found, then the call to go forth to construct theories is hollow indeed.

This reconstruction of the series of papers on the existence of a competitive equilibrium corroborates the claim that there exists a neo-Walrasian research program in the sense of Lakatos. The sequence of papers represents a hardening of the hard core of that program. *Progress, for this sequence, is a sequence of interpretations of the terms of the hard core such that (1) each successive interpretation is manifest in a consistent model, (2) each successive interpretation contains the interpretation of the predecessor, and (3) each allows a concept uninterpreted by that predecessor to be interpreted.*[1] This corresponds quite well to what Lakatos called a theoretically progressive problem shift. It does not, of course, correspond to the Lakatosian notion of progressivity, which requires that there be empirical testing – corroboration – of the excess content or extended interpretation.

What is general equilibrium theory?

I have argued that there is a neo-Walrasian research program. I have further argued that the sequence of papers discussed in the case study represents the hardening of the hard core of that program. The hardening process proceeded like any mathematical investigation; consequently, we have to appraise it as we would appraise any research line in mathematics. We have to ask about the strength of the theorems that were proved and the counterexamples that were produced along the way, as well as how these counterexamples were incorporated into the theorem structure as a sequence of lemmas. The theorems in the sequence of papers we have considered, which have been seized upon by economists and philosophers alike as a testament to the unscientific character of economics, instead represent a natural progression in the development of any scientific research program. A. Leijonhufvud (1976) alluded to the fact that the hardening of the hard core would, if we could identify it, look suspiciously like programmatic degeneration. His insight has been insufficiently appreciated. The sequence traced in the case study has appeared to economists and philosophers alike as an example of everything that is wrong with economics.

Falsificationists of various views, Blaug (1980) for instance, have argued that work on general equilibrium models is wasted energy that could better be spent developing falsifying instances of previous GE models. For such Popperians the production of new existence proofs is itself proof that the theory lacks empirical content. In their view, the activity substitutes mindless mathematizing for hard scientific analysis. This view is mistaken. *What seems like "more and more of the same old model" is rather a set of interpretative*

---

[1] I am using "interpretation" in the sense of a *bijective mapping* between a set of mathematical concepts and a set of economic concepts (where the concepts *may* be functions, relationships, or propositions). Thus, under a particular interpretation, by definition an economic proposition is true if and only if the corresponding mathematical proposition is true. "Consistent interpretations" is therefore redundant: Consistency is relevant for *propositions* given an interpretation. (I am grateful to Dale Stahl for noting this point.)

extensions of the terms of the programmatic hard core. What appears to be non-chalance about the empirical content of the existence-proof models is instead a sensible division of labor between hard core and belt.

Some theorists develop interpretations that frame the basic facts about our daily economic life – time matters, expectations matters, money matters, inflation matters, exhaustible resources matters, and so on. Other theorists and applied economists test those frameworks. This work is "located" in the protective belt. The fact that the analyst places such realistic topics on an agenda for general equilibrium modeling is an act of intellectual heroism. It shows a willingness to expose the models to worldly tests, in which real events are predicted using the theories that make up the protective belt of the neo-Walrasian program.[2] It is nonsense to speak of a theory about the demand for electricity in the state of North Carolina, a theory related to the theory of demand for durable goods, if there is no consistent model that interprets both "capital goods" and "equilibrium." Consider the effect of changing the electricity rate structure for residential users from declining block rates to time-of-day rates. Analysis requires that equilibrium usage change in a predictable fashion as rates change; it is a general equilibrium model that allows that particular set of inferences to be drawn. It is within the neo-Walrasian program that such partial equilibrium theorizing makes sense.

Thus the arguments of the philosopher Rosenberg (1980, 1983) are only

---

[2] Recall that HC6 asserted that *observable outcomes are coordinated*. The usual interpretation of this claim proceeds by assuming that *actual* states are equilibrium states. In practice, this means that, for one working in the program, analysis is conducted as if, or assuming that, equilibrium must be present in any *model*. This usually has the force of making the economist work from the perspective that as much as possible should be analyzed from the equilibrium mindset. This position has been defended most recently by Reder (1982) in his discussion of Chicago-school economics, and by Lucas (1980a, p. 288), who stated that a synthesized model involving free parameters "cannot fit facts worse than the original version on which it is based. One seems to be led, then, not to equilibrium models as a class, but to a vastly larger class of disequilibrium models. Now I am attracted to the view that it is useful, in a general way, to be hostile toward theorists bearing free parameters, so that I am sympathetic to the idea of simply capitalizing this opinion and calling it a 'Principle.'" In my language, this is not a principle but a hard-core proposition.

To further emphasize this point, I note Sheffrin's (1983, p. 150) remarks: "It is interesting to remark on the intellectual motivation for much of this new research.... A theory of market efficiency is first formulated based on some very simple models of equilibrium returns. After some initial successful tests, more intensive and sophisticated empirical investigation reveals that the particular efficient markets model does not fit the data as precisely as was first thought. This, in turn, gives rise to new models of equilibrium returns and subsequent testing.

"What is important is that the disconfirming evidence is used to argue against a particular model of equilibrium returns. It is not used, as it could be, to make blanket statements about the inefficiency of financial markets."

In other words, equilibrium (efficient) outcomes are a hard-core proposition. The "theory of efficient markets" is in the belt of the neo-Walrasian program.

partly correct. He has fairly characterized the activity associated with creating extended interpretations of the hard core of the program as a mathematical activity. He has accurately represented the sequence of papers on the existence of equilibrium as a kind of applied mathematics. What he has failed to notice is that those activities form only a part of the program of neo-Walrasian economics. Examining only the hard core of the program, he has criticized the program for not being empirical; he should instead have been looking in the protective belt to see the activity of corroboration and falsification – of improvement – of theories. In confusing the axiom structure with the interpreted theorems, he has looked at the lemma trees and missed the programmatic forest.

Hence we have two separate criteria for appraising general equilibrium analysis: First, we use criteria appropriate for gauging mathematical progress to measure the growth of knowledge associated with the hardening of the core of the neo-Walrasian program. Second, we use traditional (e.g., falsificationist) appraisal techniques to evaluate the work in the belts of that hard core. These derived theories – such as demand theory, human capital theory, or the theory of effective protection – must indeed be tested and corroborated. It is they that form the sequence of theories or models in a particular portion of the protective belt. It is thus appropriate to ask whether the theory of demand is progressive in the sense of both theoretical *and* empirical progress. It is not appropriate to ask that the theory of general equilibrium be empirically progressive, since that "theory" – if one is referring to the various papers on the existence, uniqueness, or stability of equilibrium in ever more richly interpreted models – is not a theory at all. *To ask about the falsifiability of the Arrow–Debreu–McKenzie model is not to be hard-headed, positivistic, or rigorous. It is to be confused.*

On not falsifying the unfalsifiable

We have seen that two separate issues are related to the appraisal of the neo-Walrasian research program. First, work in the hard core of the program is appropriately evaluated according to the rules of appraisal usually applied to the development of mathematical theories. That is, the general model for appraisal is that of Lakatos's *Proofs and Refutations* (1976) and not that of Popper's *Conjectures and Refutations* (1972). The idea of Lakatos's book is that theorem creation is an activity in which the mathematician simultaneously attempts to prove and disprove the theorem; proofs are based on lemmas, and the attempts at disproof proceed through a search for counterexamples to the main theorem. With this procedure, some counterexamples and exceptional cases are built into the revised versions of the theorem or into the lemmas that structure the proof itself. The process of proving a theorem is thus a process of discovery. The final theorem that emerges from this back-and-forth movement between proof and preliminary theorem may lead to a final version that bears little resemblance to the original.

Theories in the protective belt of the program, theories developed out of the hard core by the heuristics, are appraised by the method that is appropriate for any empirical science. Thus, it is entirely reasonable to ask that demand theory, production theory, or the theory of household labor supply be evaluated according to Popperian methods of sophisticated falsificationism. It is sensible to ask whether the theory of black–white earnings differentials is progressive. Has it been theoretically progressive in the sense that successive variants have explained the corroborated content of the predecessor? Has there been excess content in the sense that successor theories have made new predictions? Progressively requires that there be empirical progress as well, so it must be the case that at least some of the successor's excess content is corroborated.

It may be argued that this dualistic approach to appraisal is too lenient, that it permits too much to be packed into the hard core and insulates too much analysis from the rigors of the testing–corroboration–falsification process. Is it not the case, some might argue, that what has been here presented is fine for the period during which the hard core is hardening but is no longer appropriate during the time periods, which are relatively longer, when the hard core is fixed and serves as an immutable generator of theories in the protective belt? The answer to this question is simple. The history of the papers from 1930 to 1954 on the existence of equilibrium shows that the hard core took a long time to form. The basic propositions of the hard core were not really developed, were not richly interpreted, until the early 1950s. It is certainly not the case that the hard core of the neo-Walrasian program has been fixed since the time of Walras. The terms of the core, like "agent," functioned in 1900 in a way that hardly resembles the way they functioned in the 1960s. It is inconceivable that the way Roy Radner introduced uncertainty into the structure (Radner 1968) was a possible research strategy for even a clever analyst in the year 1910. The monetary-theoretic models or theories that were developed by Patinkin cannot be located in the organizing center of Cassel's book.

The hard core is not as fixed as Blaug and Rosenberg seem to believe. They have mistaken the form of the hard-core proposition, such as "agents optimize," for its interpretation, *which is not fixed*. As the core has evolved, its terms have been interpreted in ever-more-flexible ways. This process should be familiar to economists and philosophers who have read

Thomas Kuhn, for Kuhn showed how concepts when first presented contain little of the packed content, the associated interpretations, of the finished version. The meaning of a concept like "agent," which must be interpreted in the hard core of the neo-Walrasian program, evolved over time.

The refinement of the hard core, the hardening, was not even completed by 1954. It continues today. The New Classical Economics is a good example of how theories in the protective belt of the neo-Walrasian program are generated when the hard core is reinterpreted without being amended. If the hard-core proposition "agents optimize" of circa 1954 is now packed with the concept that one of the objects of the optimizing choice is the set of expectations of the future values of the choice variables, then the hard core supports theories of rational expectations. The literature on rational expectations contains many existence proofs that, in outline, show that the idea of optimization in the extended interpretation is consistent with the corresponding idea of equilibrium as a coordinated outcome. The idea of a rational expectations equilibrium is appropriate for this kind of interpreted model. The hard core needs to be represented by a new model if one wishes to test whether the new interpretations of the terms of the core are mutually consistent. There is no a priori reason why they must be. Indeed, if the "richer" hard core precludes a sensible concept of equilibrium, then rational-expectations *theories* of the supply of an agricultural commodity are flawed. They cannot be redesigned based on falsification if the theory generator, the hard core, is inconsistent and thus incapable of supporting a theory sequence in the belt.

A suggestion

The analysis of this chapter shows that Rosenberg correctly identified the quasimathematical nature of progress in one area of work in general equilibrium analysis. Yet work that reinterprets the terms of the hard core of the neo-Walrasian program is different from work on the theories in the protective belt of that program. And because the tasks are not the same, neither is the mode of appraising the products. Falsification is appropriate to the one but not the other. "General equilibrium theory" is thus a term that has not only outlived its usefulness but has also confused too many people for too little reason. It is not a theory, and it is not an axiom system. It is an outmoded term used to describe not only some hard-core elements of the neo-Walrasian research program, but also some of the models in the protective belt of that program. It is thus not surprising that methodologists have believed that a single appraisal structure would serve to evaluate "general equilibrium theory." They have been misled. Just because Lakatos ignored the hardening of the hard core does not mean that it is unimportant.

There is no referent for "general equilibrium theory" that is sufficiently well defined to justify use of the phrase. The term should be demoted to the adjectival "general equilibrium," which should be used to modify only words like "model" (in which case it suggests that the model is multi-market interrelated) and "approach" (in which case it suggests that the analyst favors the creation of general equilibrium models). In no case should it modify "theory," "theorist," or "economics." This change would constitute progress too.

CHAPTER 8

Classroom interlude III

Student β: I'd like to introduce a discussion topic by noting the words of a distinguished economist: "The view that we require an equilibrium notion to make precise the limits of economics and think accordingly, seems to me to be sound. The fact that our evidence is always from the past makes it important to be able to say in what sense and in what circumstances we can expect the past to shed light on the future" (Hahn 1973, pp. 38–39). Yet in my view the usual concept of equilibrium in the Arrow–Debreu –McKenzie (ADM) model appears to be clumsy and overly restrictive.

In earlier classes for the applied economics students it was argued that general equilibrium analysis serves both to reinforce arguments from partial equilibrium theory and to limit the scope of certain claims. My concerns about that argument are the following: (1) For most purposes the ADM model determines the scope and nature of general equilibrium analysis. (2) The concept of equilibrium used in the ADM model is unrealistic. (3) This unrealistic equilibrium concept is used to limit economic discourse. (4) Consequently, the ADM equilibrium rules out of economic analysis many topics and problems of real importance. (5) The result is that general equilibrium analysis biases the discussion of economic issues in the direction of a limited set of problems that can be well posed using the ADM formalism.

Teacher: I think such concerns are important ones and central to much controversy in economics. I would go further and suggest that much of what appears to be disagreement over economic policy is in fact disagreement over economic theory along the lines β has suggested. Let us thus examine β's argument in some detail.

Student α: I would like to make sure we have a context for this discussion. Consider β's fifth point. One manifestation of this bias appears in the microfoundations of macroeconomics literature. Specifically, Post Keynesians have maintained that general equilibrium models require market clearing as a feature of equilibrium. Consequently, they argue that general equilibrium analysis cannot evaluate Keynesian concepts like unemployment equilibrium. Presenting a Keynesian equilibrium in market-clearing terms forces the conclusion that a market failure induces Keynesian results. Keynes's concerns are thus shunted aside – Keynes lies on the Procrustean bed of Arrow, Debreu, and McKenzie.

Student β: One prominent Post Keynesian argued that "the intellectual auxiliary baggage of gross substitution, Walras's Law, Say's Principle, optimality of reconciled choices of all agents via the price system, etc., are so closely identified with the concept of general equilibrium, while this paraphernalia is so incompatible with a monetary economy, that to apply the term 'general equilibrium' to a monetary equilibrium system would seem to me to be a semantic travesty" (Davidson 1977, p. 25). Thus general equilibrium models are too limited to pose, let alone solve, real economic problems.

Student γ: What confounded confusion and nonsense. After all our classwork and discussions, do you still have the idea that general equilibrium analysis is coextensive with the ADM model?

Student α: Don't you?

Student γ: Of course not. I see that I have to convince you that general equilibrium analysis is not to be identified with any single general equilibrium model.

Teacher: Which is not to say, however, that general equilibrium models don't bear a *family* resemblance.

Student γ: Precisely. Perhaps we can return to Lakatos, since α and β haven't *really* grasped the central point, namely, that general equilibrium models are best thought of as interpretations of the hard core of a research program. The protective belt of that hard core consists primarily of theories that both extend and restrict a specific general equilibrium model.

Student α: What is a general equilibrium model that is *not* an ADM model?

Student γ: Let me suggest a list: Leontief input–output models, von Neumann expanding-economy models, the uncertainty ADM models of Radner, Edgeworth exchange models associated with the core, macro-models of the four-quadrant variety, Patinkin monetary-theory models, Brunner–Meltzer models, rational-expectations models, temporary–equilibrium models, neo-Keynesian disequilibrium models, etcetera.

Teacher: I think this list is a good start. Now I'd like α and β to defend the proposition they advance – that general equilibrium analysis is too narrow in its formulation to address real economic issues.

Student α: I see that I'm forced to identify the unifying theme of all these models and their variants. I have to argue that *any* model that is a variation on the theme is necessarily flawed – that it limits discourse unreasonably.

Student β: In Lakatos's terms, this exercise will identify the hard core of the program. This task looks difficult since the models differ in form and structure.

Teacher: I am reminded of Wittgenstein's analysis of the word "game."

Trying to define "game" from a study of actual games may leave no set of attributes that is possessed by every game. He used the metaphor of a rope, made up of many strands of fiber, no single fiber extending the length of the rope, but all fibers interwoven and overlapping. If we substitute "general equilibrium analysis" for "game," each model is a fiber. Still, there might be a guide to the construction of the models. Lakatos suggested that the construction guide be called the positive heuristic of the research program. Let's give the program a name: "the neo-Walrasian program." Can we here identify the positive heuristic of the program?

Student α: I can't really find an assumption that is common to all the models. Certainly not Walras's Law, or Say's Principle, or market clearing, or Pareto optimality or the like.

Student γ: The positive heuristic is more subtle. It might consist of statements or rules like these: Create models in which optimization plays a role, or build models that can pose questions about the coordination of economic activity, or develop analyses in terms of properties of equilibrium states of interdependent systems.

Student β: But Lakatos also argued that the construction guide stipulates what models should *not* be developed; he called this the negative heuristic of the research program.

Student γ: The negative heuristic would include rules like these: Don't build models that assume irrational choices, don't construct analyses based on changing tastes of agents, and so on.

Student β: I see where that Post Keynesian's view of a "semantic travesty" comes from. Can we stipulate, at least for our conversation, that we will talk about the neo-Walrasian *program*, and not general equilibrium theory? If so, then we can talk about general equilibrium *models* that are associated with the neo-Walrasian program.

Teacher: Granted. Henceforth we shall distinguish between the neo-Walrasian program and general equilibrium models like the ADM model. Can we now interpret β's assertion that "general equilibrium theory biases the discussion of economic issues in the direction of an extremely limited set of problems that can be well posed during the ADM formalism?"

Student γ: There is now only one possible interpretation: The ADM *model* may bias discussion in the precise sense that it is designed to illuminate a narrow range of issues. There is no reason, however, why the neo-Walrasian *program* need introduce any such bias. Will you concede the point, β?

Student β: I'm afraid I must concede your first point at least; it is incontrovertible that the ADM *model* is not coextensive with the neo-

Walrasian program. It is rather an interpretation of the hard core of that program. On the second point, I'm not so sure I can agree. Perhaps we can return to this notion later.

Student α: In any event, why is the ADM model represented to us by textbooks as the culmination of general equilibrium analysis?

Teacher: Textbooks usually lag behind professional knowledge by a generation; the neo-Walrasian program has grown enormously over the past fifteen years and has facilitated the construction of many families of models.

Once we recognize that the neo-Walrasian program encompasses a hard core and heuristics, or an investigative logic with a set of rules for generating theory sequences in the belt, then we see that what we used to call general equilibrium theory becomes not an end but a means, a style, of model construction.

Now what can we say about β's other questions, related to the unrealistic notion of *equilibrium* that the ADM model imposes on argumentation?

Student γ: We have to be quite clear whether we are talking about a program or a model. The difficulty as I see it is that "equilibrium" has distinct meanings. If we are speaking of the ADM *model*, I am prepared to admit that the competitive equilibrium that can be inferred in that model *is* unrealistic. Yet even so, it was useful in an earlier class as a device to evaluate the claim that resources are allocated efficiently over time. The method we used then was to define the claim by means of a well-specified model and to interpret that claim by means of the logic of the argument generated by the model. With a different model, perhaps, the evaluation of the claim would have been different, but no matter. What counts is that the ADM model is well suited to the posing of economic efficiency claims: We could at least find one context in which (a) the claim made sense and (b) the claim was false.

Teacher: But if we understand β's question to mean that *any* equilibrium notion of *any* general equilibrium model unduly biases economic discourse, we are talking on a different level: We are then methodologists, not economists. To argue the point in this way we have to defend the proposition that (a) the concept of equilibrium is intrinsic to the neo-Walrasian program, (b) any theory associated with the program requires an argument about equilibrium, (c) the *concept* of equilibrium itself introduces bias, and thus, (d) the program is biased.

When Kaldor (1972) presented his critique "The Irrelevance of Equilibrium Economics," a reader was entitled to believe that Kaldor's concern was with the program associated with general equilibrium analysis, what we are calling the neo-Walrasian program. Yet careful reading of Kaldor rebuts this notion: "The notion of equilibrium to which I refer is that of the general economic equilibrium originally formulated by Walras, and developed with ever-increasing elegance, exactness, and logical precision by the mathematical economists of our own generation, of whom the French economist Gerard Debreu is now regarded as the most prominent exponent" (p. 1237). In other words, despite Kaldor's title, he attacked the ADM equilibrium concept, a model-specific construction.

F. H. Hahn's (1973) Cambridge Inaugural Lecture, *On the Notion of Equilibrium in Economics*, gave a partial reply to Kaldor. Hahn's discussion of equilibrium in sequence economies itself refuted Kaldor's contention that the concept of equilibrium does not allow us to pose information-theoretic issues of allocative efficiency. Hahn correctly dismissed Kaldor's critique by providing a richer set of models, in which "equilibrium" had richer meanings. He did not interpret Kaldor's argument as a program critique, because Kaldor restricted his own criticism to the ADM model. Kaldor may have had a legitimate concern about equilibrium as a concept, but he never articulated this concern.

To move this discussion forward to some constructive end, I would like to ask α and β if they can develop arguments against the neo-Walrasian program's use of equilibrium as an organizing principle of discourse, as a hard-core proposition. Only arguments along these lines can define and support β's original argument.

Scene: Several days later.

Student α: β and I have spent a few days trying to develop a critique of equilibrium as an organizing principle of economic explanation. We have run into several problems. First, and most significantly, it appears that attacks on equilibrium as a concept, independent of its interpretation in an ADM model, say, must be developed from the perspective of a competing research program.

Student γ: You've provided additional support for my Lakatosian view that general equilibrium analysis is associated with a research program, since coherent attacks on a hard-core proposition must be developed from a *competing* hard core.

Student β: That appears to be correct. There are, we suspect, only two separate well-developed programmatic critiques of equilibrium; we can identify these as Post Keynesian and neo-Austrian.

Student α: Or else they reduce to attacks on the ADM equilibrium notion, which, I believe we've now agreed, is not a legitimate line of argument with which to oppose general equilibrium analysis.

Teacher: Castigation by taxonomy makes me uncomfortable. Can you be more specific in your claims?

Student α: Consider the following argument (Moore 1978, pp. 121–2): "One of the key theoretical constructs that [we] have reluctantly abandoned as useless for analyzing reality is 'general equilibrium.' The very concept of a position of balance towards which a system is tending, and from which there is no further tendency to change, is inappropriate to historical time,...which moves irreversibly towards...[and] reflects external shocks to the system which change, in ways not easily analyzed by the use of purely deductive methods, the path that will henceforth be followed. In the context of a historical process that has no long-run equilibrium position to which it is tending, what is the meaning or sense of general equilibrium?"

Or listen to this: "This mode of thought [neoclassical or equilibrium analysis], which is enshrined in the subjective theory of value, first creates for us a realm where disembodied minds hold communion with etherealized objects of choice and then, unmindful of the distance between this abstract world and reality, seeks to represent the [equilibrium] relations which it finds in this realm as governing the relations which hold in actual economic society.... To emancipate economic thought from this heritage is a task that is long overdue" (Dobb 1937, p. 81).

Or consider the following: "There are essentially two types of economic models which may be developed – equilibrium models and historical models.... All equilibrium models by their very nature of focusing on the equilibrium position are unable to handle situations of disappointment" (Davidson 1972, p. 26).

Finally, let me read this longish excerpt: "There is much to be learned from *a priori* comparisons of equilibrium positions, but they must be kept in their logical place. They cannot be applied to actual situations; it is a mortal certainty that any particular actual situation which we want to discuss is not in equilibrium. Observed history cannot be interpreted in terms of a movement along an equilibrium path nor adduced as evidence to support any proposition drawn from it.... In a model depicting equilibrium positions there is no causation. It consists of a closed circle of simultaneous equations.... The vice of the 'vulgar' economics that dominated academic teaching before Keynes (and still flourishes in some fields) was in drawing practical conclusions from equilibrium analysis" (Robinson 1968, pp. 25–7).

Student β: You can appreciate what α and I have been faced with here. These economists, most of them self-identified Post Keynesians, posit two separate modes of inquiry, historical-time modeling and equilibrium modeling. The latter appears to mean the same as working in the neo-Walrasian program. It is not at all clear what role historical-time models can play, but from these excerpts our impression is that such models examine themes first adumbrated by Ricardo and Marx. One such theme might be that historical social, production, and power relationships cannot be separated from market analysis.

Teacher: Let us pause to see what we have here. It seems as though these critics indeed object to the concept of equilibrium as an organizing theme of economic explanation. They appear to believe that a general equilibrium state is not to be found in the world.

Student γ: This objection is silly. I thought that we had progressed in our discussions beyond such cries for descriptive realism and factual truth.

Teacher: Your complaint has some merit. Perhaps we can discuss it at another time. But a more subtle point may be present in their critique. Specifically, perhaps the *focus* on equilibrium can lead an economist to a belief that equilibrium positions are the important states to investigate.

Student α: But this is a problem for the economist and not the program, isn't it? If "develop models with well-defined equilibrium states" is a proposition associated with the positive heuristic of the neo-Walrasian program, the value of the concept of equilibrium can be judged by the theory sequences, in the belt, that it generates.

Student γ: Exactly. And we can go further. If we analyze the states of a particular model, we can study the behavior of the model even out of equilibrium. Once we have an equilibrium as a benchmark, we can ask questions about adjustments, processes, and failures to achieve the equilibrium state. Frankly, I see nothing in this kind of historical model that can't be developed within the neo-Walrasian program.

Teacher: You're going too far. Certainly you can't frame a causal argument in the general equilibrium program.

Student γ: In the commonsense use of cause and effect, I am quite sure that I'd never want to create such an argument; I'm interested in explanation, not causation.

Teacher: Let's steer clear of this philosophical minefield. If you agree that you're not interested in causal explanations, will you agree that arguments that depend on temporal precedence are more easily constructed using historical time instead of the artificial time that separates a perturbation of a systemic state and the return to the equilibrium state?

Student γ: I'm willing to grant that.

Teacher: Are you further willing to grant that the concepts of power and social relationships do *not* generate classes of models in the general equilibrium program?

Student γ: Of course I grant that. Such concepts are too fuzzy, too soft, to be worth anything except as they can be defined concretely in a model in the protective belt of the neo-Walrasian program.

Student α: As in the Aumann (1964) model, power could be defined using the measure of the subset of traders taking action: We could say that two subsets of traders have equal power if, as subsets of [0, 1], they have equal measure.

Student β: But power is an unimportant issue for the neo-Walrasian program taken as a whole.

Teacher: Yes, and that is the point I want to stress. The question of what is in the hard core of a program, of whether proposition X should be an organizing feature of a research program, is not a matter of logic.

Student α: Unless of course X and Y are *both* present and are logically inconsistent.

Teacher: True, but ignoring that eventuality, we have to appraise the research program as a whole. It makes no sense to compare a neo-Marxian program, organized around the concept of power or relationships of production, with a program organized around the concept of equilibrium by examining the organizing concepts alone.

Student γ: Are you saying that one must formulate critical experiments to judge between competing research programs?

Teacher: Not necessarily, but it makes sense to compare competing programs with respect not only to the scope of their theories, but also with respect to the events or facts that the theories in separate programs attempt to explain.

Student β: We have some examples of this. A simple issue like the price of gasoline is explained in the neo-Walrasian program using a supply –demand model. That same price might be explained by some Post Keynesians in terms of the power relationships of the large firms and the various governments involved. The relationship between race and earnings is also explained differently by the two programs: The neo-Walrasian program will explain the differences in terms of education, productivity, and similar ideas from human-capital theory, whereas the Post Keynesians may explore exploitative power relationships. We are all familiar with such alternative explanations.

Student α: Before we get too far afield from our original concern about the use of equilibrium as an organizing concept, let me introduce some neo-Austrian views on the subject, for such writers are also opposed to the *idea* of equilibrium as it appears in the neo-Walrasian program. They do not, however, object to equilibrium as a feature of explanation. Rather, they tend to argue that a great deal of economic activity cannot be understood with equilibrium models.

"An equilibrium situation is one that exhibits no tendency to change and that can be derived logically from a model that incorporates the operation of opposing forces.... Equilibrium theorizing in the context of explanation is more likely to succeed than in the context of prediction.... Suppression of surprise is only possible *ex post*,...[and this] is a necessary element in economic explanation.... The notion of equilibrium, as both Machlup and Mises have stressed, is 'only' a mental tool without any direct operational significance....

"The great and crucial virtue of the Hayekian view of equilibrium is that it lays emphasis on the teleology of the adjustment process rather than viewing each step on the adjustment path as a lagged response to what happened in the previous period. Disequilibrium adjustments are, in a very important sense, forward- and not backward-looking activities. Lack of coordination implies hitherto unexploited opportunities for mutually advantageous exchange" (Rizzo 1979, pp. 4–6).

Student β: I, too, have found similar statements. For example, "Austrian contributions...focused attention on the element of adjustment time and consequently adopted the causal-sequential analysis of classical economics rather than the technique of mutual determination.... Their approach was a by-product of a concern with market processes rather than equilibrium states.... Hayek argued that a successful analysis of economic disequilibrium required a reformulation of the concept of equilibrium.... All Hayek's work may thus be seen as flowing from a conception of social interaction with emphasis on economic allocation" (O'Driscoll 1977, pp. 7, 9).

Similarly, "Kirzner's criticism of equilibrium theory goes deep. He doubts that maximizing behavior...will sustain a realistic theory of the market.... Maximizing presupposes that everyone *knows* which ends to pursue and which means to employ" (High 1978, p. 1).

Finally, "A set of pre-reconciled actions can be called a *general equilibrium*. It consists of actions *all chosen at the same time*. What of actions to be chosen in time-to-come? There must be no such actions. In order to have a general equilibrium, *time-to-come must be abolished*. The general equilibrium, where every person's action springs from fully informed reason, can exist only in a timeless world, a world of a single moment with no future" (Shackle 1976, p. 24).

Student γ: It almost sounds as if the Post Keynesians fault the concept of equilibrium because it denies the influence of the historical past while the neo-Austrians mistrust it because it denies the teleological future.

Teacher: We now have two distinct criticisms of equilibrium as an organizing concept, as a hard-core proposition. I think we must agree that these objections are not directed to specific models but rather concern the program itself.

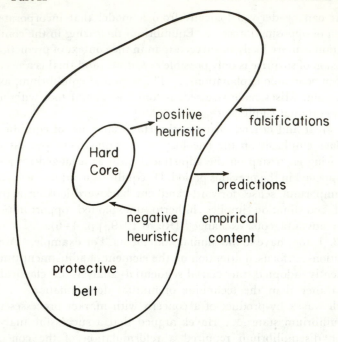

Figure 8.1

Student γ: I'm quite comfortable living with such criticisms. I realize that other economists are working within a different program to provide explanations and predictions of economic phenomena. Personally, I believe that the neo-Walrasian program is a more progressive one, richer in its falsifiable predictions and more willing to subject its conclusions to tests using data than either of the two alternatives mentioned.

Student α: That's not much comfort to me. I don't see much testing, or attempts at falsification, in the neo-Walrasian program.

Teacher: What about the work mentioned earlier, such as the influence of race on earnings?

Student α: Tests of significance seem primarily designed to compare the putative hypothesis with a null hypothesis of the form "There is no significant effect." Rejecting a null hypothesis is not the same thing as accepting an alternative explanation. We are a long way in economics from having distinct models, in either the same programs or different programs, competitively predict a specific relationship. There is insufficient theoretical sharpness: We have few tests that will lead to rejecting one theory and provisionally accepting an alternative.

Student γ: Are you suggesting that one's degree of scientific and intellectual

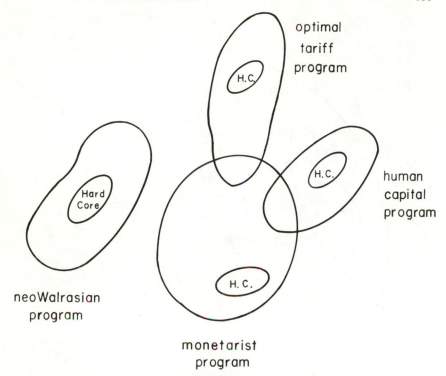

optimal
tariff
program

H.C.

H.C.

human
capital
program

Hard
Core

H. C.

neoWalrasian
program

monetarist
program

Figure 8.2

trust in the neo-Walrasian program is directly related to its falsifiability?
Student α: I've certainly heard it argued that, "without throwing away the
general equilibrium construction, what may be doubted is the notion that
it provides a useful starting point from which to approach a substantive
explanation of the workings of an economic system. Its leading character-
istic has been the endless formalisation of purely logical problems without
the slightest regard for the production of falsifiable theorems, which, we
insist, remains the fundamental task of economics" (Blaug 1980, p. 192).
Teacher: We've almost come full circle in our discussions. We've agreed
that the general equilibrium analysis provides support for falsifiable
partial equilibrium models. We've seen how it functions in a negative
fashion to rule out certain lines of analysis as illogical. Finally, we agreed
that as representations of the hard core of the neo-Walrasian research
program, general equilibrium models are not in principle falsifiable.
Student β: As I see the position we've arrived at, it comes down to one's
understanding of what a scientific research program is and what constella-
tions of theoretical constructs in economics merit the term "program."

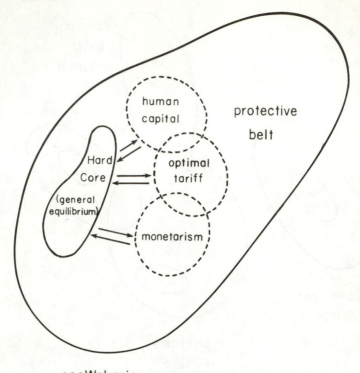

neoWalrasian program

Figure 8.3

Teacher: What do you mean?

Student β: If we think of every group of models as a program, then we could speak of the "new-home-economics program," the "monetarist program," and the "optimal-tariff program." In that case we would be forced to compare the progressivity of these programs each to each other.

Student γ: But that is exactly what I thought we agreed was not the case for the neo-Walrasian program. I have been thinking of a picture like Figure 8.1. With such a picture, general equilibrium models represent the hard core, and, say, human-capital theories are in the protective belt. My reason for saying this is that writings by human-capital analysts use equilibrium, stable preferences, optimization under constraints, etcetera.

Thus I count as an empirical success of the neo-Walrasian program any corroborations of the human-capital hypothesis.

Teacher: On β's alternative view, it would appear that the picture would be drawn as in Figure 8.2. Specifically, the neo-Walrasian program would have no empirical success, and if the optimal tariff and monetarist programs have had mixed successes, at least they are generating falsifiable theorems.

Student α: This view cannot be entertained seriously. I thought that we were willing to grant a special role to general equilibrium analysis because it was associated with the hard core of a program from which demand theory, human-capital theory, optimal tariff theory, and other theories appear in the protective belt. I thought our consensus picture was like Figure 8.3.

Teacher: In other words, groups of models in the protective belt, all linked to the hard core by the heuristics of the neo-Walrasian program, cluster naturally on occasion into what we call theories or literatures.

Student α: Precisely.

Student γ: This certainly clears up the confusion that results from comparing the empirical reach of general equilibrium theory with that of, say, the new home economics.

Teacher: It also reaffirms the centrality of general equilibrium analysis to the concerns of most working economists.

Part III

The two previous parts have addressed the main issues associated with appraising general equilibrium analysis. This part examines two questions related to that appraisal: What do economists have to contribute to philosophers' models of the growth of knowledge, and what role does mathematics play in the growth of economic analysis?

CHAPTER 9

An aside to methodologists

This chapter will not be a long one. I am not a philosopher, and thus my observations about that discipline and how it should approach economic analysis are those of an outsider. Nonetheless, I believe that economics has been ill served by models of appraisal that structure discussion about progress or its absence in physics.

The obvious defect in philosophers' attempts to explain what goes on in economics is their appalling ahistoricality. Their analyses of microeconomic theory, for example, are logical or rational reconstructions. Philosophers take the terms used in the economic theory at their present values, as it were. How is understanding served by claiming that Wald and von Neumann developed the existence theorems that were perfected by Arrow and Debreu? What sense is to be drawn from a statement that general equilibrium theory is untestable and thus unscientific? The former reflects ignorance of the history, while the latter confounds historical inaccuracy with a category mistake. Because the case study of Chapter 6 is the first historical treatment of the existence of equilibrium, I infer that methodologists have been making pronouncements about general equilibrium analysis in the absence of best evidence about its development. Appraising scientific work on the basis of its instantiation in textbooks is the worst kind of straw-man murder. One can hardly examine the claim that general equilibrium models represent the hard core of the neo-Walrasian research program if one restricts attention to textbook definitions and theorems.

Lakatos opened one of his essays with a playful paraphrase of Kant: "Philosophy of science without the history of science is empty; history of science without philosophy of science is blind" (Lakatos 1978a, p. 102). Philosophical activity, appraisal activity (at least that which examines economics), is too often a survey of current contributions; there is too little concern with historical reconstructions. The survey appraisal in economics keeps track of lines of research that are promising while identifying those that are played out or are degenerating. But these surveys, although important to scientific practice, differ from appraisals offered by philosophers of science with respect to physics, say. More is needed to evaluate progress in economics than a comparative study of current contributions to the literature. Program assessment requires studying the development of the literature, and placing that work in a context by identifying arguments, techniques, and connections to other work in the subject area.

In brief, there is no substitute for the kind of histories that historians of economic thought can produce. Yet historians are less concerned with issues of appraisal than the methodologist. It would be heartening were the historian to be concerned with episodes in the development of economic analysis that present problems of interest to the methodologist. This is not often the case. *Appraisal* concerns current themes and problems. *History* concerns the past. How can these two activities be joined? What obstacles bar a synthesis?

I have no subtle insight to offer on this point. On the one hand, it is obvious that historians of economic thought must be comfortable with modern work in economics. That is, the history of economic thought should not exclude an interest in the tools of mathematics, econometrics, and "modern high theory." It is a minor scandal that there is no comprehensive history of either the rise of econometrics[1] or the mathematization of economics. Without such studies, there can be no reliable history of modern economics. With no such history, any appraisal of modern economics is limited indeed. On the other hand, methodologists cannot continue to ignore historical evidence pertaining to the development of the work they evaluate (Kuhn 1977). Blindness to origins and lines of progress obfuscates the logic of the program itself. The resulting interpretative errors will be apparent to the scientific workers, who will correctly dismiss the appraisal as arrant know-nothingism.

On the methodology of scientific research programs

Part II provides some evidence that Lakatosian appraisals have merit. Yet this conclusion should be approached with caution by economists, as it was in *Method and Appraisal in Economics* (Latsis 1976), which reported on the first attempts to apply the MSRP framework to economics. I have argued that some of the history of general equilibrium analysis can be reconstructed as the hardening of the hard core of the neo-Walrasian program. This hardening process was ignored by Lakatos. His concept of a program was dynamic, but the core was a static notion. Yet hardening takes place in time; the core is not present fully developed at the program's inception. I know of no studies of this hardening process in physics, the subject that usually provides the case-study materials for the philosopher of science.

---

[1] Some work in England by Mary Morgan, sponsored by the Social Science Research Council and guided by Professor David Hendry, could rectify this problem.

If the ideas of Part II generalize to other disciplines, it will be seen that the hardening process is analogous to the process that generates a sequence of theories in the protective belt. Lakatos showed that the unit of appraisal was the program and not the theory. Because the program was to be appraised for progress or its absence, Lakatos introduced a dynamic element into the appraisal of theories, for the theory sequences were the referent of the progress test. *What our case has suggested is that it is false to think of a fixed core and a dynamic belt. The core is modified in time, and in predictable ways. The propositions of the core remain fixed, but the interpretations of the terms of the core change as the core hardens.* "Hardening" refers to the growing fixity of the meaning of the terms of the hard-core propositions. One of the most interesting aspects of the process is that it is only in a well-developed program that the core can in fact be hardened: The process requires modeling, and providing consistency tests of, the core propositions. *Thus true hardening requires mathematization of the program*; and it is only in this century that economics was formalized well enough for that to take place. It is in that sense that neo-Walrasian economics is better developed than theory sequences in other social-science disciplines. Its guiding principles, its core propositions, have gone through the hardening process.

Programs and subprograms

There is another problem with the Lakatosian scheme, one that may be phrased as a question: How large is a program? For physics, is mechanics a program? Or is it a subprogram of some larger program? Blaug speaks of the "human-capital research program" and suggests that it is a subprogram of neoclassical economics. I have identified the neo-Walrasian program; are there any other scientific research programs in economics? *I claim that demand theory, human capital theory, and marginal productivity theory are theories and not separate research programs. They are theories in the protective belt of the neo-Walrasian program and thus share a common hard core. They differ one from the other in the auxiliary hypotheses used to augment the hard-core propositions. They are to be appraised like any theory sequence, by the corroborations and falsifications of their excess content.* Often the augmenting hypotheses are several, and tests cannot falsify the predictions, and thus the hypotheses, except jointly. This kind of problem is a common one in scientific work and has received much attention from philosophers of science as the Duhem–Quine thesis (see Blaug 1980). I have nothing to add to the views of the philosophers about the *testing* of theories except to observe that, like Blaug and Coddington, I sense too little of it in economics; and what little there is is too often innocuous.

This said, it remains true that human-capital theory resembles a

program. Consider its augmenting hypotheses, one of which is certainly
that "people spend on themselves in diverse ways, not only for the sake of
present enjoyments but also for the sake of future pecuniary and non-
pecuniary returns" (Blaug 1980, p. 225). This assumption, added to the
core of the non-Walrasian program, is itself like a core proposition. That
is, all derived human-capital theories will share that set of augmented
propositions as a hard core. In an excellent study of this problem of
separating programs from theories in the protective belt, Joseph Remanyi
(1979) distinguished between cores and demicores, arguing that the
development of subdisciplines reflects the interaction between core and
demicore. There is great merit in this extension of Lakatos's theory, and I
see no reason to duplicate Remanyi's analysis; I shall simply adopt it as
the solution to the question of whether human-capital theory is a theory or
a program. It is a theory, and it is of sufficient stature that some of its
hypotheses serve for the human-capital theory sequence as auxiliary core
propositions; they form the demicore.

Other questions

The case study of Chapter 6 raises several other problems that rest
uneasily in a Lakatosian bed. For example, there was seen to be a fundamental interconnection between progress in economics and progress in
mathematics. What exactly is the economic methodologist to make of this
fact? Does the mathematics lead the economist to the problems, or does
economic analysis generate the demand for specific tools to solve economic
problems? What is the relationship between tools and reasoning about
problems? This issue arises in appraising work in physics; quantum
theory showed progress after the formalization of some of its propositions
by the theory of group representations. Newtonian mechanics is inconceivable without Newton's calculus. Riemannian geometry aids interpretations of relativistic mechanics.

What can be said of the interaction of mathematics and the development of the neo-Walrasian hard core? This topic will be addressed in later
chapters, but I note here that the interaction is a real one and presents
problems for any theory of appraisal. If a scientific theory never, or
seldom, is independent of the collection of tools used to develop the
theory, the appraisal cannot be a local one. It must account for the
interaction as well as the theory. Thus economic methodologists, and
philosophers of science more generally, must study the development not
only of the theories but also of the tools that shape those theories. For
economics this requires attention to the development of mathematics, and
economic methodologists must better understand mathematical activity.

It is inconceivable that an evaluation of the literature on growth theory can proceed without an express understanding of the development of optimal-control theory.

Sociology?

The case presents another problem. The role of external influences in the history was left out of the rational reconstruction, but this does not mean that such influences are historically unimportant. The Lakatosian strategy accounted for the historical development by assuming that science proceeds as a sequence of rational choices by the scientific community. The other parts of the story are supposed to be, if not "externalist rubbish," at least of less interest to the methodologist. My Lakatosian reconstruction granted, it is still of some interest to evaluate the influence of the Cowles Commission, say. The history also has too many lines that lead back to John von Neumann to let him remain of interest only to mathematicians. The role of priority for, or the simultaneous discovery of, the proofs of existence for the general competitive model present complex issues for the historian if not for the methodologist. In my own writing I have used the term "Arrow–Debreu–McKenzie model," while others have referred to the "Arrow–Debreu model."[2] The history suggests that my own usage can be justified as easily as the more common one. This totting up of points to be awarded for genius, for real contributions to economic analysis, is unseemly, although it occurs all the time; the chief scorekeepers among us are the methodologists for whom reputations provide reasons for appraising the work of the reputable.

Other programs

There remains another problem associated with the Lakatosian framework. It can be broached by a question: Are there any other programs in economics besides the neo-Walrasian program? This is a major issue, because if there are no other programs, then there can be no relative progress or degeneration of the neo-Walrasian program itself. In that event there can be no critical tradition except for those critical remarks that neo-Walrasians make to one another as they go about their business of proving new theorems and extending as best they can the theory sequences in the belt of the program.

As I have argued, both here and in the documentation I tried to provide

---

[2] Most recently, the 1983 Nobel Memorial Prize in economics was awarded to Gerard Debreu.

in a previous book (Weintraub 1979), there exists at least one other program, the Keynesian program. If there are still other programs, they might include those that can be termed neo-Marxian or neo-Ricardian, Post Keynesian, and neo-Austrian. For a variety of reasons, chief among them that I consider human capital to be a theory and not a program, I do not think that it is meaningful to speak of other programs in economics, with the possible exception of two rather new, and currently ill formed, programs associated with individuals: the embryonic "behavioral" program of Herbert Simon and the "evolutionary" program of Sidney Winter and Richard Nelson and their respective collaborators. In any event, although it may be useful later to document the differences between the various hard cores of the programs, my own task has been to establish the outlines of the neo-Walrasian program, for it is this program that dominates most teaching and research in American economics.

CHAPTER 10

Classroom interlude IV

Student β: I would like to return to a comment that α made in a previous class. α said that journals in which mathematical economists publish their results give no indication that the concepts developed in the papers have an economic context beyond the hermetic world of the abstract models. I would like to ask you, Teacher, why this is so. Is this a necessary feature of mathematical economics?

Teacher: I don't know what you're really asking. If you want to know why more articles do not have more elaborate discussion of the literature, for example, I would respond that good articles usually do have such discussions. If they appear compressed, it is because those who read the papers are generally familiar with the literature and need only a sketch of the context in which the problem arises.

Student α: I want to rephrase β's question. Look at any standard piece in the mathematical-economics genre. What do we find? First, a sketch of the background to the problem that frequently cites *only* other pieces of mathematical economics. Next, a model is presented as a series of definitions and interrelationships among those terms. Then, one finds a theorem stated, with the definitions and interrelationships as hypotheses and a new interrelationship or implication as a conclusion. Finally the conclusion is interpreted. Effectively, one first sets up a correspondence, a bijective mapping, between certain mathematical objects and economic objects; an example might be "let X, a commodity bundle, be an element of R_+^n, the non-negative orthont." When a variety of such terms have been presented, the interpretive framework is suppressed, and the analysis is carried out in the mathematical structure. The results of that analysis, the conclusions of the new theorems, are then reinterpreted in the language of economic objects.

Let me thus ask a variant of β's question: To what degree does the interpretation depend on the specific mode of mathematical analysis?

Teacher: Do you mean to question the initial correspondence between mathematical structures and economic objects, the basic framework of postulates?

Student α: No, not really. I am aware that some argue that the indivisibility of commodities makes the postulate $x \varepsilon R_+^n$ a "poor" assumption. To such individuals I preach tolerance; they ought to ask whether models using this postulate provide a rich set of potentially falsifiable conclusions. I'm asking a different question, however. Somewhere in the analysis there appears a piece of mathematical machinery. This external result (external, at least, to the interpretative structure) drives the analysis to the mathematical conclusion. Did the interpretation suggest this tool, or did the internal logic of the mathematical structure suggest it?

Teacher: Can you·give me an example?

Student α: A simple one would be, say, in the proof of the existence of a competitive equilibrium in a linear-programming general equilibrium model like that given by Dorfman, Samuelson, and Solow (1958, in Chapter 13). Once a correspondence between the economics and a mathematical structure is set up, the mathematical structure at some point "cries out" for a fixed-point theorem to be applied. After its application, the resulting conclusion can be interpreted. Now, the *statement* of the fixed-point theorem must be in terms of the assumptions of the model; otherwise it could not be applied. My question, then, is whether that theorem itself has a reasonable interpretation. If it does *not*, then I feel uneasy letting it appear in the analysis.

Student β: Let me rephrase this pictorially:

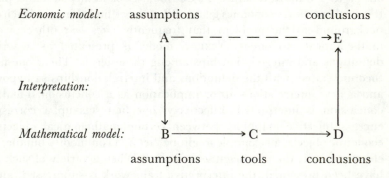

We would like to go from A to E. What we do, in fact, is go from A to E indirectly, identifying A with B, then proceeding from B to D (using C) and reidentifying D with E. The problem with this procedure seems to be with C. If it is brought in from outside the economics chain, it appears artificial. Further, I think many economists are convinced that B itself is selected not to model A, but rather to allow C to be introduced. In the example I cited, for the Kakutani fixed-point theorem to apply certain mappings must be upper semicontinuous. These mappings "live" in B. They thus model "stuff" in A. That stuff is really the demand correspondence. Did this way of setting up demand occur naturally in A, or was it forced upon the economist by the needs of C? We are now accustomed to thinking of preferences in such a way that the demand correspondence can be modeled as an upper semicontinuous mapping. But where is the economic logic in this?

Student α: My point exactly. In any presentation of an analysis of existence of a competitive equilibrium, early in the analysis – in block A, in fact – you'll find that preferences and choice sets are presented with quite complicated restrictions. These restrictions serve quite precisely to conclude, in B, that the demand correspondence is upper semicontinuous. Then (hey, presto!), such a property fits the requirements of a theorem, something in C, which allows D to be derived. Are mathematical economists so clever that they had precisely the right theorem at hand? Or rather has the whole thing been rigged to allow C to be introduced?

Teacher: γ, you have been unusually quiet. Perhaps you would like to respond?

Student γ: It appears to be a real problem, this relationship between the A and B blocks. Frequently, what one needs in B was *actually* in A though somewhat hidden, like competition in a previous discussion. I'll grant, though, that it may sometimes be the case that, in order to make the arguments work, we must select just the right elements of A to work with, to be modeled in B. This seems to be Koopmans's point made earlier, and I know of no solution except sensitivity and intellectual integrity on the part of the analyst.

Student α: But you believe that the chain B–C–D is unidirectional, that in the model, at least, we proceed deductively?

Student γ: Of course.

Student α: Then you believe that definitions and propositions come first, then come theorems, and then come proofs, in that order?

Student γ: That's how articles and books are sequenced.

Student α: That's not what I asked. Is that how mathematics works?

Student γ: If by that you mean, Is that how mathematicians proceed? of course the answer is no.

Teacher: Explain yourself, γ.

Student γ: Mathematics doesn't develop deductively. It never has. The important questions really have to do with *discovery*. How do new mathematical results get discovered? In reality, mathematics is developed by a complicated process of conjecture, proof, refutation, refining of the conjecture, and then new proofs and refutations in a back-and-forth interaction between naive, basic, or primitive conjectures and simultaneous proofs and refutations of those conjectures. This process, familiar to working mathematicians, is beautifully described by Lakatos (1976) in *Proofs and Refutations*. Definitions and restrictions that appear in developed mathematical work have their origins in this process of proofs and refutations. For example, a "peculiar" hypothesis of a known theorem might have been developed to eliminate a "monstrous" counterexample that arose during the early proof and analysis stages of discovery.

Teacher: This is both comforting and confusing. The presentation of mathematical results seems deductivist.

Student γ: Lakatos (1976, p. 12) said it well: "In deductivist style, all propositions are true and all inferences valid. Mathematics is presented as an ever-increasing set of eternal, immutable truths. Counterexamples, refutations, criticism cannot possibly enter. An authoritarian air is secured for the subject by beginning with disguised monster-barring and proof-generated definitions and with the fully-fledged theorem, and by suppressing the primitive conjecture, the refutations, and the criticism of the proof. Deductivist style hides the struggle, hides the adventure. The whole story vanishes, the successive tentative formulations of the theorem in the course of the proof-procedure are doomed to oblivion while the end result is exalted into sacred infallibility."

Teacher: One implication of your argument, or Lakatos's, is that written mathematics is misleading. To write up mathematical work in a way that respects the heuristic "would require the rewriting of textbooks, and would make them so long that one could never read them to the end. Papers would become much longer, too" (Lakatos 1976, p. 144).

Teacher: What are the implications here for mathematical economics?

Student β: Let me see if I can answer. An important problem, one that α and I have been attempting to identify, has been what we termed the irrelevance of mathematical economics. Our objections were not those of the applied-economics class, which were satisfied by the linking of the theories to simpler modes of economic reasoning. Instead, α and I tried to argue that the form of presentation of mathematical economics biases the discussion about economic problems in the direction of a more limited set of problems that could be well posed mathematically. (I for one am still uncomfortable about this point, but I'll move on for now.) Further, the deductivist mode of presentation of mathematical economics serves to *hide* this bias. Mathematical theorists, accustomed to this style, see no bias, only normal stylistic conventions. Nonmathematical theorists see a mathematical conspiracy of silence. γ has argued that there is no conspiracy, that in fact mathematical theorists are as concerned with real economic content as nonmathematical economists, no matter what appears to be the case from outside the subdiscipline. He further argued that the subdiscipline is governed by the canons of peer evaluation and self-policing.

At this point I want to suggest that professional integrity seems to require that the subdiscipline be opened to all economists so that professional standards can be *widely* appreciated. For too long our profession has been full of calls by the mathematically literate for higher mathematical literacy rates in the economics profession and calls by the unsophisticated for more surveys and translations of standard mathematical results.

Student γ: This is reminiscent of C. P. Snow's "two-cultures" problem. The professional solution seems to have taken the form of more mathematical training in graduate education. The informal solution seems to be infrequent attempts at translation by a small number of mathematical theorists; the best of them *want* their work to be read and appreciated.

Student α: Is this enough? I believe from what has been said today that all economists need to be allowed into the discovery process in mathematical economics; it is not sufficient for special translators to interpret the assumptions and conclusions, the B and D boxes, in terms of A and E. This translation hides too much.

Teacher: I suspect the only solution is to *write* the mathematics heuristically, not deductively.

Student γ: Certainly not all mathematical theorists can do this, but it is just as certain that some of them could. Historians of our discipline might play a role, too. Must they continue to argue over Marshall's footnotes, or Ricardo's correspondence, when they could apply their training to the solution of more pressing current problems? Why has there been no "rational reconstruction" of general equilibrium theory, stability analysis, or social choice theory?

Student α: I wish we had some models of this kind of heuristic presentation to work from.

Student β: Perhaps we could attempt it ourselves.

Student γ: What do you mean?

Student β: It occurred to me that two of our professors, G and W, were going to begin talking tomorrow about an idea that W had mentioned quite casually in class yesterday. W said, "You know, I should really talk to G about this: It seems interesting."

Teacher: Let's do the following. I'll ask G if they'd allow me to set up a tape recorder tomorrow. Perhaps if we had a recording of their conversation, we could see the heuristic process at work.

Student α: Wouldn't it be interesting if their talks led to a paper, a collaborative paper written in the deductivist style? Then we would have a case study of both the deductivist paper, the minitranslation that the discussion section of the paper would provide, and the actual heuristic of discovery.

Teacher: Let's adjourn now. I'll find G and ask about our plan.

A transcript.

W: Good morning, G. I'm glad you want to talk about this idea I had. The problem is, I don't know if there's anything to it. At any rate, remember our talks about Aumann's papers and how we recognized that there was now an alternative characterization of the competitive equilibrium? Do you also recall our distress at the fact that standard dynamic theory was so ad hoc, so limited?

G: Of course. The tatonnement adjustment is one of the few known dynamic processes. We can test the competitive equilibrium for stability using that process, but the restrictions needed to ensure stability seem forced; they also seem irrelevant to the concerns of general equilibrium theorists that those models be applicable to monetary theory, say.

W: Right. Briefly my idea is this: Stability has dealt with the convergence, under some dynamic like the tatonnement, of allocations to the competitive (equilibrium) allocation. In Aumann's continuum of traders model, the competitive allocation is identical with the core allocation. Could we explore, or create, a dynamic mechanism that converges to the core? If so, we have an alternative to the usual tatonnement adjustment.

G: What would be the advantage of this?

W: As I see it, the core is defined independently of *prices*, and thus independently of organized markets. There are only lots and lots of traders. If we can create a reasonable dynamic process that converges on the core, we have a strong argument that the competitive allocation is stable without having to depend on a price-adjustment dynamic brought in from outside the trading process.

G: I see your point, but without prices and markets I am not sure that we have enough structure to conclude that the core is stable.

W: This point bothered me also, but I've come to see a result along *those* lines as an important one, too; for if it's impossible to convergè to the core *without* price adjustment, then the tatonnment of something like it cannot really be ad hoc.

The difficulty as I now see things is that we don't have a dynamic process available for discussion; we don't have a process that changes allocations in a price-independent fashion and that we can test for either convergence or lack of convergence.

G: That has to be our first step. Let's each of us think about this overnight. Tomorrow let's get together and see if we can write down, using Aumann's model and its notation, some mechanisms that change allocations. Maybe we can come up with a process, call it *P*, and prove a theorem like "the *P* process converges on the core."

W: Or "the *P* process cannot converge to the core."

G: Of course. What an interesting problem! We'll be simultaneously trying to prove and disprove any conjecture.
W: See you here tomorrow.

Scene: The next day.

W: I think I've got it.
G: Great. Let me see your argument.
W: Recall Aumann's model. There is continuum of traders, as many traders as there are points in [0, 1]. A coalition of traders is any subset of that set. An allocation is an allowable assignment of goods to traders; that is, the assignment simply redistributes initial holdings. Thus an allocation models a permissible trade. Aumann says that an allocation x dominates another allocation y if some set T of traders gets more desirable stuff with x than they do with y and, further, if they can actually *get x*.
G: So that if y is the allocation *initial stocks to all*, and x is *all goods to traders* $[0, \frac{1}{8}]$, then x fails to dominate y via the coalition $[0, \frac{1}{8}]$.
W: Correct, since the set $[0, \frac{1}{8}]$ doesn't have *all* the goods in the economy.
G: The core, of course, is the set of all allocations that are undominated via *any* coalition.
W: That's right, and we know that in Aumann's model the core is a *single* allocation (if the competitive equilibrium is unique).
G: Tell me about your dynamic process.
W: Begin with an arbitrary initial allocation, like *initial holdings to everyone*. Call this i^0. Because the core *is* an allocation, call it i. How can we get from i^0 to i?

Consider the following argument: Begin with i^0. If this is the core, then stop: We're done. If not, there is some allocation i^1 and some subset of traders, call it s^1, such that i^1 dominates i^0 via s^1. If i^1 is core, stop. If not, then continue. Thus we have defined a sequence of allocations $\{i^0, i^1, i^2, \ldots\} = \{i^n\}_{n=1,2,\ldots}$.
G: Does this sequence converge on i, the core?
W: I don't know.
G: Let's see, now. Each i^n is an allocation, so it assigns a certain basket of goods to each trader in [0,1]. It's a function whose domain is [0,1] and whose range is commodity space, or R^n_+. We're thus asking a question about the convergence of a sequence of vector-valued functions. What else do we know?
W: We know some things about those functions. They are Lebesgue measurable by Aumann's assumption.
G: Intuitively, then, they're almost continuous, so I'll think of them as continuous functions.

W: Further, each is an allocation, or a redistribution, so the amount of stuff the entire group of *all* traders gets under allocation i^n is the same as the amount that the group started with. Formally, $\int_{[0,1]} i^n = \int_{[0,1]} i^0$ for all n. Frankly, I have a hard time remembering that i^n is really $i^n(t)$, for $t \,\varepsilon\, [0,1]$, and that $i^n(t)$ is a vector with as many components as there are tradable goods. Oh, well!

Do you think this process converges?

G: Nope. I'm sure, in fact, that it won't.

W: Prove it.

G: Suppose the first coalition is s^1, the second is s^1, and the third is s^1. Thus i^1 dominates i^0 via s^1 or, in new notation, $i^1 D_{s^1} i^0$; also $i^2 D_{s^1} i^1$ and $i^3 D_{s^1} i^2$. Then i^3 is unambiguously best among i^0, i^1, i^2, i^3 for s^1. But suppose s^1, s^2, and s^3 have *no* traders in common; suppose, that is, they are disjoint sets. Then we have no best for *all* traders. Some prefer i^1; some prefer i^2; some prefer i^3. We can even generate cycles. It might be that $i^1 D_{s^1} i^0$, $i^2 D_{s^2} i^1$, and $i^0 D_{s^3} i^2$ if the coalitions are disjoint.

W: Rats. I thought we could "climb up" transitivity chains of dominating allocations until we reached the core, an *un*dominated allocation.

G: I have a different idea, one based on your difficulty. Your proof went astray because at the nth iteration only a few traders – namely, those in s^n – were involved; the difficulties seemed to occur because the omitted traders at the nth stage could "come back in" at the $(n + 1)$th stage. What happens if we require all traders to receive a new allocation at each iteration?

W: Do you mean we force every single trader to trade at every single instant? That's a poor economic assumption. In the real world, my trade with the grocer is independent of your trade with the butcher.

G: If I'm not trading with someone else when you are trading, I'm really "trading" with myself, or keeping my previous holdings of goods.

W: Oh, I see. The adjustment process would then be described as follows: If i^0 is core, stop. If i^0 is not, then it is dominated by, say, x^1 via s^1. Define i^1 to be equal to x^1 for traders in s^1, and let it be equal to i^0 for traders not in s^1. Consider i^1 so defined. It it is core, then stop. If not, iterate the argument. We then produce a sequence $\{i^0, i^1, i^2, \ldots\} = \{i^n\}_{n=1,2,\ldots}$ of allocations with a stronger property than we had before: i^n is at least as good for everybody and strictly better for s^n; further by redistribution i^n is always feasible, so $\int_{[0,1]} i^n = \int_{[0,1]} i^0$.

G: It certainly seems as though this sequence, if it converges, should converge on the core.

W: Let's think about the economic meaning of this process. It seems to say that if an allocation like i^n isn't in the core, then there exists some coalition s^{n+1} that could suggest an allocation to its members alone, say, x^{n+1}. All members of s^{n+1} would prefer x^{n+1} to i^n, and they could actually achieve it. My mental picture is of many traders milling about in a marketplace shouting out their holdings and trying to make trades, in groups as large as needed, to make themselves better off. They continue milling and shouting until no more trades are possible.

G: They actually trade and achieve each i^n.

W: That's right. They trade, but out of equilibrium.

G: What happens if a trader could join either of two coalitions at the nth iteration, each of which, with that trader in it, could dominate i^n?

W: I don't think it should matter. If the one the trader ends up in yields a core allocation, the process ends. If not, it continues, at least provided the conjecture is true that this stops at the core and only at the core.

I suppose we can't avoid the question anymore. Let's call what we have the G process. We're conjecturing that the sequence $\{i^n\}$ defined by the G process converges on i, the core. Is it true?

G: Let's work on proofs overnight and see what we have tomorrow.

Scene: The next day.

G: I've found...

W: ...a proof.

G: You go first.

W: Okay. Well, it's not really a proof, but I've found some evidence for the truth of the conjecture.

We have a sequence of Lebesgue measurable functions. They're all Lesbesgue integrable, and their integrals are all equal to $I = \int_{[0,1]} i^0$, which is a vector of constants, the vector of initial amounts of goods in society. Certainly *no* trader can ever get more than I. Thus for every trader t, at any iteration (say, the nth) it must be true that $i^n(t) \leq I$.

I now appeal to the standard Lebesgue dominated convergence theorem of analysis, which says that if a sequence of Lebesgue integrable functions, $\{i^n\}$, converges *pointwise* to a limit function called $\hat{\imath}$, and if, further, there is some Lebesgue integrable function I such that $i^n \leq I$, then (1) $\hat{\imath}$ is Lebesgue integrable and (2) $\int \hat{\imath} = \lim \int i^n$.

G: I'm glad I never took measure theory. How is this supposed to help?

W: Pointwise convergence may not be so hard to prove. It involves *fixing* a trader $\bar{\imath}$ and looking at a sequence of *numbers* (in R_+^n actually), namely, $\{i^0(\bar{\imath}), i^1(\bar{\imath}), \ldots\}$. I've reduced the problem of convergence of a sequence of functions to the convergence of a sequence of numbers. If we can show this convergence, then we know by the theorem that the function $\hat{\imath}$ is, by (2), an allocation.

G: I see this: Because $\int i^n = I$ for any n, $\lim_n \int i^n = \lim_n I = I$, so $\int \hat{i} = I$ makes $\hat{i}$ an allocation.

W: Yes, and further, $\hat{i}$ is the same kind of allocation as those in the sequence: It's Lebesgue integrable and thus just as "nice" as any allocation at any iteration.

G: Is this as far as you've gotten?

W: Yes. I still need to prove two results. First, I must prove pointwise convergence. If I can prove this, then I will have to prove that $\hat{i}$ is actually equal to i, the core.

But tell me about your proof.

G: Okay, but it too is only a partial proof. I'm a bit embarrassed at the lack of sophisticated mathematics. *I* don't have the training you have.

W: Knowing theorems is different from being a mathematician. We're both *doing* mathematical economics; let's forget labels.

G: I was just teasing you. I, too, tried to simplify the conjecture. I know lots of facts about convergence of sequences of numbers, and my strategy was to try to have the process generate a real number at every iteration. This resulting sequence could then be tested for convergence. The limit would then be reinterpreted, and the core, I hope, would be the reinterpreted limit.

W: So you've created a model of a model.

G: What do you mean?

W: I'll draw it:

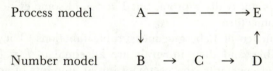

A is the sequence of functions and E the limit of that sequence. You model A by B, a sequence of numbers. You analyze that sequence by some technique, called C. Your limit number is D, which you reinterpret as E.

G: Is this relevant to my proof?

W: No, but it's interesting. Tell me your results.

G: I tend to think pictorially. Thus, when I think of a sequence of points, I think of them on a line. Convergence means that they get bunched up closer and closer to *one* point on that line. My idea has to do with creating the line.

First, note that at each stage of the iteration, say, the nth, society (the set of all traders) has preferences over aggregate bundles. That is, some bundles of goods are regarded by traders as better than what they have, and some are considered worse. Here "better" and "worse" have to do with preferences over goods. Specifically, for any trader t, $y \precsim_t x$ means (as

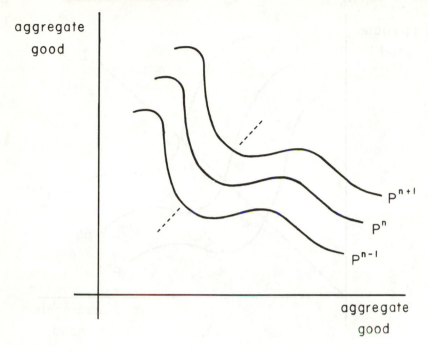

aggregate
good

P^{n+1}

P^n

P^{n-1}

aggregate
good

Figure 10.1

it usually does) that for t bundle x is at least as desirable as bundle y. We thus know from the construction of $\{i^n\}$ that $i^0 \lesssim_t i^1 \lesssim_t i^2 \lesssim_t \cdots \lesssim_t i^n \lesssim_t \cdots$ for every t.

Now, each i^n is a vector, not a number; how, then, can we "pull" a number out? My idea is as follows: Define the aggregate preferred set with respect to an allocation as the set of all aggregate bundles (to all traders) that *no* subset of traders views as less desirable than the given allocations. If i^n is the allocation, the set p^n is defined by $P^n = \{ \int x : i^n \lesssim_t x$ for all $t \}$. Look at the sequence $P^0, P^1, P^2, \ldots$. This is a sequence of *sets*.

W: Oh, my. I thought that you were going from sequences of allocations to sequences of numbers, but you're going instead to sequences of sets.

G: I'm not done yet.

W: Carry on.

G: These aggregate preferred sets are like upper contour sets for indifference curves. Specifically, (1) they are continuous, connected, and nonintersecting; and (2) $P^0 \subseteq P^1 \subseteq P^2 \subseteq \cdots \subseteq P^n \subseteq \cdots$. Note also that *if i* is the core, P^i is contained in every one of these sets.

I have this picture in mind (Figure 10.1).

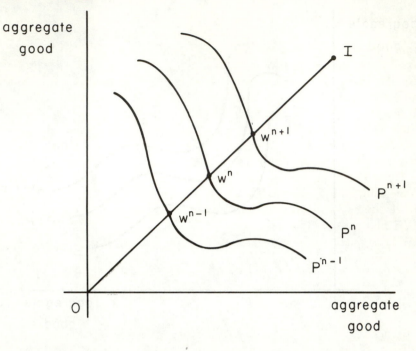

aggregate
good

w^{n+1}

w^n

w^{n-1}

P^{n+1}

P^n

P^{n-1}

I

O

aggregate
good

Figure 10.2

I'm thinking of aggregate amount of goods on the axes and of each P^n as containing its contour and everything above the contour.

W: But certainly *one* point on the contour of P^i is the core.

G: Correct. Let's call it $\int i = $ I.

W: What a neat idea. We can then imitate the idea of deriving a utility scale from indifference contours.

G: Exactly. Draw a line from the origin to I, as in Figure 10.2. Label the intersections of the line with the contours in conformity with the labels on the contours. Thus we get $\{w^0, w^1, w^2, \ldots, w^n, \ldots\}$, which is a sequence of real numbers.

Intuitively, since the P^n sets "move out," the sequence $\{w^n\}$ is monotone increasing. Further, each w^n has I as an upper bound.

W: Certainly the $w^n \rightarrow I - $ I think. Maybe. Or does it?

G: I haven't gotten that far. Give me another day.

W: Done.

Scene: The next day.

G: I've got it. I need to show several things. First, I show that, if W is the line segment connecting 0 and I, then i^n is a core allocation if and only if $P^n \cap W = I$. Next I show that if $w^n < I$, then $w^{n+1} > w^n$. Finally I show that the sequence $\{i^n\}$ converges on the core.

W: Interpretation, please.

G: The first result says that the aggregate preferred sets stop "nesting" only and exactly at the core. The second result says that if the nth iteration is not at the core, the aggregate preferred sets nest some more. Putting these two results together says that the sequence does reach the core.

In other words, the second result says that if you're not at the core, you move closer to it. The first result says that you stop when you get there.

Here; look at my formal derivations using no more than set theory and some limiting arguments. It's only five pages.

W: I don't need to look at it. I have a counterexample.

G: I find that hard to believe.

W: Trust me. Draw a line, and mark one end with i^0, the other with i, and the middle with $\hat{\imath}$.

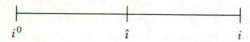

Put i^1 halfway between i^0 and $\hat{\imath}$. Put i^2 halfway between i^1 and $\hat{\imath}$. Put i^3 halfway, and so on.

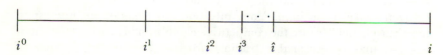

Certainly one keeps moving closer to i at each iteration. This was your second result. Your first said that you stop when you reach i. Your theorem *doesn't* follow. The sequence $\{i^n\}$ converges on $\hat{\imath}$ not i.

G: I see. Both lemmas are true, but the theorem doesn't follow. What would it mean to stop at $\hat{\imath}$?

W: In which model?

G: In the economics.

W: I think it means that at every iteration the society of traders is getting better off but for some reason they are not ever getting as well off as they could be.

G: You realize that that result makes good economic sense. Suppose that two traders, A and B, are in the large market. A has just what B needs, and B has just what A needs. Now suppose that A and B *never* meet. Each will go on trading, and getting better off, but their *potential* gains from trade are never realized. In my picture, the line segment from w^n to I represents the potential gains from trade remaining after the nth iteration.

What makes us think that traders will, in general, realize the maximum gains from trade?

W: This will take some more thought. See you tomorrow.

Scene: The next day.

W: I've got a problem.

G: Me too. You go first.

W: It's the core. I don't think our process converges to it.

G: Another counterexample?

W: Something worse. The core doesn't exist.

G: What?

W: That's correct. The core was defined with respect to a given initial allocation. Once we change that allocation via trade – from i^0 to i^1, say – the core itself changes. All we can ask are questions about being core *with respect to* the most recent allocation. Put another way, our sequence of allocations is characterized by the idea that a move from i^n to i^{n+1} makes at least some traders better off and *no* trader worse off. What we do have is a sequence of Pareto-improving trades. The core has nothing to do with anything in our analysis *or* model.

I think we should agree to rephrase our conjecture as follows: Does the sequence $\{i^n\}$ converge on a Pareto-efficient allocation? I was simply mistaken in my belief that the core would be approached.

G: Don't take it too hard. Your intuition did generate an interesting mechanism; and because the competitive equilibrium is Pareto efficient, if we find that no reasonable trading process generates a sequence of allocations that converges on a Pareto allocation, we have ruled out convergence to competitive equilibria. On the other hand, if we *can* find such a nice process, it is certainly worth exploring further. We should have recognized that any disequilibrium trade perturbs the static model. That's why Edgeworth ruled them out by "recontracting" and Walras by his "tickets."

But I too have a problem.

W: I'm all ears.

G: I am increasingly uncomfortable using Aumann's continuum-of-traders model. All our arguments pertain to "a trader like A" or a "bunch of individuals." In Aumann's terms, such traders have *no* goods: They have measure zero.

I think we should forget Lebesgue measure, forget integrals, and talk instead about allocations of goods to traders as x_m for *finite m*. We can then require that $\Sigma_m x_m = \Sigma_m i^0$, where each x_m is a vector with as many components as there are tradable goods.

W: Now I'll never have a chance to use the Lebesgue dominated convergence theorem in economics.

G: Sorry. Let's see if we can get our sequence to converge.

W: We've already seen that it can't. At least, it can't until we rule out "premature stopping," or the failure to exploit potential gains from trade.

G: My thoughts exactly. And the key word here is...

W: ...perfect information.

G: Right. We have somehow to interpret the economic condition of perfect information in our model. We both now believe that this will prevent the premature stopping of trading activity.

W: It seems that what we need to do is to make the *nonrealization* of gains from trade an unlikely event.

G: Suppose the gains from trade remaining at the nth iteration are modeled by $G^n = I - w^n$. We want to ensure that these gains are potentially realizable.

W: We seem to need probabilities here.

G: You're right. If we define m^j to be the unique solution to $w^{n+1} - w^n = m^n G^n$, then m^n represents the fraction of the potential gain from trade that is *actually* realized on the $(n + 1)$th iteration. Certainly $m^n \varepsilon [0, 1]$ for all n.

W: I see where you're heading. Suppose we create the *information assumption*: If $G^n > 0$ at the nth iteration, $\lim_{\varepsilon \to 0} \text{Prob}(m^j < \varepsilon) = 0$.

G: Okay. This says that the event "The fraction of the gains from trade actually realized is arbitrarily small" is an event of zero probability.

W: Yes.

G: This is nice since our previous lemmas still stand. We just create two more lemmas. The first says that $\lim_{n \to \infty} w^n = L \leq I$. We had this before except we thought that $L = I$. It didn't. Now we introduce our information assumption to show that $L = I$.

W: Of course all we can hope for is that $\text{Prob}(L < I) = 0$.

G: Right. We want to show that $L = I$ with probability 1. Then we're done.

W: Let's try that tomorrow.

Scene: The next day.

G: The more I played around with our information assumption last night, the unhappier I got. There seems to be some difficulty with the limiting argument in it.

W: My thoughts exactly. What we need is that $\text{Prob}(m^n < \varepsilon) \to 0$ *uniformly* in n; that is, this limit is independent of the stage of the iteration. If it is not, we can get precisely the same bunching-up problem.

G: Let's see. Because w_n is monotone increasing and bounded from above, it has a limit. Call this limit v. If, for some k, $w^k = 1$, then no further gains from trade are possible; we're at a Pareto-efficient allocation. We thus want to show that $v = 1$. This should be impossible without perfect information, so we need to show that $\text{Prob}(v < 1) = 0$. But $\text{Prob}(v < 1) = \lim_{u \to 1} \text{Prob}(v \leq u) = \lim_{u \to 1} \lim_{m \to \infty} \text{Prob}(w^m \leq u)$.

W: But the gains from trade realized after the $(n + 1)$th iteration are $w^{n+1} - w^n$. Also, $1 - w^n$ is the potential gain from trade after the nth iteration. We want to assert that

$$``m_n \equiv \frac{w^{n+1} - w^n}{1 - w^n} \quad \text{is small''}$$

is an event of low probability uniformly in n.

G: What happens if $1 = w^n$ so that the denominator is zero?

W: We have a problem then. Let's ask instead about $1 - w^{n+1} > (1 - \varepsilon)(1 - w^n)$ since this is true, for $1 - w^n > 0$, whenever

$$\frac{w^{n+1} - w^n}{1 - w^n} < \varepsilon.$$

G: Excellent. Thus our perfect information assumption now reads, For any $\delta > 0$ there exists an $\varepsilon > 0$ such that $\text{Prob}[1 - w^{n+1} > (1 - \varepsilon)(1 - w^n)] < \delta$, for all n.

W: If $0 < u < 1$ and $w^m \leq u$, then the condition $1 - w^{n+1} \leq (1 - \varepsilon)(1 - w^n)$ tells us how many iterations, or "jumps" of at least ε distance, are needed to get the sequence to w^m.

G: What?

W: Suppose the first jump is ε. The remaining distance is thus $1 - \varepsilon$. If there are r jumps, the distance remaining *after* those jumps is $(1 - \varepsilon)^r$. Thus the distance already covered is $1 - (1 - \varepsilon)^r$. If u is the distance covered, then $(1 - \varepsilon)^r = 1 - u$, so $r = [\ln(1 - u)]/[\ln(1 - \varepsilon)]$ is the number of jumps of at least ε in the sequence.

G: Put another way, if $w^m \leq u$, it follows that $1 - w^{n+1} \leq (1 - \varepsilon)(1 - w^n)$ at most $r = [\ln(1 - u)]/[(\ln(1 - \varepsilon)]$ times between $n = 0$ and $n = m - 1$.

W: Thus *at least $m - r$ terms in the sequence must involve jumps of length less than* ε. Hence by our information assumption, for a given $\delta < 1$ and the associated ε and r,

$$\text{Prob}(w^m \leq u) < \delta^{m-r}.$$

Thus $\lim_{m \to \infty} \text{Prob}(w^m \leq u) = 0$, which suffices to show, as you noted earlier, that $\text{Prob}(v < 1) = 0$.

G: Let's see if I can put things together. I know that the sequence $\{i^n\}$ converges.

W: How? I thought this was hard.

G: No. The set of allocations is a compact subset of Euclidean space. Thus there exists a limit to the sequence, which I'll call i^*. Now, w^n depends on allocations, so I'll write $w(i^n)$ instead of w^n. We have $\{i^n\} \to i^*$.

W: We can bypass some lemmas, I now realize.

G: How?

W: Because w is a continuous function since preferences are continuous. Thus $w(i^*)$ is the limit of $\{w(i^n)\}$. We've just proved that $w(i^*) = 1$ with probability one. Therefore i^* must be a Pareto-efficient allocation if $w(i^*) = 1$.

G: That really was my first lemma.

W: Granted, but we also need to show that i^* is the limit of $\{i^n\}$ when $w^n \to 1$.

G: This is a form of my second lemma.

W: You're right, but the statement and proof both look different now.

G: I think we're done. How shall it be written up? I presume we'd like to publish our result. It's not a major piece, but it is new, interesting, and connected to some recent themes in the adjustment-process literature. I think a short note would suffice.

W: Okay. I'll try writing the work up as a journal article. It does seem to have taken a very different form from my initial idea and your initial analysis. No matter – I've enjoyed this collaboration.

G: Me too.

Reprinted from THE REVIEW OF ECONOMIC STUDIES, Vol. XLII (3), July, 1975, DANIEL A. GRAHAM and E. ROY WEINTRAUB, pp. 469-472.

On Convergence to Pareto Allocations [1, 2]

DANIEL A. GRAHAM and E. ROY WEINTRAUB
Duke University

1. INTRODUCTION

The recent book by Arrow and Hahn [1] provides an admirable survey of the work on non-tatonnement adjustment processes developed by Uzawa [4], Hahn and Negishi [2] and others. Such processes permit disequilibrium trading as long as successive allocations are Pareto-better, so that all agents have non-decreasing utility indicators through trading periods. In this paper we formalize a similar process which focuses upon the coalition formation problems at the heart of all such trading processes. While our process is somewhat less descriptive of the role of the decision calculus of individuals in determining successive allocations than the bidding process of Hurwicz, Radner and Reiter [3], for example, we do admit such processes as special cases and our coalition formation framework appears to emphasize more naturally the problem of inter-agent communication. Under a particular assumption regarding the implications of costless intercommunication, we show that successive coalition formation must eventually lead to a Pareto allocation with probability one.

2. THE MODEL

Consider the Euclidean space E^k, where the dimensionality k represents the number of commodities to be traded. We use the usual vector notation: $x > y$ means $x^i > y^i$ for all i; $x \geq y$ means $x^i \geq y^i$ for all i; $x \geq y$ means $x^i \geq y^i$ for all i and $x^j > y^j$ for some j. A commodity bundle, x, will be a point in E^k_+, the non-negative orthant of E^k.

Let T denote the set of traders:

$$T = \{1, 2, ..., s\}.$$

An assignment of commodity bundles to traders will be a function x from T to E^k_+ each coordinate of which is bounded. We assume a fixed initial assignment of goods to traders, i^0, where

$$I = \sum_T i^0(t) > 0,$$

and define an allocation to be any assignment that is feasible given i^0, i.e. x is an allocation if x is an assignment and

$$\sum_T x(t) = I.$$

For each trader $t \in T$ there is the usual quasi-order $\gtrsim_t$ called preference-or-indifference, from which we may typically define $>_t$ and $\sim_t$, called preference and indifference. We assume,

[1] *First version received June* 1972; *final version accepted May* 1974 *(Eds.).*
[2] The authors are indebted to James Mirrlees for his generous help in improving several clumsy arguments in an earlier version of this paper. We also benefited from the comments of Marjorie McElroy, David Peterson and Morris Weisfeld.

Desirability. $x \geq y$ implies $x >_t y$ for all t in T.

Continuity. For each $y \in E_+^k$, and all t in T the sets $\{x:\ x >_t y\}$ and $\{x:\ y >_t x\}$ are open relative to E_+^k.

Strict convexity. For any commodity bundle, x, and all t in T the set $\{y:\ y >_t x\}$ is strictly convex.

Given an existing allocation i, an allocation y dominates or blocks an allocation x via a coalition R, $R \subset T$, if $y(t) >_t x(t)$ for all $t \in R$ and $\Sigma_R y(t) = \Sigma_R i(t)$. The core is the set of all allocations that are not dominated via any non-null coalition. If x and y are two allocations, x is Pareto-better than y if there exists a non-empty coalition R such that $x >_t y$ for all t in R and $x \gtrsim_t y$ for all t in $T - R$. An allocation x^* is Pareto if there is no allocation that is Pareto-better than x^*.

3. THE ADJUSTMENT MECHANISM

The adjustment process we wish to consider may be introduced informally; the latter part of this section will make matters precise. Assume any initial allocation of goods to the various traders. If this is not a Pareto allocation, there will be a set of coalitions and their corresponding allocations which could block the given initial allocation. (One of these allocations will, of course, be Pareto.) We suppose that one of these feasible coalitions does form, and that trade takes place according to a corresponding allocation. Consider this new allocation: traders in the blocking coalition have received a new allocation, while traders not in the coalition have retained their original allocation. Is this new allocation Pareto? If it is, the process terminates and an equilibrium has been attained (any individual made better off under any new allocation would not be able to find a trading partner or coalition to help him effect the new allocation by trading, since they would be made worse off by such an exchange). If, however, the new allocation is not Pareto, iterate the above argument. This process defines a *blocking sequence* where, at the nth iteration, the existing allocation is modified according to:

$$i^n(t) = \begin{cases} x^n(t) & t \in R^n \\ i^{n-1}(t) & t \in T - R^n \end{cases} \qquad n = 1, 2, 3, \ldots$$

if given i^{n-1}, x^n blocks i^{n-1} via R^n.

What factors affect coalition formation? At any non-equilibrium stage of the exchange process there is a potential gain from trade. How much of that gain is actually captured by the participants in the next exchange depends upon the specific allocation effected by the coalition that forms. But coalition formation depends crucially on the cost of contacting other traders at that stage of the trading process.[1] What are the implications of costless intercommunication on coalition formation? Clearly infinite costs preclude any coalition formation and the realization of any gains from trade. On the other hand, costless intercommunication assures that some fraction of the potential gain from trade should be captured. How large will that fraction be? We shall simply assume that with costless intercommunication the realization of an arbitrarily small fraction of the potential gain is most unlikely: that is, this event has a probability close to zero. This can be made more precise as follows. For any allocation, i, let

$$w(i) \equiv \inf \{w \in E_+^1:\ wI = \Sigma x(t),\ x(t) \gtrsim_t i(t) \forall t,\ x(t)\ \text{an assignment}\},$$

---

[1] The existence of markets and prices might be viewed as facilitating coalition formation. What is required here is that one set of prices supplant another only if the new prices lead to further exchange. Since the participants in such an exchange have demonstrated a preference for the new allocation, the requirements for a blocking coalition and allocation are satisfied.

that is, $w(i)I$ is the smallest aggregate endowment in the proportions of I that would suffice to make every trader as well off as with allocation i (the smallest endowment in the proportions of I that belongs to the aggregate preferred set corresponding to allocation i). Now define $w_n = w(i^n)$ $n = 0, 1, 2, \ldots$. (Obviously $\{w_n\}$ is a nondecreasing sequence on the closed unit interval and thus has a limit.) We can interpret $1 - w_n$ as a measure of the potential gain from trade remaining after the nth iteration of the trading process. The quantity $w_{n+1} - w_n$ can similarly be regarded as a measure of the gain from trade actually realized on the $n+1$st iteration. Finally notice that for $1 - w_n > 0$, $(w_{n+1} - w_n)/(1 - w_n) < \varepsilon$ if and only if $1 - w_{n+1} > (1 - \varepsilon)(1 - w_n)$. While the former expression is more easily recognized as a statement that the fraction of the potential gain from trade actually captured on the $n+1$st iteration is less than ε, its indeterminateness when $w_n = 1$ makes it more convenient to state our costless intercommunication assumption in terms of the latter expression.

Costless intercommunication. For all $\delta > 0$ there exists $\varepsilon > 0$ such that

$$\text{prob} \left[1 - w_{n+1} > (1 - \varepsilon)(1 - w_n) \right] < \delta,$$

for all n.[1]

4. CONVERGENCE

We can now state and prove our principal result.

Theorem. *Under costless intercommunication a blocking sequence converges to a Pareto allocation with probability one.*

Proof. We have already remarked that $v = \lim_{n \to \infty} w_n$ exists. We need next to establish that $\text{prob}\,(v < 1) = 0$. Let $0 < u < 1$. Then if $w_m \leqq u$, it follows that

$$1 - w_{n+1} \leqq (1 - \varepsilon)(1 - w_n)$$

at most $r = \ln(1 - u)/\ln(1 - \varepsilon)$ times between $n = 0$ and $n = m - 1$, i.e. in the sequence of m terms there are *at most* r terms of ε or larger jumps. (If $w_0 = 0$, u would be reached after r successive ε jumps.) Accordingly, there must be *at least* $m - r$ terms of less than ε jumps. By costless intercommunication we then have for a given $\delta < 1$ and the associated ε and r

$$\text{prob}\,(w_m \leqq u) < \delta^{m-r} \to 0 \text{ as } m \to \infty.$$

Thus

$$\text{prob}\,(v < 1) = \lim_{u \to 1} \text{prob}\,(v \leqq u)$$

$$= \lim_{u \to 1} \lim_{m \to \infty} \text{prob}\,(w_m \leqq u) = 0.$$

Now let i^* be a limit point of the blocking sequence $\{i^n\}$. That there is at least one such limit point follows from the fact that the set of allocations is a compact subset of Euclidean space. This combined with the fact that $w(i)$ is continuous (from continuity

---

[1] At any given stage in the trading process the requirement that for any positive δ there exists a positive ε such that $\text{prob}\,(A < \varepsilon) < \delta$, where $A = (w_{n+1} - w_n)/(1 - w_n) \in [0, 1]$, is quite weak. Any continuous distribution on the unit interval satisfies it as well as any discrete distribution provided only that $\text{prob}\,[A = 0] = 0$. Thus for a given stage in the process the assumption might be put "The probability of no further trade given an allocation that is not Pareto is zero". The only problem with this interpretation is that the probability distribution on the realized fraction of the potential gain from trade need not be independent of the stage of the trading process and this produces complications. Consider, for example, the "lumpy" distribution $\text{prob}\,(A = 1/n) = 1 - 1/n$, $\text{prob}\,(A \neq 1/n) = 1/n$ with all $A \neq 1/n$ equally likely. For any given stage in the exchange process, n, this distribution satisfies the requirement that $\text{prob}\,(A = 0) = 0$ but as n becomes larger a limit is approached in which there is a "lump" of probability at zero. The force of the costless intercommunication assumption is to rule out such "irregular" limits.

of preferences [1]) means that $w(i^*)$ is a limit point of $\{w(i^n)\}$ and thus that $w(i^*) = 1$ with probability one.

The allocation i^* must be Pareto if $w(i^*) = 1$ because if it were not there would necessarily exist another allocation, i', such that $i'(t) >_t i^*(t)$ for all t.[2] Since

$$i'(t) \in \text{int } \{z \in E_+^n: z \gtrsim_t i^*(t)\}$$

for all t, it follows that

$$I = \Sigma_T i'(t) \in \Sigma_T \text{ int } \{z: z \gtrsim_t i^*(t)\} = \text{int } \Sigma_T\{z: z \gtrsim_t i^*(t)\}.$$

This combined with the fact that $I > 0$ entails the existence of $w' < 1$ such that

$$w'I \in \Sigma_T\{z: z \gtrsim_t i^*(t)\}.$$

Thus

$$w(i^*) = \inf \{w: \ wI = \sum x(t), \ x(t) \gtrsim_t i^*(t) \forall_t\} \leqq w' < 1$$

contradicting $w(i^*) = 1$.

It remains to show that i^* is the limit of $\{i^n\}$ when $w^n \to 1$. It is sufficient in this regard to rule out the existence of any limit points other than i^*. If i^{**} were another limit point of $\{i^n\}$ then $i^{**}(t) \gtrsim_t i^*(t)$ for all t and vice versa, i.e. if $i^*(t) >_t i^{**}(t)$ for *any* t, then $i^{**}(t)$ could not be a limit point. Thus $i^{**}(t) \sim_t i^*(t)$ for all t. If, moreover, $i^{**} \neq i^*$ then the allocation $1/2 i^{**} + 1/2 i^*$ would be Pareto-better than either i^{**} or i^* (from convexity of preferences) contradicting the fact that both i^* and i^{**} must be Pareto when $w_n \to 1$. Thus, with probability one, $\{i^n\}$ tends to a limit which is a Pareto allocation.

REFERENCES

[1] Arrow, K. J. and Hahn, F. H. *General Competitive Analysis* (San Francisco: Holden-Day, 1972).

[2] Hahn, F. H. and Negishi, T. "A Theorem on Non-tatonnement Stability", *Econometrica*, **30** (1962).

[3] Hurwicz, L., Radner, R. and Reiter, S. "A Stochastic Decentralized Resource Allocation Process", School of Management, Northwestern University, mimeo (1970).

[4] Uzawa, H. "On the Stability of Edgeworth's Barter Process", *International Economic Review*, **3** (1962).

[1] Consider any sequence of allocations $\{i^n\} \to i$. To establish continuity of $w(i)$ at i we need to show that $\{w(i^n)\} \to w(t)$. But

$$\lim_{n \to \infty} w(i^n) = \lim_{n \to \infty} \inf \{w: \ wI = \sum_T x(t), \ x(t) \gtrsim_t i^n(t) \forall t\}$$

$$= \lim_{n \to \infty} \inf \{w: \ wI \in \sum_T \{z: z \gtrsim_t i^n(t)\}\}$$

$$= \inf \{w: \ wI \in \sum_T \lim_{n \to \infty} \{z:, z \gtrsim_t i^n(t)\}\}$$

$$= \inf \{w: \ wI \in \sum_T \{z: z \gtrsim_t i(t)\}\} \ \text{(by continuity of preferences)}$$

$$= \inf \{w: \ wI = \sum_T x(t), \ x(t) \gtrsim_t i(t) \forall t\}$$

$$= w(t).$$

[2] If i^* were not Pareto optimal there would exist a Pareto better allocation j such that $j(t) \gtrsim_t i^*(t)$ for all t and $j(t') >_{t'} i^*(t')$ for some t'. Since $j(t') \geqq 0$ by continuity of preferences there exists a vector $\delta \geqq 0$ such that

$$i'(t') = j(t') - \delta >_{t'} i^*(t')$$

and

$$i'(t) = j(t) + \frac{1}{s-1}\,\delta >_t i^*(t) \quad t \neq t'$$

by desirability.

Afterword

It is extremely gratifying to rewrite "history" to make oneself look clever. In reconstructing a real collaboration from memory, notes, and various drafts of a paper, much has been left out. Readers should not hold the division of insights between characters G and W necessarily to reflect words spoken by Dan Graham and Roy Weintraub. In fact, Graham is nobody's straight man. I have told him that if it is justice he seeks, he will have to write his own book.

More serious is the omission of other "characters." James Mirrlees, then the editor for our manuscript, effectively showed us how to rewrite a lengthy piece of confusion into what was at least short and clear. He also suggested the need for, and the form of, the information-cost assumption and sketched out for us one method of proof for our theorem.

A final point. One distinguished economist who read a draft of this chapter noted, "The difficulty is that W and G should have known that the Edgeworth process converges onto a Pareto-efficient allocation which, by Aumann's Theorem, must be in the core and hence it should have been clear to them that...." Several "shoulds" do not make a "was."

That reader's embarrassment at my confession of our ignorance will perhaps be an antidote for less sophisticated readers impressed by the perspicacity of G and W.

CHAPTER 11

Mathematics and economics

The physicist E. P. Wigner (1969) once wrote an essay titled "On the Unreasonable Effectiveness of Mathematics in the Physical Sciences." Wigner did not ask how mathematics was useful. Instead, he argued that mathematics was unreasonably successful: It is not obvious why mathematical reasoning should be associated with successful physical theories. Can the same be said for economics?

There was once a concern about the role of mathematics in economics. The professional rise in the post–World War II years of a new generation of mathematical economists, such as Arrow and Samuelson, and econometricians, including Koopmans and Klein, engendered controversy. Although Frisch and Tinbergen had done remarkable work in mathematical and econometric modeling through the 1930s, work for which they received Nobel Prizes, the economics profession was relatively innocent of, and ofttimes hostile to, mathematics.

The roots of this "math phobia" are easy to locate. Among English speaking economists, Cambridge was the intellectual center before World War II. Marshall and Keynes had some mathematical skill. Yet each had little use for mathematics. As Marshall (1949, p. 781) wrote, "A training in mathematics is helpful by giving command over a marvellously terse and exact language for expressing clearly some general relations and some short processes of economic reasoning." Such a view takes for granted that the economics comes first. Mathematics can best clarify, at worst dress up, an economic argument. Marshall and Keynes believed that mathematical models could do little except express fundamentally economic arguments in a compact and tidy form.

Perhaps this was a Cambridge view; in the early part of the twentieth century British mathematics appeared to be in decline. Some younger mathematicians, such as Hardy, blamed this state of affairs on the examination system. He railed against the Tripos examinations as they were then administered; students spent all their time cramming, and arcane topics crowded out new theories. In any event, the leading Cambridge economists did not believe that mathematics was necessarily connected to economic theory. The American tradition, institutionalist at the time, was similarly nonmathematical. Irving Fisher's difficulty (noted in Chapter 6) in finding people to form an Econometric Society confirms the math phobia among American economists in the early part of this century.

Yet the two revolutionary episodes in economics in this century, Keynesian and neo-Walrasian economics, are linked with mathematics and statistics or, as the terms were used by economists, mathematical economics and econometrics. Skimming the journals of the late 1940s and early 1950s, one is struck by discussion of the need for increasing mathematical literacy in the profession. There were calls for curriculum reform at both the graduate and undergraduate level to improve the mathematical skills of those who wished to become professional economists. These calls were not unopposed. Several economists sounded alarms about the alien and untoward influence of mathematics.[1] This controversy was the context for Koopmans's (1957) essay titled "On the Interaction of Tools and Reasoning in Economics."

It had two themes. First, it cautioned of the dangers of tools getting in the way of economic reasoning. Second, it reviewed the best current practice in both mathematical economics and econometrics. Koopmans assessed various lines of enquiry and showed that the analysis of the economic problems was driven by good mathematics. Koopmans showed that the economic analysis could not proceed if theorists eschewed mathematics and statistics, for those tools, and only those tools, could define certain questions whose answers were worth having. This essay provided one kind of answer to the problem implicit in its title. The interaction of tools and economic reasoning posed no danger as long as the interaction continued to be as fruitful as it then was.

This answer is unsatisfactory. The instrumentalist response, which justifies the theory by the claim that it works, gives no clue to the origin of the theory, nor does it suggest what one is to do when the theory no longer works. Appraisal requires an answer to the question, Why does it work? as well as the assertion that it does indeed work. Wigner's observation is quite apposite: It is agreed that mathematical analysis is extremely important in the construction and evaluation of economic knowledge, but why *should* this be the case? Put another way, *must* mathematics and statistics be integral to economic argumentation?

Theory versus facts

To appreciate the tentative answers I shall suggest to the questions just posed, it will be useful first to sketch an argument that is sometimes used

---

[1] See the partial bibliography presented by Koopmans (1957, p. 172).

to deny any necessary connection between mathematics and economics. It is sometimes suggested that there is a disjunction between theory and the reality of economic life. My straw man argues that there is a real world somewhere "out there," a world of economic behavior and economic fact. This world is to be explained by the economist using economic analysis developed from theories and hypotheses. On this view, the task of the economist is to discover the "truth" about the real economic world. The real world provides the data for the analyst. It provides facts, some of which can be woven together into a coherent tapestry on the loom of a theory. This theory, separate from the facts themselves, permits us to position a new thread. It guides the weaving but it is separate from the materials themselves.

I reject such views. In particular, I deny that there is any worthwhile distinction to be drawn between the facts out of which economic knowledge is constructed and the theories that define the construction process.

This is not a radical position. The physicist and philosopher Eddington wrote in 1934 that "it is also a good rule not to put too much confidence in the observational results that are put forward *until they are confirmed by theory*" (Judson 1979, p. 93). The biologist Francis Crick has remarked that "the point is that evidence can be unreliable, and therefore you should use as little of it as you can.... People don't realize that not only can data be wrong in science, they can be misleading. There isn't such a thing as a hard fact when you're trying to discover something. It's only afterwards [when a theory has been created] that the facts become hard" (Judson 1979, p. 113).

What is an economic fact? If pressed to give an example, some people might offer the statement that the unemployment rate was 9.8% in the United States on September 15, 1983. They believe that this is a characterization of an independent economic reality about which economic theories are to be developed. On such a view I, as an economic theorist, am to construct a theory to explain that fact. I should be pleased if my theory can also explain why the U.S. unemployment rate was higher than 9.8% in June 1983. I should be delighted if my theory could explain why the rate was higher still in the Netherlands on that same September day.

This kind of answer is as common as it is naive. For many years philosophers of science have appreciated that the basic facts about our physical world are theory dependent. To say that the weight of a particular physical object is 764 grams is to make a conjunctive statement about the object and certain meter readings. Theories about the operation of the meters, theories about a class of objects, and suppositions about the relation between theories of meters and objects – all are bound together in the observation statement. How does this statement about weight differ from the "fact" of the unemployment rate? A moment's reflection shows that it differs not at all. The unemployment rate is a theoretical concept. The rules by which it is constructed are derived from a macroeconomic theory and refined by theories of labor-market behavior. A proposition about the unemployment rate is as much a theoretical proposition as is a statement about the mass of an electron.

Even if it is granted that some economic observation statements are theory dependent, this might not be true for all observation statements. Consider two other statements: (1) The business cycle is found in all capitalist countries. (2) The price of 2% fat-content milk in Durham, North Carolina, on September 15, 1983 was $2.29 a gallon. We are taught that each of these propositions is an economic fact to be explained by an appropriate theory. We might search for theories to explain the link between business cycles and capitalism, and we could try to explain why the equilibrium price of milk should indeed have been $2.29 in that local market.

We could push the question back a step or two. If the basic fact is that Roy Weintraub paid $2.29 for a gallon of milk in the Kroger supermarket at Lakewood Shopping Center on September 15, 1983, then the observation statement *appears* to be more primitive. But then the quest for an explanation must take a different tack, for such an observation statement could be explained by a psychological theory of my behavior or by an economic theory that explained my optimizing choice. The fact of the business cycle is itself problematic; there are reputable economists who deny that the business cycle is anything other than a policy failure on the part of government. We could, of course, push the putative observation statements back to even more primitive statements like "Person X (a collection of sense impressions noted by observer Y) reported (made noises that were heard by observer Z) that he was unemployed (was observed to fill out form BLS ABC)." It is not clear what this reduction would accomplish; the price of separating theories from fact is tedium.

We cannot make a clear distinction between theories and facts. Yet we can and do *define* "theory" and "fact" independently. The problem appears when we identify a particular proposition as theoretical or factual. The solution to this is obvious. If we accept that all facts are theory dependent, we can argue that any particular fact is relatively more theorylike or observationlike. We can certainly agree that the fact about business cycles is theorylike whereas the fact about the price of milk is observationlike. Just because economic facts are not pure does not mean that the scientific enterprise is doomed to provide circular chains of reasoning.

The conflation of theories and facts confuses arguments that theories are created to rationalize facts, and facts are used to develop and corroborate theories. There is an implication for mathematics and economics: *If there is no clear demarcation between facts and theories, then it is a mistake to believe that mathematical arguments come into economics only at the "higher" theoretical level.* Instead, if mathematics is associated with theoretical argumentation, then mathematics is linked to even the most primitive level of discourse about economic life. *As facts and theories are linked, and mathematics and theories are linked, so mathematics and low-level facts are linked.* Mathematics is indeed inseparable from economic discourse, and this conclusion is stronger the further that discourse is from primitive description. This argument presupposes that mathematics and theorizing are bound together. Let us for the moment accept this position. What does acceptance imply?

Mathematics and economic theory

If mathematics and economic theory are interwoven, then to understand the practice of economics we must understand the practice of mathematics. Put another way, if an appraisal of some work in economics requires attention to the best gambits of economists, what informed professional opinion considers to be the best lines of progress in the discipline, then that study cannot ignore the parallel lines of mathematical progress. If we seek to identify progress in economics, it is unreasonable to separate the mathematics, to put it aside as it were, for the duration of the appraisal. The mathematics must be appraised jointly with the economic theory.

Appraisals must attend to the growth of mathematical knowledge. What methods have philosophers of science devised to appraise mathematical work? Clearly, appraising mathematical work is different from appraising (empirical) science because there is no sensible correlation with the idea of empirical progressivity. There is a correlate to the idea of theoretical progress, but ideas of corroboration and falsification are inappropriate. Mathematics is not science. Models from the philosophy of science have to be replaced by those more appropriate to the structure of the mathematical enterprise. Leaving aside for the moment any consideration of what that enterprise might be, we can nevertheless approach the appraisal of mathematics by stripping away the empirical components from science. That is, we can initially think of mathematics as nonempirical science. On such a view, progress in mathematics is associated with a process that in science would be called hypothesis development.

Recall that, for empirical science, the Popperian process of conjectures and refutations is one in which initial conjectures or hypotheses are refined by the refutations that the empirical work provides. What is left of this process for a nonempirical science? What does it mean to say that there can be a process of conjectures and refutations in the absence of empirical work? For mathematics, we must interpret the Popperian dogma to mean that the initial conjectures of the mathematician are refined by the process of creating proofs and finding that certain of those proofs do not suffice to establish the original conjecture. From an initial failure comes refinement not only of the proof but also of the conjecture. Problematic elements of the proof point the way to defects in the original conception. There is a to-and-fro movement between the conjectures, in the form of theorems, perhaps, and proofs and refutations of those theorems, out of which develop more refined theorems and more informative proofs. This idea of progress in mathematics, first developed in Lakatos's Ph.D. thesis, is called the method of proofs and refutations, after Lakatos's (1976) book of that title. For Lakatos, any appraisal of work in mathematics must specify, and rationalize, the interaction between primitive conjecture, proof or refutation of all or part of the conjecture, and refinement of the naive conjecture.

Mathematics is not a deductive enterprise. It is false and misleading to suggest that first come the definitions, then come the propositions and lemmas, and finally, in all their glory, come the theorems. In fact, all these develop together. They are refined out of the initial primitive conjecture (which may not resemble the final form of either theorem or definition). For Lakatos, mathematics books and articles mislead students by suggesting that mathematics develops sequentially, when in fact its development is chaotic. Mathematics suffers from a myth of deductivism just as physics suffers from a myth of inductivism.

If we accept this view of the mathematical enterprise, our argument leads to a dilemma: (1) We accept that mathematics must be intertwined with economic theory. (2) We accept that both the mathematics and the theory must be appraised. (3) We accept that those methods are not identical and thus each must be appraised separately, or at least independently. (4) Yet they cannot be easily separated. One horn of this dilemma skewered the philosopher Alexander Rosenberg, who reached the conclusion that formal economic theory must be appraised *as* a branch of applied mathematics. Gored by the other horn are those who believe that the mathematics in mathematical economics must be ignored. That is, they seem to argue that mathematical theory must be appraised by the same criteria used to appraise any empirical science. Each of these two views, taken by itself, is misleading. It is impossible to reconstruct the neo-Walrasian program along Popperian lines; it is foolish to reconstruct the New Classical Economics as a branch of applied mathematics.

There is another difficulty. Consider existence proofs for competitive models on the one hand and time-series analyses of actual economic data on the other hand. These appear to be polar cases in economic analysis; in the usual language, the former is theoretical work and the latter is empirical work. Most economic analyses mix the two; they are hardly ever separated perfectly. A separation in any appraisal is foolhardy. Appraising a piece of economic analysis thus requires unusual sensitivity to the ways in which the best gambits of the economists are implemented in the programmatic shifts and modifications. Some problem shifts are mathematical and must be appraised with relatively more emphasis on the proofs-and-refutations model of the growth of mathematical knowledge. Other problem shifts are more closely tied to empirical corroborations or falsifications, and those shifts are appropriately appraised using the methodology of scientific research programs.

Another lesson from the case

Using the case study of Chapter 6, it is possible to give an account of the mathematical progress that was linked to the development of the competitive equilibrium theorems. The naive conjecture might be the belief of economists that equilibrium could be inferred in systems that had the requisite number of behavioral restrictions. Proofs of this, by counting equations, led to the recognition that the special cases of negative or zero prices had to be barred from the equation system.

The refined conjecture involved characterizing the system with inequalities, not equations. The first Wald proof of this refined conjecture required that there be a single good and no production choice. The improved conjecture required an assumption akin to the (aggregate) weak axiom of revealed preference.

Von Neumann's proof of a related theorem showed that fixed-point techniques were appropriate for the theorem's proof, and subsequent work by Kakutani and Nash extended this line of attack. The production-choice problem was developed by Koopmans in a manner that recalled the consumption-choice problem, and the fixed-point techniques allowed both problems to be embedded as lemmas of the proof of the existence of equilibrium.

Such a sketch, to be sure, hardly qualifies as an appraisal, a rational reconstruction, of the mathematical developments. It does suggest, however, that the logic of the mathematical process cannot be separated from the sequence of papers that led to the Arrow, Debreu, and McKenzie theorems. Mathematical progress occurred simultaneously with the progress in economic analysis. The core of the neo-Walrasian program could not have been hardened without that mathematical progress.

The idea that progress may occur on several levels is documented by the work of Arjo Klamer on New Classical Economics. Klamer (1981) found that argumentation could be carried out on several different levels; he called them *discourses*. Some of these were mathematical; some were theoretical; some were econometric; still others were practical. Confusion, or controversy, occurs when one kind of argument confronts another, as when a policy argument is met by a theoretical one. The gambits of the economists engaged in developing the New Classical program could not, in such cases, be reconstructed using an MSRP framework. Appraisal was problematic. This is not to say that Klamer agreed with McCloskey (1983) that there can be no critically rational appraisal of work in economics. It is misleading to suggest that economics *is* rhetoric. We can reconstruct developments in economic analysis using the ideas of appraisal developed in Chapter 7, bearing in mind that progress in economics must be treated differently from progress in mathematics (since mathematics has no use for empirical progressivity). Following Klamer, however, I accept that there may be gambits that are best interpreted as rhetoric, as attempts to engage discussion across discourses. Thus in appraising work in a subdiscipline in economics, we should be alert to the possibility that a full appraisal may require separate attention to the mathematical work, the theoretical work, the empirical work, and the rhetoric associated with each; each requires evaluation, perhaps by different methods. In the case of the hard core of the neo-Walrasian program, an appraisal can be more focused. General equilibrium analysis is easier to evaluate than the New Classical Economics; its discourse is theoretical. Its rational reconstruction requires attention only to the economic theory and the mathematics. It is often the case that the mathematics is hidden in the theory. As what we are accustomed to call theory becomes more and more developed, as it has progressed (in the MSRP sense) further from its initial formulation, the mathematical structures associated with it become more rooted in the basic construction. The mathematical structure becomes part of the framework of thought, and its own problematic nature is buried in unpublished working papers. For example, when one says that commodities are represented by non-negative real numbers, one has subsumed a lengthy historical chapter treating free goods versus economic goods and the duality of prices and quantities. The more developed an area of economics is, the more the appraisal of the mathematical structure is necessary, for it is further under the surface. The more the mathematics is hidden, the more important it is to assess its role, for the mathematics may force the economics along certain paths that the unwary, attempting an appraisal, could misinterpret. What might appear to be a degenerative problem shift could, in fact, be progressive were the mathematical substructure sufficiently well understood. The introduction of game-theoretic ideas into the existence proof of Arrow and Debreu could be considered degenerative were there no realization that the fixed-point theorems had an interpretation, through the work of Nash, as interdependent optimization.

We can now address one part of the problem suggested by Wigner's question. Surprise at the effectiveness of mathematics for economic theorizing is unwarranted to the extent that the mathematics and the theories have developed symbiotically. Imagine a rope with two intertwined strands; each was present at the start and each supports the other. Neither can be understood without the other. Appraisals of the one are linked to appraisals of the other. Judging the effectiveness of theories forces attention to the mathematical work that is linked to the theory.

This said, there remains the question of why. Why has mathematics played the role it has in economics? What is there about mathematics that leads economists as if by an invisible hand to express their ideas in mathematical form?[2] Is mathematics natural and, if so, in what sense? Pointing out that mathematics has been and continues to be linked to progress in economics is not an explanation of why this is necessarily the case, if indeed it is necessarily the case. It is thus time to address the curious and difficult question that Wigner posed: Why is mathematics so effective?

Speculations on mathematics

This section is almost entirely speculative, concerning as it does those properties of brain, mind, and mathematics that seem to go together in humans.[3] The argument, as we have brought it to this point, requires an answer to the question why mathematics is natural. What is it about humans that leads their analytic skills to be made manifest in the activity of doing mathematics? To discuss this question, we must be clearer about the activity of doing mathematics, for resistance to the idea that mathe-

---

[2] It was once argued that economic variables are quantitative, like physical variables and unlike anthropological ones. On such a view, measurability admitted mathematicization into economics. This view is hopelessly naive. We have seen that "the real world" does not present us with measurability. We impose that structure on the phenomena. Measurability is not the issue at all. Donald Katzner's (1983) *Analysis Without Measurement* presents a lucid case for the use of mathematics even when quantitative measures of variables are absent.

[3] I am not, of course, a neurobiologist; neither am I a specialist in any area of artificial intelligence. The following speculations are based on a perspective that, from Kant to Chomsky, has been seriously entertained by many philosophers.

matics is a *natural* activity is rooted in fundamental misperceptions about the nature of mathematical activity.

The most common fallacy is to suppose that mathematics is a deductive enquiry. The previous chapter was really an extended plea to the reader to abandon that view of mathematics. My argument is a gloss on the arguments put forward by Lakatos in *Proofs and Refutations*. I submit that mathematical activity is no different from any other mode of enquiry. Ideas are put forward in an imperfect form, criticized and modified, and refined into new ideas. The process continues as long as the ideas that emerge are of value. Doing mathematics is no different from any other human activity (Davis and Hersh 1981).

Mathematical activity is not austere. It is not sublimely rational. It does not stand apart from an activity that has as its end an understanding of the impact of the Black Death on Christian–Jewish relations in medieval France. Mathematicians and historians each start with ideas and evidence all mixed together and proceed through a process of conjectures and refutations to a conclusion. In the case of mathematics the conjecture, as well as the argument that got the analyst to the conclusion, is then hidden from view as the material is presented to the relevant public, but the false starts of the historian, too, are hidden from the final readers. The final drafts are clean. The historian presents ideas, marshals evidence, and links ideas and evidence in such a way that seams in the argument hardly show. Such is an explanatory success for an historian. A clear historical paper that unravels a complex problem is akin to a clean final draft to the mathematician. The false leads are invisible; the blunders are not proclaimed.

The activity of doing mathematics is not *intrinsically* different from the activity of doing history, or doing physics. Neither does it differ from writing a novel; ideas, or Jamesian streams of thought, are touched by other thoughts, ideas, impressions, and even feelings, which combine to redirect the flow of the stream, to channel it into new courses (Barzun 1983). The process is recognizable. The activity is human.

Is it reasonable to claim that to be human is to be a mathematician? Why the ubiquity, and the success, of mathematical activity in physics, chemistry, biology, economics, and other fields?

I cannot give definite answers to these questions. I can, however, offer two separate arguments that may alleviate the discomfort that such questions often produce. First, if it is granted that the problem-solving activities of the human mind are associated with the process of conjectures and refutations, then mathematical activity *is* that process in its purest form. That is, the process of proofs and refutations that characterizes mathematical activity is intrinsic to any investigatory activity. The nature of mathematical progress is a model of the growth of knowledge. Because the meaning of "the growth of knowledge" is clear in the empirical sciences, it is not surprising that mathematical activity models this growth process quite well. The clarity of the successful mathematical argument, when written up in deductive form, masks the development of that argument, in which ideas were presented, modified, and modified again. It is the activity of modification – the back-and-forth flow among naive conjecture and examination and modification of that conjecture (consistent with the study of the conjecture's failure) – that models the growth of knowledge; the model is not the deductive form of the final argument. The process of proofs and refutations requires not only that modifications be made; it also suggests exactly why, and how, those modifications must be incorporated.

Recall the puzzle faced by a falsificationist. Once a falsifying instance has been identified, how does one incorporate this knowledge into the process? How does evidence lead to modification of hypotheses? *We do not abandon falsified conjectures: We modify them in light of our experience.* This process is often ignored in the rationalist's theories of the growth of knowledge, perhaps because it permits psychology to intrude on philosophy. It is clearly unsatisfactory to claim that the *creation* of conjectures is a problem for psychologists to study while the *appraisal* of conjectures can be guided by philosophers of science.

Conjectures do not emerge *de novo*. They develop from more-primitive conjectures that have faced evidence and have been modified in accord with the lessons of that evidence. This claim is supported by case studies of the development of mathematical ideas, including Lakatos's study of the Euler theorem, or my own study in Chapter 10 of a minor convergence theorem. Case studies of the growth of knowledge in the natural sciences have tended to focus on episodes in which there was a sharp break between the original conjecture (or established theory) and a revolutionary alternative. The back-and-forth nature of conjecture, refutation, and refined conjecture is, for all its omnipresence, curiously missing in many accounts of the growth of scientific knowledge. It surfaces most clearly in those autobiographical accounts by scientists whose object is to make scientific practice understandable, congenial even, to the layperson. Such a purpose forces their narratives to evoke their readers' own experiences in solving complicated problems. Pirsig's (1975) *Zen and the Art of Motorcycle Maintenance* is a better guide to actual scientific practice than is the initial chapter of an economics book in which the scientific character of economics is declared desirable – and present.

My first speculation in response to Wigner's questions can be stated briefly. Mathematics is a model for the kind of human problem-solving activity that has been successful in furthering the interests and actions of the species. In the language of sociobiology, the ability to be a mathematician, in the sense of the preceding paragraphs, has survival value. Mathematical ability in the sense of conjectures and refutations promotes fitness. It enables individuals to learn from experience; those who do learn survive to pass on their peculiar talents to their offspring. The ability to do mathematics, facility with the mathematical activity of sequential reformulation, is naturally human.

Mathematics and structure

Even if mathematical thinking is inextricably linked to the process by which humans engage experience in order to learn, to promote the growth of knowledge, why is mathematics the *form* in which that growth is expressed? My response to that question is again less an answer than a speculation. In brief, I believe that mathematics itself is the study of structures. The structures that concern mathematicians are the fundamental building blocks of knowledge. Thus the human activity known as doing mathematics is connected to the sources of human knowledge. And economics, concerned with knowledge about the economy and the economizing behavior of individuals, is a fit subject to have its insights developed in mathematical form.

Such claims require argument. We can agree that the richness and complexity of our ideas – indeed, the process of thought itself – requires the presence of a person who thinks. There is no knowledge "out there." Knowledge grows as the ideas of humans grow. To say this is to admit that between the perceptions and the theories stands a human mind. The sensations of the world are organized; the organization is what allows us to claim that we understand something. We structure experience ourselves. It does not come to us preconfigured. The Swiss "genetic epistemologist" Jean Piaget argued in his many books that the child is extraordinarily able to organize experience: Ideas of conservation, cardinality, order, continuity, geometry or spatial relationships, and time seem to develop in all children, in all cultures, in an orderly fashion (e.g., Piaget 1971). One of the implications of this order is that as humans we appear to be "programmed" (or hard wired!) to search for structure unceasingly. We *necessarily* impose structure upon our various perceptions. These structures do not seem to vary much from person to person or from group of people to group of people. If our human reality, including all our thoughts and ideas, is configured to accord with the inherent structures of our minds, it is no accident that so much of what we find to be useful knowledge is mathematical in form. It can be none other, for mathematical activity seeks knowledge of structures, often abstract structures to be sure, but structures nonetheless. If all knowledge is structurally organized, is developed out of some basic and unchanging mental structures, the connection between mathematics and the growth of knowledge is not accidental. It is a manifestation of the duality between an activity that is concerned to analyze structures, mathematics, and an activity that is concerned to organize experience structurally, problem solving. In this sense economic analysis, or economic problem solving, is a mathematical activity, and surprise at the success of mathematics in economics is unwarranted.

References

Arrow, K. J. 1951. "An Extension of the Basic Theorems of Classical Welfare Economics," in J. Neyman (ed.), *Proceedings of the Second Berkeley Symposium on Mathematical Statistics and Probability*. Berkeley, Cal. Reprinted in Newman, 1968, Vol. 1, pp. 365–90.

Arrow, K. J., and Debreu, G. 1954. "Existence of an Equilibrium for a Competitive Economy." *Econometrica* 20: 265–90.

Arrow, K. J., and Hahn, F. H. 1971. *General Competitive Analysis*. San Francisco: Holden Day.

Aumann, R. 1964. "Markets with a Continuum of Traders." *Econometrica* 32: 39–50.

Ayer, A. J. 1977. *Part of My Life*. New York: Harcourt Brace Jovanovich.

Barzun, J. 1983. *A Stroll with William James*. New York: Harper & Row.

Baumol, W. J., and Goldfeld, S. M. (eds.) 1968. *Precursors in Mathematical Economics*. LSE Series of Reprints of Scarce Works on Political Economy, No. 19. London: London School of Economics.

Bilimovic, A. 1938. "Einige Bemerkungen zur Theorie der Planwirtschaft." *Z. Nationalökonom*. 9: 147–66.

Blaug, M. 1980. *The Methodology of Economics*. Cambridge: Cambridge University Press.

Cassel, G. 1899. "Grundriss einer elementaren Preislehre." *G. Staatswissen.*
   1932. *The Theory of Social Economy*, 2nd ed., S. L. Barron (transl.). New York: Harcourt Brace.

Christ, C. 1952. *Economic Theory and Measurement*. Chicago: Cowles Commission.

Clare, G. 1982. *Last Waltz in Vienna*. New York: Avon.

Coddington, A. 1975. "The Rationale of General Equilibrium." *Econom. Inquiry* 13: 539–58.

Davidson, P. 1972. *Money and the Real World*. New York: Halsted.
   1977. "Money and General Equilibrium." *Economie Appl.*

Davis, P., and Hersh, R. 1981. *The Mathematical Experience*. Boston: Birkhauser.

Debreu, G. 1951, "The Coefficient of Resource Utilization." *Econometrica* 19: 273–92.
   1952. "A Social Equilibrium Existence Theorem." *Proc. Nat. Acad. Sci. U.S.A.* 38: 886–93.
   1954. "Representation of a Preference Ordering by a Numerical Function," in R. M. Thrall, C. H. Coombs, and R. L. Davis (eds.), *Decision Processes*. New York: Wiley. Reprinted in Newman, 1968, Vol. 1, pp. 267–63.
   1959. *Theory of Value*. New York: Wiley.

Debreu, G., and Scarf, H. 1963. "A Limit Theorem on the Core of an Economy." *Internat. Econom. Rev.* 4: 235–46.

De Marchi, N. B. 1976. "Anomaly and the Development of Economics: The Case of the Leontief Paradox," in S. Latsis (ed.), *Method and Appraisal in Economics.* Cambridge: Cambridge University Press.

Dobb, M. 1937. "The Trend of Modern Economics," reprinted in E. K. Hunt and J. G. Schwartz (eds.), 1972. *A Critique of Economic Theory.* Baltimore: Penguin, pp. 37–82.

Dorfman, R., Samuelson, P. A., and Solow, R. 1958. *Linear Programming and Economic Analysis.* New York: McGraw Hill.

Edgeworth, F. Y. 1881. *Mathematical Psychics.* London: Routledge.

Eichner, A. (ed.) 1978. *A Guide to Post-Keynesian Economics.* White Plains, N.Y.: Sharpe.

Feyerabend, P. 1975. *Against Method.* London: Verso. Reprinted 1978.

Graham, D. A., and Weintraub, E. R. 1975. "On Convergence to Pareto Allocations." *Rev. Econom. Stud.* 42: 469–72.

Graham, F. 1948. *The Theory of International Values.* Princeton: Princeton University Press.

Gram, H., and Walsh, V. 1980. *Classical and Neoclassical Theories of General Equilibrium.* New York: Oxford University Press.

Hahn, F. H. 1973. *On the Notion of Equilibrium in Economics.* Cambridge: Cambridge University Press.

Hahn, F. H., and Negishi, T. 1962. "A Theorem on Non-tatonnement Stability." *Econometrica* 30: 463–69.

Handler, E. W. 1980. "The Logical Structure of Modern Neoclassical Static Microeconomic Equilibrium Theory," *Erkenntnis* 15: 33–53.

Hands, D. W. 1983. "Second Thoughts on Lakatos." Unpublished working paper. Tacoma, Wash.: University of Puget Sound, Department of Economics.

  1984. "What Economics Is Not: An Economist's Response to Rosenberg." Unpublished working paper. Tacoma, Wash.: University of Puget Sound, Department of Economics.

Haslinger, F. 1982. "Structure and Problems of Equilibrium and Disequilibrium Theory," in Stegmüller, Balzar, and Spohn, 1982, pp. 63–84.

Herstein, I. N., and Milnor, J. 1953. "An Axiomatic Approach to Measurable Utility." *Econometrica* 21: 291–7. Reprinted in Newman, 1968, Vol. 1, 264–70.

Hicks, J. R. 1939. *Value and Capital.* Oxford: Oxford University Press.

Hicks, J. R., and Weber, W. (eds.) 1973. *Carl Menger and the Austrian School of Economics.* Oxford: Oxford University Press.

High, J. 1978. "Equilibrium." *Aust. Econom. Newslet.* 1: 3.

Hurwicz, L., Radner, R., and Reiter, S. 1970. "A Stochastic Decentralized Resource Allocation Process." Mimeograph. Evanston, Ill.: Northwestern University, School of Management.

ICF 1981. *Developing a Least-Cost Energy Strategy.* Washington, D.C.: ICF, Inc.

Janik, A., and Toulmin, S. 1973. *Wittgenstein's Vienna.* New York: Simon and Schuster.

182   References

Judson, H. F. 1979. *The Eighth Day of Creation.* New York: Touchstone.

Kakutani, S. 1941. "A Generalization of Brouwer's Fixed Point Theorem." *Duke Math.* 8: 457–9. Reprinted in Newman, 1968, Vol. 1, 33–5.

Kaldor, N. 1972. "The Irrelevance of Equilibrium Economics." *Econ. J.* 82: 1237–55.

Katzner, D. 1983. *Analysis Without Measurement.* Cambridge: Cambridge University Press.

Keynes, J. M. 1936. *The General Theory of Employment, Interest, and Money.* New York: Harcourt Brace.

  1973. *The Collected Writings,* Vol. XIII: *The General Theory and After: Part I – Preparation,* D. Moggridge (ed.). London: Macmillan.

Klamer, A. 1981. *Levels of Discourse in the New Classical Economics.* Ph.D dissertation, Durham, N.C.: Duke University, Economics Department.

Knight, F. 1921. *Risk, Uncertainty, and Profit.* Chicago: University of Chicago Press.

Koopmans, T. (ed.) 1951a. *Activity Analysis of Production and Distribution.* New York: Wiley.

  1951b. "Analysis of Production as an Efficient Combination of Activities," in Koopmans, 1951a, pp. 33–97.

  1957. *Three Essays on the State of Economic Science.* New York: McGraw-Hill.

  1964. "Economic Growth at a Maximal Rate." *Quart. J. Econom.* 78: 355–94. Reprinted in Newman, 1968, Vol. 2, pp. 239–78.

Koopmans, T., and Reiter, S. 1951. "A Model of Transportation," in T. Koopmans, 1951a, pp. 222–59.

Kötter, R. 1982. "General Equilibrium Theory: An Empirical Theory?" in Stegmüller, Balzar, and Spohn, 1982, pp. 103–17.

Kuhn, T. S. 1962. *The Structure of Scientific Revolutions.* Chicago: University of Chicago Press.

  1977. *The Essential Tension.* Chicago: University of Chicago Press.

Lakatos, I. 1970. "Falsification and the Methodology of Scientific Research Programmes," in I. Lakatos and A. Musgrave (eds.), *Criticism and the Growth of Knowledge.* Cambridge: Cambridge University Press. Reprinted in Lakatos, 1978b, Vol. 1, pp. 8–101.

  1976. *Proofs and Refutations.* Cambridge: Cambridge University Press.

  1978a. "History of Science and Its Rational Reconstructions," in I. Lakatos, 1978b, pp. 102–38.

  1978b. *The Methodology of Scientific Research Programmes: Philosophical Papers,* Vol. 1, J. Worrall and G. Currie (eds.). Cambridge: Cambridge University Press.

Lange, O., McIntyre, F., and Yntema, T. (eds.) 1942. *Studies in Mathematical Economics and Econometrics.* Chicago: University of Chicago Press.

Latsis, S. (ed.) 1976. *Method and Appraisal in Economics.* Cambridge: Cambridge University Press.

Leijonhufvud, A. 1976. "Schools, 'Revolutions,' and Research Programmes in Economic Theory," in Latsis, 1976, pp. 65–108.

Leijonhufvud, E. C. 1985. "The Emigration of the Austrian Economists." *Hist. Polit. Economy.*

Lucas, R. E. 1980. "Methods and Problems in Business Cycle Theory," in R. E.

Lucas, *Studies in Business Cycle Theory*. Cambridge: MIT Press, pp. 271–96.

Marschak, J. 1950. "Rational Behavior, Uncertain Prospects, and Measurable Utility." *Econometrica* 18: 111–41.

Marshall, A. 1949. *Principles of Economics*, 8th ed. New York: Macmillan.

McClosky, D. N. 1983. "The Rhetoric of Economics." *J. Econom. Lit.* 21: 481–517.

McKenzie, L. 1951. "Ideal Output and the Interdependence of Firms." *Econom. J.* 61: 785–803.

1953–4. "Specialisation and Efficiency in World Production." *Rev. Econom. Stud.* 21: 165–80.

1954. "On Equilibrium in Graham's Model of World Trade and Other Competitive Systems." *Econometrica* 22: 147–61.

1974. "Why Compute Economic Equilibria?" in J. Los and M. Los (eds.), *Conference on Computing Equilibria: How and Why*. Torun, Poland, pp. 1–19.

1981. "The Classical Theorem on Existence of Competitive Equilibrium." *Econometrica* 49: 819–41.

Menger, K. 1952. "The Formative Years of Abraham Wald and His Work in Geometry." *Ann. of Math. Stat.* 23: 14–20.

1973. "Austrian Marginalism and Mathematical Economics," in Hicks and Weber, 1973, pp. 38–60.

Miedema, A. K., White, S. B., Clayton, C. A., Alexander, B. V., and Kumm, M. S. 1981. *Time of Use Electricity Price Effects, North Carolina*. Research Triangle Park, N.C.: Research Triangle Institute.

Moore, B. 1978. "Monetary Factors," in Eichner, 1978, pp. 120–38.

Morgenstern, O. 1935. "Vollkommone Voraussicht und Wirtschaftliches Gleichgewicht." *Z. Nationalökonom.* 6: 337–57. Reprinted as "Perfect Foresight and Economic Equilibrium," F. H. Knight (transl.), in Morgenstern, 1976a, pp. 169–83.

1941. "Professor Hicks on Value and Capital." *J. Polit. Econ.* 49: 361–93. Reprinted in Morgenstern, 1976a, pp. 185–217.

1951. "Abraham Wald, 1902–1950." *Econometrica* 19: 361–7. Reprinted in Morgenstern, 1976a, pp. 493–7.

1968. 'Karl Schlesinger," in *International Encyclopedia of the Social Sciences*, Vol. 14. New York: Macmillan. Reprinted in Morgenstern, 1976a, pp. 509–11.

1976a. *Selected Economic Writings of Oskar Morgenstern*, A. Schotter (ed.). New York: NYU Press.

1976b. "Collaborating with von Neumann." *J. Econom. Lit.* 14: 805–16.

Nash, J. 1950. "Equilibrium Points in *N*-Person Games." *Proc. Nat. Acad. Sci. U.S.A.* 36: 48–9.

Neisser, H. 1932. "Lohnhöle und Beschäftigungsgrad im Marktgleichgewicht," *Weltwirt. Archiv.* 36: 413–55.

Nelson, R., and Winter, S. 1982. *An Evolutionary Theory of Economic Change*. Cambridge: Harvard University Press.

Neumann, J. von 1928. "Zur Theorie der Gesellschaftsspiele." *Math. Ann.* 100: 295–320. Reprinted in von Neumann, 1963. Translated and reprinted in Tucker and Luce, 1959, pp. 1–27.

1936. "Über ein ökonomisches Gleichungssystem und eine Verallgemeinerung des Brouwerschen Fixpunksatzes," in K. Menger (ed.), 1937, *Ergebnisse eines Mathematischen Kolloquiums, 1935–36*. Leipzig and Vienna: Franz Deuticke. Reprinted as G. Morton (transl.), 1945–1946, "A Model of General Economic Equilibrium." *Rev. Econom. Stud.* 13: 1–9. Reprinted in Newman, 1968, Vol. 2, pp. 221–9; Baumol and Goldfeld, 1968, pp. 296–306; von Neumann, 1963, pp. 29–37.

1963. *Collected Works.* New York: Macmillan, Vol. VI.

Neumann, J. von, and Morgenstern, O. 1947. *Theory of Games and Economic Behavior*, 2nd ed. Princeton: Princeton University Press.

Newman, P. (ed.) 1968. *Readings in Mathematical Economics.* Baltimore: Johns Hopkins Press, Vols. 1 and 2.

O'Driscoll, G. 1977. *Economics as a Coordination Problem.* Kansas City: Sheed Andrews and McMeel.

Patinkin, D. 1949. "The Indeterminacy of Absolute Prices in Classical Economic Theory." *Econometrica* 17: 1–27.

1965. *Money, Interest, and Prices*, 2nd ed. New York: Harper & Row.

Pearce, D., and Tucci, M. 1982. "A General Net Structure for Theoretical Economics," in Stegmüller, Balzar, and Spohn, 1982, pp. 85–102.

Piaget, J. 1971. *Structuralism.* London: Routledge and Kegan Paul.

Pirsig, R. M. 1975. *Zen and the Art of Motorcycle Maintenance.* New York: Bantam.

Popper, K. 1959. *The Logic of Scientific Discovery.* New York: Harper & Row. Reprinted 1965.

1972. *Conjectures and Refutations: The Growth of Scientific Knowledge.* London: Routledge and Kegan Paul.

Public Staff of the North Carolina Utilities Commission 1979. *Analysis of Long Range Needs for Electric Generating Facilities in North Carolina.* Raleigh, N.C.: North Carolina Utilities Commission, Vols. 1 and 2.

1981. *Analysis of Long Range Needs for Electric Generating Facilities in North Carolina.* Raleigh, N.C.: North Carolina Utilities Commission.

Quirk, J., and Saposnik, R. 1968. *Introduction to General Equilibrium Theory and Welfare Economics.* New York: McGraw Hill.

Radner, R. 1968. "Competitive Equilibrium Under Uncertainty." *Econometrica* 36: 31–58.

Rapoport, A. 1980. "Game Theory in Biology." *Evolutionary Theory* 4: 249–63.

Reder, M. 1982. "Chicago Economics: Permanence and Change." *J. Econom. Lit.* 20: 1–38.

"Referee's Report on Kakutani Paper" 1941. *Arch. Duke Math. J.*

Remanyi, J. 1979. "Core Demi-core Interaction: Toward a General Theory of Disciplinary and Subdisciplinary Growth." *Hist. Polit. Economy* 11: 30–63.

Rizzo, M. 1979. "Disequilibrium and All That: An Introductory Essay," in M. Rizzo (ed.), *Time, Uncertainty, and Disequilibrium.* Lexington, Mass.: Lexington Books, pp. 1–18.

Robinson, J. 1968. *Essays in the Theory of Economic Growth.* New York: St. Martin's.

Rosenberg, A. 1980. "A Sceptical History of Microeconomic Theory." *Theory and Decision* 12: 79–93.

1983. "If Economics Isn't Science, What Is It?" *Philos. Forum* 14: 296–314.

Samuelson, P. A. 1941. "The Stability of Equilibrium: Comparative Statics and Dynamics." *Econometrica* 9: 97–120.

1947. *Foundations of Economic Analysis.* Cambridge, Mass.: Harvard University Press.

Schlesinger, K. 1933. "Über die produktionsgleichungen der ökonomischen Wertlehre," in K. Menger (ed.), 1935, *Ergebnisse eines mathematischen Kolloquiums, 1933–34.* Leipzig and Vienna: Franz Deuticke. Reprinted as "On the Production Equations of Economic Value Theory," W. Baumol (transl.), in Baumol and Goldfeld, 1968, pp. 278–80.

Schumpeter, J. 1954. *History of Economic Analysis.* New York: Oxford University Press.

Shackle, G. L. S. 1976. "New Trends for Economic Theory: 1926–1939," in S. Weintraub (ed.), 1977, *Modern Economic Thought.* Philadelphia: University of Pennsylvania Press, pp. 23–37.

Sheffrin, S. 1983. *Rational Expectations.* Cambridge: Cambridge University Press.

Shubik, M. 1959. "Edgeworth Market Games," in Tucker and Luce, 1959, pp. 267–78.

Simon, H. A. 1979. "Rational Decision Making in Business Organizations," *Am. Econ. Rev.* 69: 493–513.

Sneed, J. D. 1971. *The Logical Structure of Mathematical Physics.* Dordrecht: Reidel.

Stackelberg, H. von. 1933. "Zwei kritische Bemerkungen zur Preistheorie Gustav Cassel," *Z. Nationalökonom.* 4: 456–72.

Stegmüller, W. 1976. *The Structure and Dynamics of Theories.* Berlin: Springer-Verlag.

1979. *The Structuralist View of Theories.* Berlin: Springer-Verlag.

Stegmüller, W., Balzar, W., and Spohn, W. (eds.) 1982. *Philosophy of Economics.* Berlin: Springer-Verlag.

Szilard, L. 1969. "Reminiscences," G. W. Szilard and K. R. Winsor (eds.), in D. Fleming and B. Bailyn (eds.), *The Intellectual Migration.* Cambridge, Mass.: Harvard University Press.

Tucker, A. W., and Luce, R. D. (eds.) 1959. *Contributions to the Theory of Games.* Princeton: Princeton University Press, Vol. IV.

Ulam, S. 1958. "John von Neumann, 1903–1957." *Bull. Amer. Math. Society* 64: 1–49.

1976. *Adventures of a Mathematician.* New York: Scribner's.

Uzawa, H. 1962. "On the Stability of Edgeworth's Barter Process." *International Economic Review* 3: 218–32.

Ville, J. 1938. "Sur la Théorie Générale des Jeux où Intervient l'Habilité des Joueurs," in E. Borel et al. (eds.), *Traité du Calcul des Probabilités et de Ses Applications.* Paris: Gautier-Villars, Vol. IV.

Wald, A. 1934. "Über die eindeutige positive Lösbarkeit der neuen Produktionsgleichungen (I)," in K. Menger (ed.), 1935, *Ergebnisse eines mathematischen Kolloquiums, 1933–34.* Leipzig and Vienna: Franz Deuticke. Reprinted as "On the Unique Non-negative Solvability of the New Production Equations, Part I," W. Baumol (transl.), in Baumol and Goldfeld, 1968, pp. 281–8.

1935. "Über die Produktionsgleichungen der ökonomischen Wertlehre (II)," in K. Menger (ed.), 1936, *Ergebnisse eines mathemathischen Kolloquiums, 1934–35.*

186   References

Leipzig and Vienna: Franz Deuticke. Reprinted as "On the Production Equations of Economic Value Theory II," W. Baumol (transl.), in Baumol and Goldfeld, 1968, pp. 289–93.

1936. "Über einige Gleichungssysteme der mathematischen Ökonomie," *Z. Nationalökonom.* 7: 637–70. Reprinted as Wald, 1951.

1951. "On Some Systems of Equations of Mathematical Economics," O. Eckstein (transl.). *Econometrica* 19: 368–403.

Wallis, W. A. 1980a. "The Statistical Research Group, 1942–1945." *J. Amer. Statist. Assoc.* 75: 320–30.

1980b. "Rejoinder." *J. Amer. Statist. Assoc.* 75: 334–5.

Weintraub, E. R. 1979. *Microfoundations.* Cambridge: Cambridge University Press.

Wigner, E. P. 1969. "The Unreasonable Effectiveness of Mathematics in the Natural Sciences," in T. L. Saaty and F. J. Weyl (eds.), *The Spirit and the Uses of the Mathematical Sciences.* New York: McGraw-Hill, pp. 123–40.

Wolfowitz, J. 1952. "Abraham Wald, 1902–1950." *Ann. Math. Statist.* 23: 1–13.

Wood, M., and Dantzig, G. 1951. "The Programming of Interdependent Activities: General Discussion," in T. Koopmans, 1951a, pp. 15–18.

Zeuthan, F. 1933. "Das Prinzip der Knappheit, technische Kombination und ökonomische Qualität," *Z. Nationalökonom.* 7: 1–24.

Index